THREE
EIGHTEENTH CENTURY
FIGURES

THREE
EIGHTEENTH CENTURY
FIGURES

SARAH CHURCHILL   JOHN WESLEY
GIACOMO CASANOVA

———————————

BONAMY DOBRÉE

LONDON
OXFORD UNIVERSITY PRESS
NEW YORK   TORONTO
1962

Oxford University Press, Amen House, London E.C.4

GLASGOW   NEW YORK   TORONTO   MELBOURNE   WELLINGTON
BOMBAY   CALCUTTA   MADRAS   KARACHI   LAHORE   DACCA
CAPE TOWN   SALISBURY   NAIROBI   IBADAN   ACCRA
KUALA LUMPUR   HONG KONG

Sarah Churchill, Duchess of Marlborough was
first published by Gerald Howe Ltd. (1927)

John Wesley by Gerald Duckworth and Co. Ltd. (1933)

and

Giacomo Casanova, Chevalier de Seingalt
by Peter Davies Ltd. (1933)

Three Eighteenth Century Figures was first
published in 1962

PRINTED IN GREAT BRITAIN

CONTENTS

INTRODUCTION

It is an odd affair, this, of presenting images of people. For what is this business of biography, especially of brief biography? When a writer tackles the portrayal of anybody's life he must have some preconceived idea about the person, otherwise the incentive to write would be lacking. The danger is, that having started with this idea he will only too easily find support for it in the maze of letters, reports, memoirs, confessions and so on, to justify his picture. Perhaps he may rebel against popular notions, and that is all to the good (so long as he does not make rebellion a principle), for that will give another view of the complex being that every individual being is. With all of my figures I was aware only of enough to make me eager to investigate. My original ideas were greatly modified, sometimes very much changed, as I read more, and tried to imagine myself into the minds and circumstances of the people being by little and little revealed to me. What emerged, in my mind, was a fairly definite living object, but such as I present him or her can be relevant to myself alone; somebody differently constituted, with other knowledges and experiences, would not present the same portrait. That is why biographies need constantly to be rewritten. Each age has experiences and feelings different from the last; dwellers in it make different assumptions, and for that reason no one can really imagine himself as being an inhabitant of an earlier period. A biographer writing before 1914 will see the year 1714 differently from anyone with the experience of two world wars, of sundry revolutions, and the disruption of the social order as witnessed by a change of values outrageous to some. We can see people only through the veil of centuries, the safeguard being the probability that in essentials human beings do not vary much through the ages. Perhaps the veil may not be so thick after all.

In writing a 'brief biography' the problems are rather different from those that face the writer of a large-scale one. The value of the latter is that the reader can be given so much material that he can construct his own concept of the person in question—up to a point. For even in such great biographical quarries as Lockhart's *Life of Scott* something of Lockhart must have crept in, some heightening, some suppression, corresponding with his own view of life, not to say of his father-in-law. Again, treating the subject on a small scale means that many matters which the biographer does not feel to be illuminating of his victim have to be left out. He must tell the truth as he sees it; yes, and nothing but the truth. But he cannot tell the whole truth, for there simply is not the space. So he has to select, and that according to what he himself thinks will give the most vivid glimpse of the character he is trying to put into action. It is this selection that, apart from the writing itself, makes biography an art, a subtle art. But the biographer must avoid the temptation of distorting for the sake of art, as Lytton Strachey would have allowed him to do. Thus in my account of Wesley I have given the greater part to his earlier years, to the private rather than to the public Wesley, to the man in process of growth rather than to the finished figure. This I found the more interesting, for though I do not altogether agree with Mr. C. E. Vulliamy that the last half-century of Wesley's life is made up of 'a noble monotony', to all intents and purposes inner conflicts had been resolved. Some matters have been left out altogether, such as Wesley's experimenting with the doctrine of acting only when the spirit was free to act (I am not competent to comment upon Wesley's religious doctrine: I try to seize him as a character), and his political moves, such as his printed epistle to the American colonists, and his letter to Lord North.

Moreover, when dealing with doubtful or controversial matters, where more than one view may be held, the 'brief biographer' has to make up his mind which interpretation he will choose: he has not the space to argue pros and cons. He will present what he thinks to be probable in view of the picture he has, inevitably, formed. Thus, to refer again to Wesley, I have ventured to identify 'a religious friend' met in 1725 with Varanese, but have avoided all apocryphal stories except the one told of Wesley at the Charterhouse; for this legend, unverifiable as fact, is so true to the spirit that I have thought myself justified in including it. Where memoirs are largely relied on there must naturally be more than a little hesitation—not much, to be sure, with Wesley—as with to some degree the Duchess of Marlborough. With Casanova the case is plainer still.

'There are few more delightful books in the world than Casanova's *Mémoires*', as Havelock Ellis declared, but they have been debated as fiercely as any writings of the kind, both by those who regarded them chiefly as a tissue of lies, and by the others defending their veracity. The questions, however, are gradually being settled by ardent scholars of many nations, and it would appear that where Casanova's statements can be checked, they are often found to be true. After all, while he was writing his confessions he was between the ages of sixty-four and seventy-three, and though a multitude of notes and a prodigious memory enabled him to construct a coherent tale, he often muddled his dates, confused sequences, and mis-interpreted facts. Thus in using his memoirs I have corrected his most glaring mis-statements in the light of recent research.

Frank as he was, he occasionally glozed over certain incidents in his past; he often confessed to dubious dealings, but at other times concealed unpleasant facts. Perhaps his memory was kind to him, but his critics have been more ruthless. Where it is impossible to check his statements—for even scholarship cannot always draw back the curtains of the bed—his story must, with reservations, be taken as it stands. And though, naturally, he vaunted his prowess and spread his tail, there is no reason to be too sceptical; and if he heightened his scenes (after all, he was an artist, so much so that his work was at one time ascribed to Stendhal), we may gratefully accept his drama. Since he could in his mind invent staggering improbabilities, as in his magical sabbaths, so he could, and very probably did, put them into effect. There was nothing within to stop him.

The three famous or notorious figures here sketched constitute part of the picture we have built up for ourselves of 'the eighteenth century', though, to be sure, the Duchess of Marlborough belongs in part to the seventeenth. But how far are they typical of the idea of the century we have so long been invited to accept? What is this myth of The Age of Reason? Looking at these personalities we may well ask what it was that urged them. Reason? The first two at least were deeply passionate, in their own very different realms, and might well

exclaim with Dryden's Serapion, 'Poor reason! What a
wretched aid art thou!', and nobody will claim that a sweet
reasonableness directed Casanova's variegated existence. The
truth is, we are far too prone to make easy generalizations
about centuries, or periods, or even decades—how grossly
superficial the term 'the naughty 'nineties' turns out to be on
the most cursory examination!—as though people living in any
age took its 'colouring'. Human beings are diverse creatures,
and do not act in accordance with what we have come to
pigeon-hole and think of as 'the spirit of the age', but are led
or driven by their passions, their desires, their illuminations.
Men, as suggested earlier, do not much change; conditions at
any given time may to some extent vary their manner of
working, how they strive to attain their objects, what names
they give to their efforts and their ends, what jargon they use
to describe their emotions. Wesley could not work in quite the
same way as George Fox (though he sometimes did), or as
William Penn, who had other means to employ; but essentially
he is of the same mould, though Penn, if anything, was the more
'reasonable'. There are plenty of women as outstanding as
Sarah Marlborough in imposing their wills, Florence Nightin-
gale for example; it was the personal, not the secular conditions
that were different. Casanova cannot be satisfactorily matched
in other centuries, though there are in all centuries clever,
entertaining rogues deceiving themselves that they were something more. In the actual conduct of their lives eighteenth-
century folk were no more reasonable than those of any other
age. The springs of action, the motives of behaviour, are the
same in all. It is the individuals who are ceaselessly and
fascinatingly varied.

It may nevertheless be asked why the eighteenth century,
especially the first half, should so constantly be dubbed The
Age of Reason? 'Society', to use the snob phrase, was, to be
sure, better mannered than in the seventeenth century: but was
Lady Mary Wortley Montagu, for instance, more reasonable
than Dorothy Osborne? Was Gibbon more sceptical of revealed
religion than Hobbes? Had Chesterfield more common sense
than his grandfather, the Marquess of Halifax? Was the
populace that rioted at every excuse—Gin Acts, Lord George
Gordon, or prices at Drury Lane—more reasonable than the

citizenry that fought in the Civil Wars? It is true that people in the early eighteenth century (before it became The Age of Sentiment) talked a great deal about reason, but more often than not it was to try to define its limitations, and to be extremely sceptical, as Pope was, of its directive force. This fiction of The Spirit of the Age as a dominating influence ought to be gently deposed. Hazlitt's book with that title should be enough to dispel the mirage. How is Bentham like Byron? What is the binding connection between Elia and the Rev. Mr. Irving? If it is through a veil that we see people in the past, it is only that we do not know enough about them, do not quite seize their personal social ambience, do not speak quite the same language.

So I have not attempted, nor have I wished, to write about these three individuals as representing anything but themselves. These studies were not shaped to any pattern, arranged to fit in with any preconceived idea. They were written at different times, when it happened that I was asked to write about these people for one series or another, because, I imagine, those who invited me thought, more often than not mistakenly, that I already knew much about them. As already explained, I knew very little about them; but on delving into the material, rummaging about the mass of papers, I found them to be fascinating, though not all of them admirable, people, portraits of whom, as they seemed to me to be, I felt that I would like to offer to general readers because I found them furiously interesting, and hoped that they would too.

Bonamy Dobrée

SARAH CHURCHILL
DUCHESS OF MARLBOROUGH
(1660–1744)

CONTENTS

SARAH CHURCHILL

My chief aim (if I have any acquaintance with my own heart) has been, both in publick and private life, to deserve approbation; but I have never been without an earnest desire to have it too, both living and dead, from the wise and virtuous.

THE DUCHESS OF MARLBOROUGH

I

The Stage is Set

It is very rarely, and then only for a moment, that we get the sense of the real being of a person long since dead. For a second a voice rings in our ears, a raised hand flashes before our eyes, but even so it is only as a memory, not as a thing heard with the waking ear, or seen with the living eye. A series of portraits, a maze of dancing movements, passes over the screen of our minds, and here and there a figure frees itself to send out a glance of anger or a smile of invitation. It is like friends remembered after decades of oblivion, when even the tones of speech are forgotten, the features blurred and melting, and the inflections or shades of modelling have to be invented to fill in the blanks. But there are emotions, events in common, things done or endured, to link us with our friends: our sensations are grouped around one especial period. This is not so with the figures of the past; chance nodes gather to themselves the more vivid pictures: we do not see one, we see two or three or four persons, who, against all likelihood, bear the same name, and are gathered together in one coffin under one belettered tombstone.

Who, then, is Sarah Churchill, Duchess of Marlborough? What sort of person do we conjure up when we hear her name mentioned? To give a word to the qualities she always wore is not enough; it does not do to say termagant, strong-willed, grasping, or to find all her life one warfare upon earth. At first there is the girl of dazzling beauty, with a cascade of golden hair, flitting through the Stuart court, laughing among the feathers and the finery, tapping the brilliant politicians with her fan while she plots light-heartedly for her husband's advancement. The next picture is different: she is middle-aged, though still wonderfully beautiful. One watches her sitting on a throne only a little lower than Queen Anne's, and one can hardly distinguish in whose hand the sceptre is grasped. There is a touch of petulance in her look, a slight frown on her forehead, and she is plotting with indomitable energy to retain the position won for her husband. Then the last long painful phase, a grey-haired woman with her energy turned to raging rancour, and still plotting—for what? against whom? feverishly putting in order her memoirs to prove that she had always been in the right, not seeming to notice that the tide of life had gone beyond her, and that it mattered a fig to nobody whether she had been right or wrong. These are the pictures we have come to accept. Which is the real person? Who is it we mean when we say 'the Duchess of Marlborough'?

There is, naturally, a puppet whose course we trace in histories and memoirs and letters, through a number of years whose complicated events we decide to have been this or that. But to weld this person into one coherence seems almost impossible. The first vision we perhaps admire and like; we wish we could have been in a room with her, have saluted her, have felt drawn into the whirl of her amazing vitality. Of the second we should stand in some awe, as we do of a dangerous animal, but there would be admiration and liking mingled with our fear: at least, we should say, here is an extraordinarily human being against whom to pit ourselves. And finally, there is an old woman hunched in her chair, or stumping about with a stick, raging at everybody, or counting up the endless list of the houses she owns. What can we give her but the insufferable, the patronizing, pity of posterity, which sees in this figure but another object-lesson of the vanity of human wishes, knowing of her, as we do not really know of ourselves, that she had to die? What was all the pother about? we ask. Merely another life, like countless other lives. She should have been as wise as we should be, had we been dead for nearly two hundred years.

Sarah Jennings was the third daughter of Mr. Jennings, of St. Albans in Hertfordshire, and was born on the 29th May,

1660, in a suburb of that town. Her father, one of the twenty-two children of Sir John Jennings (or Jenyns), owned the estate of Sandridge in the neighbourhood, could sway elections, was, by family tradition, a friend of the Stuarts, and enjoyed an income of some four thousand a year. Her mother, the daughter and heiress of Sir Gifford Thornhurst, came of a rather more distinguished and wealthy family. She seems to have been a woman of good sense and character, and was a fair example of the best type of English gentlewoman. Thus, though Mrs. Jennings does not seem to have cared much for court life, she felt she had to provide for her daughters (her two sons would absorb the estate), so she sent her eldest daughter, Frances, to be maid of honour to Anne Hyde, Duchess of York. *La Belle Jennings* rapidly became famous as a court beauty, and was assailed for favours from every quarter of a frolicsome court. But she scornfully repelled all advances, even those of the Duke, publicly scattering his unopened billets-doux, and behaving altogether with high-spirited independence. With such an elder sister to look after her, there could be no harm in sending little Sarah also to court; and there, before her twelfth birthday, she joined Frances. No doubt she liked the court of the Duchess, who prided herself upon collecting grace and beauty about her and who was a good and sensible friend to her maids; but in 1671, not long after Sarah had joined her, she died.

Then, at the end of 1673, Sarah Jennings had a new mistress in an exquisitely beautiful and happy child, hardly older than herself, so fated as soon to be known as 'the Queen of Tears', the unfortunate Princess of Modena, who at this period married the Duke of York. Sarah does not seem to have lived at this court from the beginning so much as often to have been there, rather as a playmate to the Lady Anne, the Duke's daughter by his first marriage, than as a maid of honour. For the Duke of York's daughters did not 'come to court' officially until 1674, when Crowne's *Calisto* was played, two added parts, not in the original of Ovid, being taken by Sarah, aged fourteen, and Anne, aged ten. Sarah was not as beautiful as her renowned sister, but she had more than her fair share of good looks, and a wonderful mass of golden hair. Above all she had a winning liveliness, a quick wit, and an amazing candour of speech. She always said what she thought, and never flattered anybody. She

2

was evidently something of an imp, a laughing romp of a pretty girl with much of the tom-boy about her, though she could at will be precociously dignified. She had nothing of the servility of the courtier—her looks were far too good for that; and brought up as an equal with the highest in the land, she acquired all that independence of thought and action which is the privilege of aristocrats in all walks of life. To be able not to care a jot for anybody is the only really enviable position, and Sarah, who had a will of her own, evidently enjoyed it very much. From the very first she seems to have been able to get her way, for when in 1676 her mother wished to remove her from the dangers of a dissolute court, fearing she might follow in the tracks of two other maids of honour whose condition was unmistakable, 'the young one complained to the Duchess that if her mother was not put out of St. James's, where she had her lodgings to sanctuary her from debt, she would run away'. The affair was smoothed over for a time; but a month later Sarah gained her first decisive victory: her mother was ordered 'to leave the court and her daughter in it'. The girl of sixteen had won.

But there was a very special reason why she wanted to stay at the Duchess's court, for attached to the Duke as Groom of the Bedchamber was a young officer, some ten years her senior, Colonel John Churchill. He was admittedly a most captivating person, with every courtly charm, whom Sarah had first noticed because he danced so well: it seemed to her that 'every step he took carried death with it'. He was invariably gentle and kindly, always sensible and straightforward, not one of those smart wits to talk with whom was a perpetual and wearisome competition in repartee. He had all the generosity of strength, but if he was simple and even homely, no man was ever pert with him. He was obviously beautiful to the eye, and notoriously brave, having already distinguished himself in battle. Nor was he altogether unknown in softer battlefields than those of Tangier and Flanders, though he was no rake. In any case, Sarah loved him. He on his side was equally attracted by her, and the correspondence between them began when he was twenty-five, and she was fifteen. The worst of it was that neither made for the other what parents and the world consider a 'good match'. Sarah was not yet heiress to the Sandridge estates, and did not seem likely to become so; Churchill had practically no money at all, and was a mere commoner without much importance, who would receive nothing from his father, Sir Winston Churchill. Sarah did not care; she wanted him. She refused brilliant offers, notably one from the Earl of Lindsay, afterwards Marquis of Ancaster. Churchill was equally determined; and it may as well be said here, that whatever slurs may be cast upon the characters of these two, however much they may be accused of coldness of heart, of venality, of continual calculation, their match was a pure love match, a romance which lasted till both were dead. There can be no doubt but that they were passionately devoted to one another all their lives. She, perhaps, was more fierce and possessive than is quite pleasant to over-cultured tastes; Lord Wolseley called hers a 'tiger-like affection'; and on the other side there can be no clearer proof of the depth of Churchill's nature than his lifelong solicitude for his wife, his readiness, his desire even, at any moment to abandon his career and live quietly with her. But she was too ambitious to allow that, ambitious for him; since it cannot justly be said that she aspired only for herself. Her pride in him after his death, when she had nothing more to gain, reaches almost fantastic heights.

But during their courtship he was not quite so definite as she was: under family pressure he vacillated. He was then a young man of twenty-six with his way to make; he suffered from headaches, and probably had a mortal dislike of family rows. Miss Jennings was only sixteen; who could tell how she would turn out? Love, as far as he could see, was no lasting thing. Why shatter a career for an ephemeral passion? It sounds cold, but he was obviously struggling desperately. It is no easy situation: the romantic movement had not begun, there was no worship of love for love's sake, and it was not until his last days that he liked to see *All for Love* performed. Like a great many young men, though very much moved, he rebelled against the slavery of love, while she would have no half-measures. If she could not have him completely, she would not have him at all. In fact, to begin with, she was more in love than he was. There is no need to say, as all biographers have hitherto done, that her behaviour was petulant and proud just because she was not sweetly submissive. She was very young, very green; her flame burned brightly and ardently, and she expected much, not having reached the disillusioned tolerance of middle age. We get a glimpse of one lovers' tiff, when Churchill had evidently tried to show his independence, and she writes:

At four o'clock I would see you, but that would hinder you from seeing the play, which I fear would be a great affliction to you, and increase the pain in your head, which would be out of anybody's power to ease until the next new play. Therefore, pray consider, and without compliment to me, send me word if you can come to me without any prejudice to your health.

He, on his side, used to write such letters as this:

If your happiness can depend upon the esteem and love I have for you, you ought to be the happiest thing breathing, for I have never anybody loved to that height I do you. I love you so well that your happiness I prefer much above my own; and if you think meeting me is what you ought not to do, or that it will disquiet you, I promise you I will never press you more to do it. As I prefer your happiness above my own, so I hope you will sometimes think how well I love you; and what you can do without doing yourself an injury, I hope you will be so kind as to do it—I mean in letting me see that you wish me better than the rest of mankind; and in return I swear to you that I will never love anything but your dear self, which has made so sure a conquest of me that, had I the will, I had not the power ever to break my chains. Pray let me hear from you, and know if I shall be so happy as to see you to-night.

He had not the power to break his chains; but he tried to do so. Perhaps there were too many tiffs; like most men of action Colonel Churchill probably had a terror of scenes, hating to be nerve-wracked, and the family grew pressing. They prepared a marriage for him with the witty Catherine Sedley. He half fell in with their scheme, and the French ambassador, Courtin, wrote to Louis in November 1676, that at a ball given by the Duchess of York 'Sarah Jennings had a greater wish to cry than to dance. Churchill, who is her lover, says he is in consumption, and that he must have a change of air in France. I wish, notwithstanding, that I were as well as he is. The truth is, he wishes to get out of this love affair. His father wishes him to marry a relation, very rich and very ugly, and will not consent to his marriage to Mademoiselle Jennings. He is believed to be somewhat worldly himself.'

Sarah was deeply hurt. She begged him 'to renounce an attachment which militated against his worldly prospects'. She declared that she would herself go abroad, with her sister

Frances, now Countess of Hamilton. Again she wrote, evidently on his asking to be allowed to explain:

As for seeing you, I am resolved I never will in private nor in public if I could help it; and as for the last, I fear it will be some time before I can order so as to be out of your way of seeing me; but surely you must confess that you have been the falsest creature upon earth to me. I must own that I believe I shall suffer a great deal of trouble, but I will bear it, and give God thanks, though too late I see my error.

It was too much for him; he could not break his chains, but he could with Catherine Sedley (who consoled herself by becoming the mistress of James), though it took a great deal of passionately worded wooing before Sarah would forgive him. And for this she is called arrogant and a shrew! Was it not perfectly reasonable, and still perfectly loving, to tell him:

If it were sure that you have that passion for me which you say you have, you would find out some way to make yourself happy—it is in your power. Therefore press me no more to see you, since it is what I cannot in honour approve of, and if I have done too much, be so good as to consider who was the cause of it.

If she made him suffer for his lapse, was she not quite right? There is no space to go further into this question: the curious may see much of the correspondence in Wolseley's *Marlborough*. All goes to show that this was as sound a romantic love affair as ever there was; but it seemed practically hopeless. At last the kind-hearted young Duchess came to the rescue and provided funds; so the romance fittingly concluded with a secret marriage, probably early in 1678.

To the outside observer the next few years of Mrs. Churchill's life seem very ordinary and domestic, a routine of following her husband about from one place to another, except when prevented either by the nature of his mission—for he now began to be employed as a diplomatic agent—or by childbearing. She stayed with Sir Winston and Lady Churchill at Mintern, or at her mother's home at Sandridge, getting on as best she could on inadequate funds and imperfect sympathy. She did not live on the best of terms with her mother-in-law, but Sarah was not to blame; she did her best, as may be seen from her husband writing to her, in one of his charming love-letters:

I have received yours of the 10th, with a copy of the letter you writ my mother, which if she takes anything ill that is in that letter, you must attribute it to the peevishness of old age, for really I think there

is nothing in it that she ought to take ill. I take it very kindly that you
have writ to her again, for she is my mother, and hope at last she will
be sensible that she is to blame for being peevish.

Sarah had written to Lady Churchill asking her to be god-
mother to their first child, and had got no answer. The child
was Harriot, born at the end of 1679, who did not survive
infancy. Their next child, Henrietta, was born in July 1681;
Anne was born on the 12th of January, either 1683 or 1684;
Jack in January 1686. Another daughter, Betty, was given to
them in March 1687, Mary came in July 1689, and Charles in
August 1690. There seems also to have been another son born
to them, who died in infancy. Unfortunately, none of her letters
to her husband are preserved, as she gave him orders to burn
them, and he unluckily obeyed; but we have many of his,
breathing warm love, or full of a simple domestic bliss, and a
tremendous pleasure in playing with his children. She does not
appear to have been quite such a good correspondent as he was;
we see from some of his answers that he got well scolded if he
missed a post, while in other letters he overflows with gratitude
for the 'kindness' she expresses for him in some of her missives.
And we can see that, at any rate until 1683, they both constantly had thoughts of retiring from court life and settling
happily in the country. For they were so often separated; they
were always travelling to Holland or to Scotland, in the wake of
the exiled Duke. There seemed to be no peace, only a succession
of hazardous prospects.

Yet it is plain that these were the most important years in
the development of the future Duchess; they were her education,
for before that she had scarcely ever read a book, and had spent
her spare time at playing cards. The girl we have so far seen
probably took little interest in public affairs; but now her
husband's duties, and her care for his safety, forced her to
become politically minded. No one in their position could
afford to stand outside. It was becoming increasingly clear that
sooner or later everybody would have to make a definite choice
in the great politico-religious agitation that was shaking the
country. In the autumn of 1678 the nation was horrified,
alarmed, puzzled, by the Popish Plot, half invented, half
revealed, by the monstrously long wagging chin of Titus Oates.
There was, of course, a real Popish plot: the Duke of York

was determined to re-establish the Roman faith, and with its help govern despotically. The country was racked and rent by the brilliant intrigues of Shaftesbury, and the ambitious charm of the Duke of Monmouth, while the royal brothers were playing a double game with Louis XIV. This is not the place to discuss the extraordinarily involved and fascinating politics of the period: in the words of Archdeacon Coxe, 'We must refer the reader to the histories of the times, for an account of the religious and party feuds which agitated the parliament and nation for the remaining part of the reign of Charles.' Nevertheless there are some facts that we may notice.

The first result of the Popish Plot was to banish the Duke of York at once to Holland, and then to Scotland, in connection with which some important points emerge for us. One is that Churchill, though absolutely loyal to James, working always in his best interests, doing his utmost to moderate his sadistic rages in Scotland, made it perfectly clear to William that he would never abandon the Protestant faith, or be party to the predominance of the rival sect in England. However, throughout these times, probably on his wife's advice, he kept as far as possible out of all party strife, and on one occasion refused the offer of a seat in Parliament. There was too much intemperance in these days of Test Acts, Exclusion Bills and Rye House Plots, apart from the scandals, treacheries and executions, to tempt a careful man. The prudence practised in these years must have been of inestimable value as a training for that perilous tight-rope dancing no person of note could avoid performing immediately after the Revolution. Another point to notice is that when Sarah Churchill accompanied her husband to Holland, she in some way aroused the antagonism of the Princess Mary, who wrote to her sister Anne, then with her father in the same country, in terms which, even though sometimes polite, admit of no real doubt as to her feelings towards Mrs. Churchill.

For Anne was already attached to her with whom she had so often played as a child, and it is at this point that the extraordinary friendship, without which there would have been no great Duchess Sarah, begins to be important. It is now time to look more closely at the Lady Anne, and try to appreciate the various circumstances, social and psychological, which made possible this amazing alliance.

On the face of it, there is every reason why Anne should have liked her elder playmate, and when they were rather older, elder companion. For Anne was a trifle lumpish, and admired Sarah's liveliness. She delighted in plentiful and amusing talk, which Sarah could pour out abundantly. Above all, she wanted to be ruled, to be commanded, to be dominated: in her friendship there was more than a little of dog-like confidence: that was what she liked to feel, and if Sarah had not a will, nobody had. Moreover, the maid of honour was charming and beautiful, the sort of person one would like to have about one.

But besides these things there was something in the atmosphere in which Anne had been brought up which would develop to intensity the sentimental attachment a young girl normally has for some rather older leader. Female society was more separated from male than it has since become, and it is as though some of the girls had to play the male part in these friendships. They would give each other men's names, often taken from the male parts they had acted in theatricals. The most extreme, the most extravagant instance, is that of Anne's elder sister Mary, who fixed for support on Frances Apsley, who shortly after her royal friend's marriage became Lady Bathurst. A little before her wedding with William, Mary wrote to Miss Apsley in this strain:

I have sat up this night a great deal longer than I used, only to tell my dear dear dear dearest dear husband what she has heard so often that I am afraid she will be weary of hearing it, but still I can't choose but tell you that I am more and more in love with you every time I see you, and love you so well that I cannot express it no way but by saying I am your louse in bosom and would be very glad to be always so near you, near upon any condition.

Your affectionate friend,
MARY CLORINE

It would be absurd to scent perversity in this; it is merely a girl's natural sentimentality swollen by circumstance. Once Mary had a strong and dominating husband these expressions grew tamer. It is possible that had Anne found a husband with character, instead of a pumpkin whom Charles II tried sober and tried drunk without finding anything in him, Sarah would never have come to rule her as she did. Yet she deliberately chose Sarah, abandoning in her favour another friend, who was, no doubt, not strong enough for her.

Thus it is that the year 1683 became a crucial one in the life of Mrs. Churchill, for Anne, when she married Prince George of Denmark, begged her father to let her have her friend as one of her bedchamber women, though it is probable that her uncle, Lord Rochester, opposed the suggestion, as he hated the Churchills. However, the application was successful, and the elated Princess wrote to Sarah:

The Duke has just come in as you were gone, and made no difficulties, but has promised me that I shall have you, which I assure you is a great joy to me: I should say a great deal for your kindness in offering it, but I am not good at compliments.

It looks as though Sarah had proposed the arrangement, not necessarily from a desire to rise, but because the extra two hundred pounds a year would come in very handy with her growing family. But there can be no doubt that from this point Sarah began to be ambitious, and the idea of plain Colonel and Mrs. Churchill retiring to rustic bowers faded into the distance. To add to the incitements of fame, already at the end of 1682 Churchill had been made a Scotch peer, being given the Barony of Aymouth. Yet it is curious to watch the growth of ambition in these two women, neither of whom appears to have cared much for greatness to begin with, but who seem to have egged each other on. As yet, of course, anything more than idle hopes of power would have been mere striving after wind, since Anne's chances of succeeding were small.

At all events the friendship grew so fast and firm, Anne apparently found so little pleasure in the companionship of her husband (in which she conformed to universal opinion), that she insisted on her real domestic life being with Sarah, who was by far the best-looking and most amusing of all her ladies. Dull Anne still wanted to be entertained, and still liked those about her to be gay. No doubt Sarah liked her in return, for Anne was agreeable, a little too placid, perhaps, but she had a nice face and figure, with an extremely pleasant voice, and beautiful hands which she made the most of. Besides, she was so friendly. First of all she begged Sarah not to 'Your Highness' her at every moment: it was chilling; it made intimacy impossible. Then she suggested dropping all titles, and of this transaction we have Sarah's own account:

'A friend was what she [the princess] most coveted: and for the sake of friendship (a relation which she did not disdain to have with me) she was fond even of that *equality* which she thought belonged to it. She grew uneasy to be treated by me with the form and ceremony due to her rank; nor could she bear from me the sound of words which implied in them distance and superiority. It was this turn of mind, which made her one day propose to me, that whenever I should happen to be absent from her, we might in all our letters write ourselves by feigned names, such as would import nothing of distinction of rank between us. Morley and Freeman were the names her fancy hit upon; and she left me to chuse by which of them I would be called. My frank, open temper naturally led me to pitch upon Freeman, and so the princess took the other; and from this time Mrs. Morley and Mrs. Freeman began to converse as equals, made so by affection and friendship.'

Such an arrangement made it all the easier for Sarah to carry out her principles, for 'Young as I was,' she said later, 'when I first became this high favourite, I laid it down as a maxim, that flattery was falsehood to my trust, and ingratitude to my dearest friend.'

By this time the Duke of York was again living in London, Anne was at the Cockpit in Whitehall, so the Churchills were not separated. Lord Churchill was now beginning to become richer; he was making a reputation as a business man, and could afford to build himself a fine house at Holywell, the suburb of St. Albans where his wife had been born; and whatever the public services of both husband and wife may have been, there was at this period a very pretty background of domestic happiness. When in 1685 the Duke of York came to the throne as James II, he created Churchill Baron Churchill of Sandridge, in the County of Hertfordshire, Sarah, her brothers being dead, having succeeded to some of the family estates. When, shortly afterwards, Lady Clarendon went with her husband to Ireland, resigning the post of first lady of Princess Anne's bedchamber, the Princess promoted Lady Churchill to the office, 'with a satisfaction that was not to be concealed'. No doubt it was a happy change, for Lady Clarendon, according to her successor, 'looked like a mad woman, and talked like a scholar'.

'During her father's reign, [the Princess] kept her court as private as she could, consistent with her station.' Throughout that troubled period she held firm to the Protestant faith, resisting her father's insidious attempts to convert her: for though he twice paid her debts, she did not read the subversive books he carelessly left about her rooms. George of Denmark also remained loyal to his creed, thus easing the mind of the public, which had had a strong suspicion that he had been purposely chosen by the royal brothers for Anne's husband because he was such a fool that it would be child's play to convert him to anything.

Churchill was employed as ambassador to Paris, and in various other missions, and remained always loyal to James, even when, though made a brigadier-general, he was superseded by a foreigner, Lord Feversham, in the command of the troops sent against Monmouth. He was so loyal that he even tried to reason with James. But as the reign went on, it grew ever more plain that the King was doomed; the gods had decreed his destruction, and were rapidly sending him mad. The Bloody Assize must have disgusted Churchill, who was always humane; and things went from bad to worse at court and in council, for it was by now clear to every eye that James was becoming more and more priestridden, and was undoubtedly plotting against that State religion, which alone seemed to guarantee the freedom of the individual. Churchill could not follow him there. 'If', he had said, at the beginning of the reign, 'the King should attempt to change our religion I will instantly quit his service.' He and his wife must have had many conversations as to what their attitude would be if, or rather when, a revolution should come, and really one cannot see that there was anything dishonourable in what he did on that occasion. He should, perhaps, have declared himself a day or two earlier, and not have accepted a high command in the King's troops against William; but such a position is very delicate: at best he would only have been sent to the Tower, and perhaps he still hoped against hope that something would turn up to save the situation.

But there can be no doubt that the Princess Anne's attitude must have been, if not decided, at least strengthened, by the counsels of her chief lady and most intimate friend, and it is at this period that we see her ambition beginning to sprout, and we guess that Lady Churchill's also took firm root at this point. For it now began to look likely that Anne might after all some day succeed to the throne. The king had no son, and William and Mary were apparently going to be childless. Anne, in fact, began to see herself as queen; nothing else can account for her behaviour when the Prince of Wales was born. She attached herself violently to the party which claimed this birth was all a fake, that the babe had been smuggled in in a warming-pan, and she exulted when she thought the infant was going to die. We can definitely say that it was during the reign of James II that Sarah Churchill embarked on her strenuous and glorious career.

Whatever decision Mrs. Morley and the Freemans had come to, they had to put it into execution when William landed in November 1688. Churchill and Prince George of Denmark accompanied James to Salisbury, where we are given the picture of a gloomy, nerve-wracking meal, when the news came in of one defection after another. Whenever this occurred, the Prince to cover his uneasiness, ingenuously remarked *Est-il possible?* That night he also went. When James heard the news, he simply asked, 'Is *Est-il possible* gone too?' It did not matter; but Churchill's departure did. James began to make his way sadly back to London.

The event put the Princess Anne in a queer position, one of those where the ways divide, and the finger-posts impartially point 'To a good conscience' up either road. On the one hand was her loyalty to her husband, on the other her duty to her father. But now that from a hated step-mother she had a half-brother (officially so, whatever she might privately think), her chances of succession were even smaller than if her sister were to become queen. And then, she was a staunch Protestant. She sent for Mrs. Freeman to ask what she was to do. Mrs. Freeman was desolated, we suppose; it was a nice point. But seeing that Prince George had sided with William, could Mrs. Morley face her injured father? No, Anne declared, she certainly could not; 'she would rather jump out of the window'. But what was she to do? She could not walk out of the front door and rush over to William on her husband's heels. Mrs. Freeman, however, had no fear of the back stairs, a set of which had luckily been made only six weeks before. She was a practical woman, and had no doubts whatever as to what was to be done. Knowing where the

Bishop of London had his secret apartments, she was prepared to make all arrangements, and went over to him to get a coach, which she knew he would be ready to lend, as he had been one of those who had invited William over. The household apparently went to bed as usual, but after midnight Lady Churchill gently led the Princess down the stairs into the dark night, where Bishop Compton was waiting with the coach. All went well, save that the Princess lost a slipper in the mud. They lodged at the bishop's house that night, and the next morning moved on to Lord Dorset's place in Essex. At Copt Hall the Countess lent them coach and horses, supplied them with a generous larder, and packed them off to Northampton, with the good bishop as captain of the horse to protect them on the way. The Princess Anne was safe; and so was Lady Churchill, whose arrest had been ordered the day before.

The latter said in after years that it had all been done on the spur of the moment, because Anne had been in a great fluster at the news of her husband's defection; but as Anne had sent a letter to her sister a few days before, promising that Prince George of Denmark would go over to the invader, we are free to see a little more deliberate planning in the escape. At any rate, the adventure seems to have agreed very well with Lady Churchill, if we are to believe the account of Colley Cibber, who waited on the party when they moved on to Nottingham. 'So clear an emanation of beauty,' he wrote, 'such a commanding grace of aspect struck me into a regard that had something softer than the most profound respect in it.' During the whole entertainment his eyes 'wanted no better amusement than of stealing now and then the delight of gazing on the fair object near me'.

But the whole thing might yet turn out to be the most crazy adventure; the decision might have been wrong. One might think the world was safe for Protestantism, but from the very beginning there were set-backs. Churchill had moved at just the right moment; it might seem that he, and he alone, had been the deciding weight in the scale of the Revolution; but no sooner had James, at the second attempt, got safely across the Channel, than annoyances began to crop up. One thought one had William in one's pocket, but it soon became very clear that William was not at all the sort of person to be in anybody's pocket. He actually made terms with the people of England. Parliament was having a delightful time, debating whether James should be recalled, or Mary be made Queen with a Consort, or William be made Regent; they had invented the charming word 'abdicate'—the Whigs were so clever at coining phrases—when all at once William put his foot down, and said that if they did not make him king, he would simply go away and leave them to stew in their own juice. According to Lady Churchill, such behaviour very much surprised her simple mind. She had thought William would come over, and that once he had made them all happy, go home again. But she was soon 'taught to know the world better'. That brilliant, wise, but to many in his day, incomprehensible trimmer Halifax stepped in, and kingship was decided upon. If William was going to be so successfully high-handed, what chance would there be for the Princess Anne and her friends? Yet Lady Churchill wisely counselled Anne to agree; it would not look well to seem to grab at a crown wrested from her father; and if she did not consent with a good grace, she would have to accept with an ill. Dr. Tillotson was of the same opinion, and his services were enlisted to persuade the Princess. Mrs. Freeman showed admirable common sense, as well as a high sense of duty; in fact, she bowed to the inevitable, and it was absurd to suggest that she did so to curry favour with William and Mary.

All went well to begin with. William created Churchill Earl of Marlborough, and showered all sorts of honours upon him: he was sworn of the Privy Council, and made Gentleman of the Bedchamber. But there was no security in these things, and at the crucial moment Sarah made her real entry into politics, and showed herself amazingly clever. Her swift clear thought grasped that the Princess Anne must plainly be seen to stand apart from the usurpers. William was quickly becoming un-popular; he was dour and stand-offish, and preferred Dutchmen to Englishmen. And the less he was liked the more Anne would be welcomed if ever she came to the throne; she might even be offered the crown instead of her father, if William gave up in disgust, and returned to his dull Holland with his wife. On the other hand, if James came back, Anne, and her friends, would escape retribution. It may be easy enough to see now, it may have seemed childishly so a few months after the event, but

Lady Marlborough saw it from the very first, which is more, apparently, than her husband did.

For when she seized upon the beautifully simple means of carrying out her project, he did not stand at all hand in glove with her, and would have prevented her if he could. It appeared to him merely a silly feminine squabble based upon vanity, for the means the Countess hit upon was to make the royal sisters quarrel. It seemed to him just a sordid business, for his mind was of a larger mould, and he could not see the point of palace intrigues. The Princess Anne blandly demanded a preposterous pension. After all, Lady Marlborough suggested, was she not heir-presumptive, as it were Prince of Wales? Had she not stipulated for a princely allowance when she waived her right to the throne in favour of William should he outlive Mary? It was all perfectly plain sailing, and there must be no shilly-shallying about it; there ought to be a little court almost as brilliant as the great one, and surely there could be no difficulty. Had not the Queen said when she came over that she was extremely glad to see her sister? The scheme had the directness of genius. To Anne the matter seemed so obvious that she never even raised the issue with Mary, and was so tactful as never to be left alone with her in case the subject might crop up. But the Queen was hurt, and finally William forbade her to mention the matter to her sister. He told Shrewsbury to offer fifty thousand a year, and the payment of all debts. Shrewsbury carried the notion to Marlborough, who conveyed it, but begged that his part in it should not be made known to his wife, 'who would by no means hear of it, but was like a mad woman'. In the end the affair was settled by Parliament; but the Countess had inserted the wedge.

She drove it home in the summer of the next year, for when Anne became partially reconciled to her sister, Lady Marlborough neatly countered by suggesting to Anne that she should seize the opportunity to ask for another twenty thousand a year; and though Mary guessed in whose mind the scheme had been hatched, it did not help to make family relations cordial.

Marlborough was apparently blind to the value of all this, and was at this later phase in Ireland, where the King had left him to finish off the war after the battle of the Boyne. But he soon did see the point with a vengeance. For not only was the

King disliked, the Revolution also was beginning to be unpopular. People were forming a habit of drinking to the King
over the Water; they would go through curious antics of
squeezing oranges, and invented several strange toasts. To be
a hero of the Revolution might have its disadvantages: thus
like many another of his day Marlborough tried to be in with
Paul as well as with Peter, and took to corresponding with the
exile. Lady Marlborough, of course, saw that Mrs. Morley and
the Freemans must stick together, and in due course Anne also
wrote to her father. But the essence of these things is that they
should not be found out, and unfortunately William did find out.

He did not act at once; there were too many people doing the
same thing as his Gentleman of the Bedchamber. Yet he had
many causes to be dissatisfied with Marlborough, who, on his
side, had grievances enough in seeing foreigners continually
preferred to him in military posts. Mary did her best to detach
Lady Marlborough from Anne, and justifiably, for it was
notorious that at the smaller court William was constantly
referred to as 'the monster', or 'Caliban', or 'the Dutch
Abortion'. At last the situation grew intolerable. On the 18th
of January 1692, Marlborough was dismissed 'from all his
charges, military and other', Evelyn wrote on the 24th, 'for his
excessive taking of bribes, covetousness and extortion on all
occasions from his inferior officers'. Evelyn, of course, was
hostile and guessing; hardly anybody knew the real reason,
which was that Marlborough was going to move in the House
of Lords that all foreigners be dismissed the King and Queen's
service, a notion unbearable to William, and a setting by the
ears of English and Dutch which would please Louis above all
things. The news came to the ears of Portland, who told the
King. The public, however, those who did not agree with
Evelyn, were inclined to think that it was on account of a bitter
quarrel, a 'painful explanation' as Macaulay describes it,
between the Queen and her sister, which had taken place the
evening before, over the allowance of a thousand a year Anne
was making Lady Marlborough. It all fitted in very well for
the Countess, who knew that that was not the real reason. It
was a blow, but she could make capital out of it. Her lord
might lose the King's confidence, she would show the public
that she still had the Princess Anne's; she would also show the

Queen. Thus when the princess went to court at the beginning of February, she brazenly went with her.

The Queen was very properly furious. She wrote to her sister:

Never was anybody suffered to live at court in my Lord Marlborough's circumstances. I need not repeat the cause he has given the King to do what he has done, nor his unwillingness at all times to proceed to such extremities. . . . It is very unfit Lady Marlborough should stay with you, since that gives her husband so just a pretence of being where he ought not. I have all the reason imaginable to look upon your bringing her as the strangest thing that ever was done. . . .

She concluded the letter:

. . . it shall never be my fault if we do not live kindly together. Nor will I ever be otherwise than your truly loving and affectionate sister   M. R.

Anne wrote back a soft answer, in which, nevertheless, she pointed out that seeing her delicate state she ought to be allowed to keep her friend. Mary snubbed her by sending a message through the Lord Chamberlain to forbid the Countess to stay any longer at the Cockpit. But Anne was spirited; she insisted upon being mistress in her own house: if Sarah could not come to the Cockpit, she herself would leave it, and go somewhere where Sarah could come; and she forthwith borrowed Sion Hall from the Duchess of Somerset. Yet, still conciliatory, she went to visit the Queen, but the latter 'was as insensible as a statue'.

So the matter went on through the spring, until a worse blow fell. William, leaving Mary in charge, had gone abroad to conduct a campaign in which Marlborough would have joined but for his disgrace. At the end of April it was found out that Louis XIV was preparing an invasion of England, a secret which had been kept by hundreds of Jacobites at home. Mary at once countermanded the sailing of several regiments, and laid an embargo upon shipping. There was something like a panic in the country, and prices rose. Then a man named Young, a sort of imitation Titus Oates, an insolvent who hoped to get rich by telling tales, laid information against several peers, among whom was Marlborough, who, charged with high treason, was sent to the Tower on the 4th May. Sarah was struck to the heart, and hurried to London; and here we may

3

with probability date a scrap she wrote to her husband, a rare
and precious document:

> Wherever you are, whilst I have my soul, I shall follow you, my
> ever dear Lord Marlborough; and wherever I am, I shall only kill the
> time [until] night that I may sleep, and hope the next day to hear
> from you.

She was, without doubt, very anxious indeed as to the issue;
it made her ill; she had to be bled, and Anne's letters to her are
full of solicitude for her health. In the circumstances such a one
as the following cannot be described as fulsome, the word that
Horace Walpole later applied to her epistles:

> But let them do what they please, nothing shall ever vex me, so I
> can have the satisfaction of seeing dear Mrs. Freeman; and I swear I
> would live on bread and water between four walls with her, without
> repining; for as long as you continue kind, nothing can ever be a real
> mortification to your faithful Mrs. Morley, who wishes she may never
> enjoy a moment's happiness in this world or the next, if she ever proves
> false to you.

Luckily the evidence of Young broke down; he was whipped
and pilloried, and Marlborough was freed under the Habeas
Corpus Act, though not before the family sorrows had been
added to by the death of their son Charles.

William, however, maintained his anger against Marlborough, which he showed by not releasing him from his
recognizances for bail; and the Earl, now deprived of nearly all
his sources of income, lived mainly at Berkeley House, where
Anne dwelt as a private person. The Princess wanted to invent
a post for him at a salary of a thousand a year, but Sarah begged
her not to.

Mary, all the while, was bringing pressure on her sister to
dismiss her Lady of the Bedchamber. Anne was shorn of all
royal honours; her guard was taken away; the court was forbidden to visit her. The Queen behaved in a way that was down-
right rude, sending maids of honour to visit the Duke of
Gloucester, the hope of the Stuarts, with instructions to ignore
the presence of his mother. More than once Lady Marlborough
offered to leave the Princess so as to heal the breach between
the two sisters—a breach the Jacobites hailed with delight—
but Anne, to her credit, would not budge. Time and again she
wrote in this strain:

The last time he was here [speaking of the Bishop of Worcester, who acted as go-between for the sisters], I told him you had several times desired you might go from me, and I have repeated the same thing again to him. For you may easily imagine, I would not neglect doing you right upon all occasions. But I beg it again for Christ Jesus' sake, that you would never name it any more to me. For be assured, if you should ever do so cruel a thing as to leave me, from that moment I shall never enjoy one quiet hour. And should you do it without asking my consent (which if I ever give you may I never see the face of heaven), I will shut myself up, and never see the world more, but live where I may be forgotten by human kind.

In fact, whenever Lady Marlborough suggested it, the usually lethargic Princess fell into a passion of weeping.

The next two years were of very great difficulty and delicacy for the Marlboroughs. The Earl had a few friends at court, but no party in his favour, since he never was in any sense a party man. William knew he was a conspirator, but to proceed against him alone would have been invidious. In 1693 the position of the usurping King was terribly insecure: he could really trust only his Dutch favourites, through whom those who were jealous of their power or position, as Marlborough justly was, struck at the King's tenderest nerve. Portland, moreover, disliked Marlborough, maybe through motives of jealousy. So Marlborough plotted, but prudently, non-committally, and in powerful company. His wife, no doubt, was privy to his schemes, and perhaps held him back from dangerous moves; for Marlborough still had the relics of a loyal feeling for James, and had every cause to be angry against William. Sarah was always more Whiggish than her husband; she did not want James back again —she was looking forward to the time when Mrs. Morley should be Queen. The situation might be strained, but all the while Anne was earning popular sympathy, and more people were looking upon Marlborough, not only as an injured man, but as one who might save the country by gaining the military successes which William, with all his pedantic tactical lore, was incapable of wresting from the French.

Still, it was a risky game, and luckily, at the end of 1694, Queen Mary died. On the advice of the Marlboroughs, the Princess made overtures to William, which were accepted. She was installed at St. James's Palace, her guard and her royal honours were restored to her, and she was in short, accorded the position of heir-apparent to the throne. Sarah was once more a woman of importance in affairs. Her husband, however, was not for some time regarded as anything but a traitor in disgrace. But the new situation must have eased his mind; his policy now was so clearly unswerving fidelity to William, and though he still met Jacobite agents, they found him rather unsatisfactory, and could never get him to commit himself. Here, too, we can trace the mind of Sarah. And little by little, William, though against the grain, relented, and Marlborough was restored to high place and comparative affluence. In 1698 he was appointed governor to the Duke of Gloucester (heir to the throne after his mother), re-admitted to the Privy Council, and made a Chief Justice to rule in William's absence.

In the next years Marlborough did all he could to remove every cause of complaint against him; yet he was loyal to Anne as against William in a quarrel that arose in December 1699 over some money claimed by Prince George of Denmark. It was the Marlborough influence that established this claim, and for a time William was once more hostile to the Earl. But the cloud soon passed, and when in the summer of 1700 the Duke of Gloucester died, William wrote to his late governor, 'Je vous assure qu'en cette occasion et en toute autre je serés très aise de vous donner des marques de mon amitié.'

One thing at least Marlborough at this stage had in common with William, especially after the death of James in 1701—a determination to ensure a Protestant throne for England. The Marlboroughs induced Anne to agree to the Act of Settlement, and William, at the moment of re-organizing the Grand Alliance and embarking on the War of Spanish Succession, chose the Earl as the bearer of his political flag. The King knew that he could not live long; somebody must carry out his life work. Thus, in 1701, in spite of some opposition, he appointed Marlborough commander-in-chief of the armies in Flanders, and Minister Plenipotentiary to the States General.

It was a Churchill triumph: when William should die, an event which could not be long delayed in spite of his middle years, Sarah would be virtually Queen of England, Marlborough the reigning king. This was felt so strongly both in England and France, that at home a plot was set on foot by the Marlborough enemies to pass over Anne in the succession, and give the crown at once to the Elector of Hanover; while abroad it was suggested that the Pretender should marry one of Marlborough's daughters. It was a magnificent position, and the honour of gaining it must belong equally to husband and wife.

This is not the place to enter into the intrigues of faction, nor William's arrangements at this juncture; we must return to Sarah. During William's reign she had been steadily making her position solid; she ruled Anne altogether, ruled her almost brutally, but not at this stage without affection. She never tried to disguise her emotions, her dislike, or her fury; she carried to uncomfortable lengths the doctrine of never flattering: with those whom she held, the Princess, Godolphin, and her husband, she felt secure. Over secure: it led to her ruin, for at this time things were made too easy for her. Her sense of power waxed so great that she came to forget that she was working in material that might rebel; her sense of her own strength grew to a state of megalomania. If she wanted a thing done, it was enough, it would be done; so that when at a later date the mere wish was not enough to ensure the doing, she flew into ungovernable rages. So far no harm was observable, but there is no doubt that at this time began to germinate the seeds of that species of madness which in the end brought about her husband's downfall with her own, and seriously endangered the destinies of the country. The mere flow of time was to change a virtue into a fatal vice.

In 1698, she married her daughter Henrietta to Godolphin's eldest son, a lad of twenty. Godolphin was a boyhood friend of Marlborough's, and was a great friend of his wife's, though Mrs. Manley's scurrilous suggestion, repeated by Swift, that he was too fond of Sarah, and that Marlborough played the complaisant husband for the sake of political support, is too ludicrous to be entertained. Whatever Sarah may have been, she was honest in every sense of the word, and Marlborough was far too deeply in love with his wife to tolerate such a relationship. Godolphin had already occupied the post of Lord Treasurer, corresponding to our Prime Minister, but he was only in when the Tories were in. He was, indeed, much too Tory for Sarah's taste, but where practical things were concerned, he always put country before party.

In 1699, Lady Anne Churchill was married to Charles

Spencer, the Earl of Sunderland's eldest son. He was still mourning for a first wife, but Anne was very lovely, his father much desired the match, and the young man was soon captivated by Anne's sweetness of temper. His principles were rigid and honourable, though something too advanced and republican for even the most Whig of Whigs. But in any case, both marriages were important 'alliances', props to the Marlborough position.

Lady Marlborough, though eager enough for money, never abused her situation to make it. When she first came to court, she sold two places, which she had a perfect right to do, 'yet it was not long', she wrote afterwards, 'before I began to condemn in my own mind this practice'. And she adds: 'Had I been disposed to heap up money by the sale of employments, I should certainly not have neglected to sell those which, by virtue of my office, were in my own disposal. I might have done it with the greatest ease; and custom had given me a sort of right to do it: but I could never think of selling my own favour, any more than that of my royal mistress.' She did, of course, do what she could for her family. There was, for instance, a cousin of hers, a certain Abigail Hill, of whose existence she had not been aware until she found her working almost as a servant. She took her into her own nursery, and when a vacancy occurred in the Princess Anne's bedchamber, she successfully begged the post for her. Abigail seemed to have no ambition; she was ungainly, red-nosed, and vulgar in her manners; she could certainly be no rival, but she might very well act as a substitute for the Countess in her many absences. Sarah could not guess that in performing this act of kindness—as well as providing for the rest of the Hill family—she was preparing her own doom. Herself generous-minded, and very proud, how could she see that this dull mediocrity, deep in her debt, should, or could, repay her with ingratitude and injury?

And how could Marlborough guess that when he pressed for Robert Harley, a not too distant cousin of Abigail's, to be made Speaker in 1701, he was performing a parallel act? His was the kind of greatness that always trusted the men to whom he rendered a service. But it is a curious thing to consider, that when William died on March the 8th, 1702, leaving the Marlboroughs in possession of the Queen, with every prospect of the Earl being at last able to use his military and diplomatic genius to the full, and bring such glory to his country as it had never had before, each of them had firmly established the lesser mortals who were to eat into their stronghold, and be the instrument, not only of their downfall, but also, nearly, of their country's humiliation. That, however, is a melodramatic, not a moral reflection.

The Great Drama

It may sound monstrous to say it, yet it is largely the fact, that the history of Europe for the next few years is the tale of the relations between Lady Marlborough and Queen Anne. It was the energy of the former, her will to pursue a policy to the very end, that made the Whigs, the war party, all powerful; that thus upheld the Austrian side of the War of Spanish Succession, and would have broken Louis XIV. It was she that kept Marlborough in the Queen's service, in spite of his constant and often repeated wish to give up the struggle with stupidity abroad and malice at home. But if he asked for nothing better than to live quietly with the wife he adored, living quietly had now become impossible for Lady Marlborough. She laboured endlessly and terrifically with a vigour that was masculine, if the means she used were as purely feminine as the impulses which drove her. Her son-in-law, the Earl of Sunderland (for he had succeeded his father), may have been flattering her when he wrote in September 1705, 'I must say one thing in general upon all this, and that *very sincerely, and without the least compliment, that if England is saved, it is entirely owing to your good intentions, zeal, and pains you have taken for it*'; he may have been flattering, but he was not far from the truth.

If, then, in this part of the Duchess's life, we seem to treat of domestic scenes rather than of the great European struggle, it must all the while be borne in mind that Sarah's dominion over Anne, and the undermining of that dominion, is the key to the history historians deal with. We may see in little what was going forward on a tremendous scale over the map of Europe; we can measure the political barometer by reading the rise and fall of the mercury in a few rooms in Whitehall. This is made a point of here lest the smallness of the events recorded should blind us to their real weight; it is not offered as a comment on the queer or ludicrous workings of destiny.

Naturally, the moment Queen Anne came to the throne, the

Marlboroughs became rich and powerful. Marlborough, made a duke in 1703, rather against the wishes of his wife, who feared the extra expense, was appointed commander-in-chief; and Sarah became Mistress of the Stole, besides engrossing other offices, including, as soon as possible, that of Ranger of Windsor Park, which was granted her for life, and even to her heirs. Her daughters also had posts about the court, so much so that it was reckoned by a pamphleteer in 1704 that the Marlborough emoluments amounted to some £65,000 a year. The Duchess improved the position of the family by marrying her two remaining daughters: Elizabeth to the Earl of Bridgewater; and Mary, the loveliest of them all, to Viscount Mounthermer, son of the Earl, later Duke, of Montagu, an alliance which it was hoped would please both political parties, though it was repugnant to the Lady Mary. But before this last marriage, the Marlboroughs suffered the very heavy grief of losing their surviving son, the Marquis of Blandford, a promising and much-loved youth, who died of smallpox at Cambridge early in 1703. This was a severe blow; and as no further children were born to them, though at one time the Duke had hopes, at a later date the title was allowed to pass through the female line by special remainder. Such was the immediate family background of the Duchess of Marlborough for the first two or three years of Queen Anne's reign.

One would have thought, and no doubt Lady Marlborough thought, that Mrs. Morley on coming to the throne would be clay in Mrs. Freeman's hand. 'The intimate friendship, with which the Queen was known to honour me,' the Duchess wrote in her *Conduct*, 'afforded a plausible foundation for this opinion. And I believe, therefore, it will be a surprise to many, to be told, that the first important step which her Majesty took, after her accession to the government, was against my wishes and inclination: I mean, *her throwing herself and her affairs almost entirely into the hands of the tories.*'

The Queen, the Duchess goes on to explain, 'had from her infancy imbibed the most unconquerable prejudices against the whigs', whereas the Duchess's liking for them was equally strong. The Queen's feeling was very natural, for though the action of the Whigs had made her Queen, that very fact was a blow at the royal prerogative. What had been done once might be done again, and Anne might have to join her half-brother in exile. The Tories, on the other hand, believed like herself in the inviolable nature of kingship; like herself they were Jacobites at heart. The Whigs had supported her sister and William against her; the Tories had helped her in the affair of her settlement. The Whigs were, moreover, to her mind, little better than atheists; the Tories were at one with her in supporting the Church. Further, the Earl of Rochester, her uncle, the highest of high Tories, had always had an influence over her, an influence he was only to lose after behaving to the Queen a little too cavalierly.

Nevertheless, the Government contained both Marlborough and Godolphin, the latter Lord Treasurer, since both were by tradition Tories. Both, however, were ready to belong to whatever party would further what they believed to be the right policy, particularly the foreign policy laid down by William. The Duchess, then, an ardent Whig, made still more fiery, perhaps, by chats with Lord Sunderland, had a triple task to perform. She had to prove to her husband, to Godolphin, and hardest of all to the Queen, that their interests lay with the Whig party. The Duchess herself had no doubts: she had reached the stage where she never had any, where she was the most fully conscious of her power, where she saw everything quite plainly, and grew madly impatient of those of her friends who could not see things as simply as she did. It is during these years that she is most herself.

She was now a very remarkable women, both in looks and in character. Lovely as her daughters were, she could still vie with them in beauty; she could still be the life and soul of a ball or assembly; was still ready to be diverted, and able to amuse very much. In character she was striking, not for any qualities women do not often possess, but because she pushed the normal to heights that were above the normal. It was not any kink of brain, but sheer super-abundance of life that made her what she was. What had once been frankness she strained to rudeness; what had been a refreshing tomboyishness grew to a termagant fury; what had been an ordinary wish to lead among her friends became a passion for domination. Perhaps something of her violence at this period may be accounted for by her being at the change of life, but even so the unquenchable spleen of her rages has too much extravagance to be so easily explained. No one was safe from her, not the Queen, not Godolphin, not her husband. On one occasion, when quarrelling with the last, in a fierce, uncontrollable temper she shore off the still beautiful and luxuriant hair which she knew he adored. On coming back to the room, after a dramatic exit, she could not find the locks, and never saw them again until she came upon them on going through her husband's papers at his death. She wept then, and used to weep on telling the story, in which there is something wonderfully true of both: it illustrates her burning need to own all that she loved, as well as his deeper affection which was content with her as she was, and asked for no change or betterment. But, however wild she may appear at this period, one cannot but admire the stubborn perseverance with which she pursued her end—the triumph of Whig policy as it was directed during the first ten years of the century.

For the moment Godolphin and her husband might wait; they were at most only half-hearted Tories, and the mere force of events was dragging them the way she wished them to go. The main attack must be upon the Queen, especially upon her absurd notion that whenever things were leaning towards the Whigs, 'I shall think the Church beginning to be in danger', an idea to which she clung with a pitiful persistence, and that Stuart obstinacy which she began to develop in middle age. For however soft she may have been in her early days, now she was by no means that malleable stuff Mrs. Freeman had been used to work in. She loved the Tories, and she loved the Church; to those she would stick like a limpet to a rock.

'For my own part,' the Duchess wrote, 'I had not the same prepossessions. The *word* Church had never any charm for *me*, in the mouths of those who made the most noise with it; for I could not perceive that they gave any other distinguishing proof of their regard for the *thing*, than a frequent use of the *word*, like a spell to enchant weak minds; and a persecuting zeal against dissenters. . . .' The Tories, or the Church party, as the Queen preferred to call them, worked upon the sovereign's weakness, safe in the fact that she 'could not alter her opinion'. They twice tried to bring in the Occasional Conformity Bill, which would have kept most of the Whigs out of office; it was passed twice by the House of Commons by an overwhelming majority, only to be thrown out by the Lords on each occasion, for though the Queen could scent no atom of persecution in it, the powerful oligarchy did.

Luckily Mrs. Morley gave Mrs. Freeman full leave to speak out what she thought. 'You can never give me any greater proof of your friendship,' she wrote, 'than in telling me your mind freely in all things.' 'I did therefore', the Duchess remarks, 'speak very freely and very frequently to Her Majesty upon the subject of whig and tory, according to my conception of their different views and principles.' Fortune also favoured the Duchess, for the Tories became too violent, and disgusted the moderates of their own party by trying to tack the obnoxious measure on to a money Bill. The Earl of Rochester, who thought he could order his niece about, refused to go to Ireland, of which he was Lord Lieutenant, and was dismissed his post. The Church party, moreover, disgusted Godolphin and Marlborough by their cold attitude towards the war, and the Duchess entertainingly wrote of it all: 'The church in the meanwhile, it must be confessed, was in a deplorable condition. The earls of Rochester, Jersey and Nottingham, and Sir Edward Seymour out of place, and the whigs coming into favour. It was resolved therefore the next sessions of parliament, to tack the occasional conformity bill to the money bill, a resolution which showed the spirit of the party in its true light. But it happened that my lord Marlborough, in the summer before parliament met, gained the battle of Blenheim. This was an unfortunate accident, and by the visible dissatisfaction of some people on the news of it, one would have imagined that instead of beating the French, he had beat the church.' Parliament took its revenge for the victory, and irritated the Queen by 'ridiculously' pairing its thanks to Marlborough with those for Sir George Rooke's drawn battle with the French at sea.

This was rather too much for the Queen, who was a patriot, and who shared the delight her people so amply showed in the victory when Marlborough had his triumph later in the year. She induced Parliament to grant the Manor of Woodstock to the Duke, and arranged for the building of the palace of Blenheim, which was to take up so many years of Vanbrugh's life, and prove such a source of worry to the Duchess.

The Marlboroughs were really up now, as was fully realized

by the Grub-street hack-writers, who at this time began that paper war of which the Marlboroughs were never free until their deaths. One of them wrote in 1704:

—I'll mount to *Honour's* Stage;
My easy *Minor* ne'er shall be *of Age*.
Her *Crown* shall be the *Foot-stool* to my *Name*,
Her *Scepter* but my *Hobby-horse* to *Fame*. . . .
Nor shall she dare, at my *directing Nod*,
To *own* her *Kindred, Friends*, her *Church*, or *God*.
And, while my *Hero* does her *Foes* subdue,
My *Moderation* shall her *Friends* pursue.
Thus I the *Height* of *Glory* will attain,
And *A——* shall *wear* the *Crown*, but *S——* *reign*.
Ch——l shall *rise*, on easy *St——t's Fall*,
And *Blenheim's Tow'r* shall *triumph* o'er *Whitehall*.

The Whigs, however, delighted with the ability and energy with which Godolphin and Marlborough were carrying on the Revolution policy, lost all suspicion of them, and took them into their fold, to which the Duchess gladly led them, and they as happily followed. Little by little important Tories were ousted from their posts: the Duke of Buckingham lost the Privy Seal, and Sir Nathan Wright the Great Seal; and more than all, the new Parliament of 1705 turned out to be Whig. The Queen too, seeing from Marlborough's letters to Godolphin how much he was harassed by factious opposition, exhorted the parties to lay aside their differences, urging that they could best save the Church by vigorously waging war abroad, and making the country safe against invasion.

To complete the Duchess's victory, the Tories then made a fatal error. Pretending that the Protestant succession was in danger, they brought forward a motion in the House of Lords, in which, after insulting Marlborough, they suggested inviting to England the Electress Sophia, heir presumptive to the crown. Nothing could have been better calculated to rile the Queen, who, as she said on a similar occasion, three years later, could not 'bear to have a successor here, though but for a week'. She could not, that is, bear to have a Hanoverian successor, and be reminded that by being where she was she was ruining her family. She went to hear the debate, where insult was added to injury, for not only did Lord Haversham unfeelingly wound her by a reference to the Duke of Gloucester, but the Duke

of Buckingham, with great disrespect, blurted out that Anne
'might live till she did not know what she did, and be like a
child in the hands of others'. This was a mere side-stroke at the
Marlboroughs, the object of the Bill being to discredit the
Whigs, who it was thought must support the motion, though
in fact they stoutly opposed it. The result was exactly the
reverse of what the Tories wanted, and Mrs. Morley wrote:

> . . . I believe dear Mrs. Freeman and I shall not disagree as we have
> formerly done; for I am sensible of the services those people have done
> me that you have a good opinion of, and will countenance them, and
> am thoroughly convinced of the malice and insolence of *them*, that you
> have always been speaking against.

The final triumph was when, in the next year (1706), Lord
Sunderland replaced Sir Charles Hedges as one of the two
Secretaries of State, to the Duchess's jubilation, though rather
against the judgment of Godolphin and Marlborough, who
thought him too republican, and of the Whig party generally,
who, though they did not think him the 'properest man for the
post', 'imagined it was driving the nail that would go'. The
Duchess of Marlborough had won all along the line: she was
at the dizziest heights of her power.

But from that time there began more obviously to operate
those causes, mainly personal, which were in some five years to
bring the Duchess of Marlborough to her fall. It seems from
Swift, who would have been well informed on this point, that
the rift between the Queen and the Duchess began to appear
from the moment Anne mounted the throne, a split, that is, not
in mere opinion, but in affection. It is easy to understand why
the Queen, who 'loved fawning and adoration', began to dislike
Mrs. Freeman: she was altogether too domineering, and could
never learn to wheedle; she treated all human beings as her
tools, and moreover, she was not a good enough reader of
character to see that if she was to continue to control Anne,
she must be with her always, and not here or there looking after
her husband or her children, or politically engaged. Lord
Wolseley has made this point admirably, when speaking of the
rise of Abigail Hill: 'Daily intercourse with the Princess was
essential to the maintenance of her favourite's influence, and
Sarah might have foreseen that Anne would soon come to lean
upon the subservient woman who lived constantly in her

society, and who would slowly but surely acquire a mastery over Anne's dull and narrow mind.'

The Duchess's dislike was more complicated. Firstly, there was the almost maniacal impatience she felt against any thing or person resistant to her will; but probably much more important was the purely physical dislike she began to feel for her erstwhile playmate. Horace Walpole reported that she used to turn her head away when offering the Queen her fan or her gloves, 'as if the Queen had offensive smells'. It is more than likely, as Sarah with her radiant health and vitality must have begun to find repulsive the person of the Queen, which was becoming ungainly and gouty and gross. This nausea overcame her even before Anne's accession, as is shown by the terrible story of the gloves, here taken from Wolseley, and stated by him as an event which took place shortly after the Duke of Gloucester's death. 'The Princess Anne, having forgotten her gloves, told Abigail to fetch them from the next room, where she remembered having left them on the table. In the next room Abigail found Lady Marlborough seated at the table engaged in reading a letter, and wearing the gloves, which she had evidently put on by mistake. Abigail, in a submissive tone, pointed this out to her. "Ah!" exclaimed Sarah, "have I put on anything that has touched the odious hands of that dis-agreeable woman?" Then, pulling them off, she threw them on the floor, exclaiming with violence, "Take them away!" The door was ajar between the two rooms, and Anne heard every word. Abigail perceived this when she shut the door and handed the gloves to her mistress, but Lady Marlborough never knew that Anne had overheard her.'

To the impartial historian, Anne's faithfulness in friendship is remarkable. Indeed, as Macaulay said, 'The fondness of the Princess for Lady Marlborough was such as, in a superstitious age, would have been ascribed to some talisman or potion.' For years after this she professed, and from her princely gifts as well as from her letters she must have felt, a deep affection and respect for Sarah; in fact, her constancy is touching. 'Her friendships', the Duchess was to write, 'were flames of extravagant passion, ending in indifference or aversion'; but this is not fair, for if her passion in friendship was too exalted, the flame was not quickly burned out, as is implied, but was wonderfully constant. Her

attachment to Sarah lasted some twenty-seven years, and at the
very end, when all was over, she gave her her full due as a
loyal and honest servant. If failure in friendship is heinous, it is
Sarah and not Anne who is to blame; but constancy is not a
question of virtue, it is a matter of luck.

The tone of the letters passing between the friends does more
than anything else can to illuminate their changing relations.
Already in 1702 we find Mrs. Morley daring to differ from her
friend:

And upon my word, my dear Mrs. Freeman, you are mightily
mistaken in your notion of a true whig. . . . I can say no more to my
dear dear Mrs. Freeman, but that I am most passionately hers.

December, 1703. Nothing shall ever alter your poor, unfortunate,
faithful Morley, who will live and die with all truth and tenderness,
yours. . . .

November 17th, 1704. . . . your poor, unfortunate, faithful Morley,
who doth not at all doubt of your truth and sincerity to her, and hopes
her not agreeing in every thing you say, will not be imputed to want of
value, esteem, or tender kindness for my dear dear Mrs. Freeman, it
being impossible for any one to be more sincerely another's, than I
am yours.

Something, we see, was beginning to happen; the Duchess
scented some falling off, in spite of such violent protestations.
She suggested to the Queen that perhaps Mrs. Freeman's
letters were becoming a nuisance, and was answered on

November 21st. I am very sorry, you should forbear writing upon
the apprehension of your letters being troublesome, *since you know
very well they are not, nor ever can be so,* but the contrary to your poor,
unfortunate, faithful Morley.

There is something in Swift's statement that 'There was not,
perhaps, in all England, a person who understood more
artificially to disguise her passions than the late Queen.'

The Duchess, however, went on being very liberal with her
comments, although she felt her hold weakening. A couple of
years later she found it expedient to begin a letter:

October 20th, 1706. I must, in the first place, beg leave to remind you
of the name of Mrs. Morley and your faithful Freeman, because
without that help I shall not be well able to bring out what I have to
say, it is so awkward to write any thing of this kind in the style of an
address, tho' none, I am sure, ever came from a purer heart, nor that
can be the tenth part so serviceable to you, if you please, because they

are generally meant for compliment, which people in Mrs. Morley's post never want, though very often it turns to their own prejudice. What I have to say is of another nature; I will tell you the greatest truths in the world, which seldom succeeds with any body so well as flattery.

Having made Mrs. Morley thoroughly awake and uncomfortable, she proceeded to her political business, and recalled, parenthetically, 'every thing to my memory, that may fill my heart with all that passion and tenderness I once had for Mrs. Morley', just to show, one supposes, that two can play at the game of cooling off. Going on to speak of ill advice, she pursued:

> Though 'tis likely nobody has even spoke thoroughly to you ever upon those just misfortunes, I fear there is reason to apprehend there is nothing of this in the case of Mrs. Morley, since she has never been able to answer any argument, or to say any thing that has the least colour of reason in it, and yet will not be advised by those that have given the greatest demonstrations imaginable of being in her interest. I can remember a time when she was willing to take advice, and loved those that spoke freely to her, and that is not five years ago; and is it possible, that when you seriously reflect, that you believe you can do the business upon your hands without it? Can flatteries in so short a time have such power? or can you think it is safer to take it from those you have little or no experience of, than from those who have raised your glory higher than was ever expected? And let people talk what they please of luck, I am persuaded whoever governs with the best sense, will be the most fortunate princes.

Mrs. Morley was still docile, but she did not like being called an idiot, and with a flash of pride she answered:

> *October 30th.* If I have not answered all my dear Mrs. Freeman's letters (as indeed I should have done) I beg she would not impute it to anything but the apprehensions I was in of saying, what might add to the ill impressions she has of me. For though I believe we are both of the same opinion in the main, I have the misfortune that I cannot agree exactly in everything, and therefore what I say is not thought to have the least colour of reason in it, which makes me really not care to enter into particulars; but though I am unwilling to do it, it is impossible for me to help giving you some answer to your last letter, in which I find you think me insensible of everything. . . .
>
> But whatever becomes of me, I shall always preserve a most sincere and tender passion for my dear Mrs. Freeman to my last moment.

Towards the end of 1706 there was a distinct coldness, arising out of the struggles of the Queen not to have Lord Sunderland

4

imposed upon her as a Secretary of State. The Duchess wrote a long letter to the Queen, addressing her as Your Majesty throughout, very firmly and respectfully insisting upon her loyalty, but threatening the resignation of Lord Marlborough, Lord Godolphin, and herself. She ended significantly:

I beg Your Majesty's pardon for not waiting upon you, and I persuade myself that long as my letter is, it will be less troublesome to Your Majesty.

It was in the autumn of 1707 that the first heavy blow fell, when it was revealed to the Duchess how rickety her position had become, and who really was the royal favourite. Little by little, unheeded by her (though afterwards, putting two and two together, she saw how blind she had been), Abigail Hill had been strengthening her hold upon Anne, aided by her cousin Harley, the Tory, whom she admitted up the back stairs to many a secret conference with Her Majesty. It had been the Duchess's own fault Harley had become her enemy: he had done everything he could to ingratiate himself with her, but she could not bear the man. She always thought him a sneaking fellow, who carried the evidence of his treachery in his face, and as she never did nor could disguise her feelings, he continually felt himself snubbed, and with Abigail's help threw himself into intrigue. The Duchess was already aware that Mrs. Hill had some influence, but the way she came to discover how deeply her position was sapped, can best be told in her own words:

'The first thing which led me into inquiries about her conduct was, the being told (in the summer of 1707) that my cousin Hill was privately married to Mr. Masham. I went to her and asked her if it were true; she owned it was, and begged my pardon for having concealed it from me. As much reason as I had to take ill this reserve in her behaviour, I was willing to impute it to bashfulness and want of breeding, rather than to anything worse. I embraced her with my usual tenderness, and very heartily wished her joy; and then, turning the discourse, entered into her concerns in as friendly a manner as possible, contriving how to accommodate her with lodgings, by removing her sister into some of my own. I then inquired of her very kindly, whether the Queen knew of her marriage; and very innocently offered my service, if she needed it, to make that matter easy. She had by this time learnt the art of dissimulation pretty well, and answered with an air of unconcernedness that the *bedchamber women had already acquainted the* Queen *with it*, hoping by this answer to divert any farther examination into the matter. But I went presently to the Queen and asked her, *why she had not been so kind as to tell me of my cousin's marriage*, expostulating with her upon the point, and putting her in mind of what she used often to say to me out of Montaigne, *that it was no breach of promise of secrecy to tell such a friend any thing, because it was no more than telling it to one's self*. All the answer I could obtain from Her Majesty was this, *I have a hundred times bid* Masham *tell it to you, and she would not*.

'The conduct both of the Queen and of Mrs. Masham convinced me that there was some mystery in the affair, and thereupon I set myself to inquire as particularly as I could into it. And in less than a week's time I discovered, *that my cousin was become an absolute favourite; that the* Queen *herself was present at her marriage in* Dr. Arbuthnot's *lodgings*, at which time Her Majesty had called for a round sum out of the privy purse; *that Mrs.* Masham *came often to the* Queen, *when the* Prince *was asleep, and was generally two hours every day in private with her*. And I likewise then discovered beyond all dispute Mr. Harley's *correspondence and interest at court by means of this woman*.

'I was struck with astonishment at such an instance of ingratitude, and should not have *believed*, if there had been any room left for *doubting*.'

The Duchess again complained to the Queen that Abigail had kept such an important event in her life secret from her, but the Queen answered with one phrase. It was her 'usual way on any occasion, when she was predetermined, to repeat over and over some principal words she had resolved to use, and to stick firmly to them. She continued therefore to say, *it was very natural, and she was very much in the right*.' The Duchess then protested to Abigail of the alienation of the Queen's affection, to which the new favourite insolently replied, that '*she was sure the* Queen, *who had loved me extremely, would always be very kind to me*'. Had loved her! Would always be very kind to her! It was unbearable. A few days later the Duchess went to see the Queen,

who was obviously very uneasy, and as cold as ice. The Duchess
wrote to her respectfully:

December 27th, 1707. If Mrs. Morley will be so just as to reflect
and examine impartially her last reception of Mrs. Freeman, how very
different from what it has been formerly, when you were glad to see
her come in, and sorry when she went away; certainly you can't
wonder at her reproaches, upon an embrace that seemed to have no
satisfaction in it, but that of getting rid of her, in order to enjoy the
conversation of one, that has the good fortune to please you much
better, though I am sure no body did ever endeavour it with more
sincerity than Mrs. Freeman has done. And if I had considered only
my interest and that of my family, I might have borne this change
without any complaint. For I believe Mrs. Morley would be sincere
in doing us any good. But I have once been honoured with an open,
kind confidence and trust, and that made all my service agreeable;
and it is not possible to lose it without a mortification too great to be
passed with silence, being sure I have never done any thing to forfeit
it, having never betrayed nor abused that confidence by giving you a
false representation of any body. My temper is naturally plain and
sincere, and Mrs. Morley did like it for many years. It is not in the
least altered. But I can't help thinking those things reasonable that
appear to be so. And I appeal to God Almighty, that I never designed
or purposed any thing, but as I was thoroughly convinced it was for
Mrs. Morley's true interest and honour. And, I think, I may safely put
it to that trial, if any thing has yet proved unsuccessful, that was of
any public consequence, that Mrs. Freeman has been earnest to
persuade Mrs. Morley to. And it is not possible for me to dissemble
so as to appear what I am not.

She wound up by asking for the establishment of some footing
upon which they could meet. Either Marlborough or Godolphin
carried the letter, which after a few days was answered in a
softening manner, and Lady Marlborough appeared at court
with what ease she could. The matter, however, soon became
public, and a Whig pamphleteer balladed it thus:

> Wheneas Q—— A—— of great renown
>   Great Britain's sceptre swayed,
> Besides the Church, she dearly loved
>   A dirty Chamber-maid.

For the quarrel was not a merely personal one.

Its political importance may be judged from the fact that the
Queen and Harley now thought the time had come to break the
Freeman-Montgomery (Godolphin) clique. Marlborough and
Godolphin, alive to the situation, and knowing the value of

attack, announced they could no longer serve with Harley. The Queen did not care. She called a Council meeting for February the 9th, 1708, at which she was present, but her old friends were not. The meeting was gloomy and sullen. Harley tried to open proceedings with some matters relating to foreign affairs. There was an uneasy silence. Finally, the Duke of Somerset, referring to Harley as 'that fellow', remarked that it seemed futile to discuss anything if the Lord Treasurer and the Commander-in-Chief were not there. Anne, baffled and furious, had to break up the meeting, and two days later to dismiss Harley. St. John, who was now coming to the fore, went with him. It was again a Marlborough victory, but there was no glory about it.

It was clear to the Duchess, that though Harley had been dismissed, it had been at his own request, and that his influence and Mrs. Masham's would be as great as ever. She therefore asked to be allowed to resign her posts; but the Queen refused to let her do so, as long as Marlborough remained in her service. The Duchess then stipulated that if she should ever be allowed to go, her children should step into her posts. The Queen promised, verbally, but Sarah got her word in writing. Hardly had she put the document safe under lock and key, than she once more resigned, and once more was told to stay.

The whole Masham transaction seemed to the Duchess a betrayal; she felt bitterly that the Queen had been ungrateful, not only for all she had done for her, but also for the great victories Marlborough had won abroad. The outside world was of a different opinion, and addressing her many years afterwards, the author of *The Other Side of the Question* wrote that most believed 'That the Queen was a captive, and you her Gaoler: that she was neither Mistress of her Power, nor free to express her own Inclinations. That she was so far overawed by a length of Oppression, as to dread the very Approach of her Tormentress. That she was forced to unbosom herself by stealth; and that she durst not venture upon a Contest with your Grace, even to set herself free from your Insupportable Tyranny.—A situation so terrible, that no private Person would for any Consideration submit to it; and consequently, what a Sovereign might justly endeavour, at almost any Rate, to be delivered from!'

One can imagine how lacerated the Duchess's nerves must have been at this time. It seemed as though all the work of years was to be wasted, all the labour and constant care for, and guidance of, a great party to go for nothing. Would she now be able to keep abroad the husband whose sole desire now appeared to be to hurry on the building of Blenheim, so that he might live there in comfort with her? His wish was all the more remarkable, since she had never spared him her tantrums, as we can see from a letter he wrote to her as early as 1704, when they had evidently parted in disagreement:

Your letter of the 15th came to me but this minute. . . . I would not for anything in my power it had been lost; for it is so very kind, that I would in return lose a thousand lives, if I had them, to make you happy. Before I sat down to write this letter, I took yours that you wrote at Harwich out of my strong box, and have burnt it; but, if you will give me leave, it will be a great pleasure to me to have it in my power to read this dear, dear letter often, and that it may be found in my strong box when I am dead. I do this minute love you better than I ever did in my life before. This letter of yours has made me so happy, that I do from my soul wish we could retire, and not be blamed.

Now he was always writing in this strain, only more and more strongly. Wearied, he hankered after a quiet domestic life. But she could not allow him this until his great work was done. Godolphin was staunch, though something too timid; but the war, which seemed to drag on for ever, was becoming unpopular: the Tory forces were massing, and the acrid pen of Swift was beginning to make itself felt against the side he was deserting. It was becoming clear that, strain as they might, gain what victories they could, it was only a question of time for the Whig power to be overthrown.

The Duchess still continued to see the Queen sometimes, and often to write to her; and whatever the form of address might be, the tone was one of perfect equality: it was even said that when she went to see her, her accusing voice would rise so high, that the footman at the bottom of the stairs could hear what was being said in the room above. Sometimes the letters grew more friendly, but there was never the same intimacy, and the Queen went so far as to refer to the Duchess's *commands*. Anne still trusted Marlborough, but she grew less and less able to tolerate her ancient playmate. One imagines that she stuck to her as

long as she did from that inability profound sentimentalists
have to break a tie that has existed for a long time: it seems
terrible to people of Anne's nature that anything which has
been so real should ever crumble. But the Duchess was no
longer conciliatory or kind; she tried to force everything with
a high hand, with virulence and bluster, and continual accusation.
Never having tried to control her feelings, she could not do so
now. She was furious at the Queen's attitude, and complained
to her husband, who wrote to Her Majesty about it. Anne
answered (1709):

> You seem to be dissatisfied with my behaviour to the Duchess of
> Marlborough. I do not love complaining, but it is impossible to help
> saying on this occasion, I believe nobody was ever used by a friend as
> I have been by her ever since I came to the Crown. I desire nothing
> but that she would leave off teasing and tormenting me, and behave
> herself with the decency she ought, both to her friend and Queen, and
> this I hope you will make her do.

But he was powerless. As he used ruefully to confess, when the
Duchess was in a taking, there was nothing to do but wait until
the gale had blown itself out. In any case, Sarah herself was
quite aware of the position, for in October the Queen wrote
to her:

> It is impossible for you to recover my former kindness, but I shall
> know how to behave myself to you as the Duke of Marlborough's
> wife, and as my Groom of the Stole.

The climax came in 1710. Anne, to try her strength,
proposed to Marlborough that 'honest Jack Hill', Abigail's
brother, should be given the command of a regiment, a post
made vacant by the death of the Earl of Essex. It put Marlborough in a very difficult position, for the appointment would
be a scandal; but then, if he refused to make it, he would be
accused of being the Queen's enemy, and one determined to give
posts only to his friends. However, he stood firm, pointing out
how unjust the proposal was to senior officers who had seen
service. Anne coldly told him that he might be well advised to
consult his friends. It was almost a threat, and he absented
himself from a Council meeting. Yet the Duke's absence did not
have the same effect as it had had in 1708. There was no
awkwardness, and business went on as usual. Thus the Hill
affair seemed to the Duke, and rightly, to portend more than it

showed on the surface. Mrs. Masham, he decided, must go; the Queen must be told to dismiss her, and if she did not do so, the Captain-General would resign. He saw clearly that if Mrs. Masham stayed, the great, the ponderous, the now motley Whig organization, would crash to the ground. But Somers and Godolphin, the one moderate, the other afraid, persuaded him to accept a compromise. Abigail stayed, but Anne on her side was forced to give way over the command of the regiment, which she did grudgingly. However much she wanted to hurt Sarah, she could not yet afford to rid herself of the Duke.

The Sacheverell trial, however, came to her rescue. Sacheverell, a Tory parson, preached in terms which he should not have allowed himself, on the doctrine of non-resistance. He raised the cry, 'the Church in danger', and offensively referred to Godolphin as Volpone, the last nickname that excellent man deserved, though he had borne it for the last five years. At first Anne was huffed, then she saw that this might turn to her advantage, for the Whig oligarchy, against Marlborough's advice, and in the face of the strong tumultuary opinion of a public sick of the war and sick of the Whigs, decided to prosecute. The Queen was made more determined than ever to make the most of her chance, since while the trial was pending, a few hotheads intrigued to move in Parliament that Abigail Masham should be dismissed the Queen's service. It was an outrageous and unconstitutional plot, and naturally came to nothing; but it shows both how the Whigs were reduced to counsels of despair, and how important they considered it for Sarah to retain her mastery over the Queen. This was not to be, though Sarah made one desperate attempt, after the Sacheverell trial had, amid the most intense social and popular excitement, virtually turned out in the Queen's favour, the Whigs only daring to impose a nominal sentence.

'I learnt that the Queen was made to believe, that I often spoke of her in company disrespectfully. As I knew myself wholly free from the guilt of this charge, and indeed incapable of it, I waited on Her Majesty the 3rd of April, 1710, and begged of her that she would be pleased to give me a private hour, because I had something which I was very desirous of saying to Her Majesty, before I went out of town. I named three several hours, in which I knew the Queen used to be alone, but she refused them all, in a very unusual and surprizing manner: and at last she herself appointed 6 o'clock the next day, the hour for prayers, when she could least of all expect to be at leisure for any particular conversation. But even this small favour, though promised, was not thought advisable to be granted by her new counsellors. For, that night, she wrote a letter to me, in which she desired me *to lay before her in writing whatever I had to say, and to gratify myself in going into the country as soon as I could.* I took the first opportunity of waiting upon the Queen again, and used all the arguments I could to obtain a private hour, alleging that when her Majesty should hear what I had to say, she would herself perceive it impossible to put things of that nature into writing; that I was now going out of town for a great while, and perhaps should never have occasion to give her a like trouble as long as I lived. The Queen refused it several times in a manner hard to be described, but at last appointed the next day after dinner. Yet upon farther consideration it was thought advisable to break this appointment: for, the next morning, she wrote to me to let me know *that she should dine at Kensington, and that she once more desired me to put my thoughts into writing.*

'To this I wrote an answer, begging that Her Majesty would give me leave to follow her to Kensington; and, that she might not apprehend a greater trouble than she would receive, I assured Her Majesty, that what I had to say, would not create any dispute or uneasiness (it relating only to the clearing myself from some things which, I had heard, had very wrongfully been laid to my charge), and could have no consequence, either in obliging Her Majesty to answer, or to see me oftener than would be easy to her; adding, that if that afternoon were not convenient, I would come every day and wait till Her Majesty would please to allow me to speak to her. Upon the sixth of April I followed this letter to Kensington, and by that means prevented the Queen's writing again to me, as she was preparing to do. The page who went in to acquaint the Queen, that I was come to wait upon her, stayed longer than usual; long enough, it is to be supposed, to give time to deliberate whether the favour of admission should be granted, and to settle the measures of behaviour if I were admitted. But at last he came out, and told me I might go in. As I was entering the Queen

said, she was just going to write to me. And, when I began to
speak, she interrupted me four or five times with these repeated
words, *"whatever you have to say, you may put it in writing"*.
I said, Her Majesty never did so hard a thing to any, as to
refuse to hear them speak, and assured her that I was not going
to trouble her upon the subject which I knew to be so ungrateful
to her, but that I could not possibly rest, till I had cleared myself
from some particular calumnies with which I had been loaded.
I then went on to speak (though the Queen turned away
her face from me) and to represent my hard case; that there
were those about Her Majesty, who had made her believe that
I had said things of her, which I was no more capable of saying
than of killing my own children; that I seldom named Her
Majesty in company, and never without respect, and the like.
The Queen said, *without doubt there were many lies told*. I then
begged, in order to make this trouble the shorter, and my own
innocence the plainer, that I might know the particulars of
which I had been accused. Because, if I were guilty, that would
quickly appear; and if I were innocent, this method only would
clear me. The Queen replied, that *she would give me no answer*,
laying hold on a word in my letter, that what I had to say in
my own vindication *would have no consequence in obliging* Her
Majesty *to answer*, etc, which surely did not at all imply that I
did not desire to know the particular things laid to my charge,
without which it was impossible for me to clear myself. This
I assured Her Majesty was all I desired, and that *I did not ask
the names of the authors or relators of those calumnies*, saying all
that I could think reasonable, to enforce my just request. But
the Queen repeated again and again the words she had used,
without ever receding. And it is probable that this conversation
had never been consented to, but that Her Majesty had been
carefully provided with those words, as a shield to defend her
against every reason I could offer. I protested to Her Majesty
that I had no design, in giving her this trouble, to solicit the
return of her favour, but that my sole view was to clear myself;
which was too just a design to be wholly disappointed by Her
Majesty. Upon this, the Queen offered to go out of the room,
I following her, and begging leave to clear myself; and the
Queen repeating over and over again, *you desired no answer, and
shall have none*. When she came to the door, I fell into great

disorder; streams of tears flow'd down against my will, and prevented my speaking for some time. At length I recovered myself, and appealed to the Queen, in the vehemence of my concern, whether I might not still have been happy in Her Majesty's favour, if I could have contradicted or dissembled my real opinion of men, or things? whether I had ever, during our long friendship, told her one lie, or play'd the hypocrite once? whether I had offended in any thing, unless in a very zealous pressing upon her, that which I thought necessary for her service and security? I then said I was informed by a very reasonable and credible person that things were laid to my charge, of which I was wholly uncapable; that this person knew that such stories were perpetually told to Her Majesty to incense her, and had beg'd of me to come and vindicate myself; that the same person had thought me of late guilty of some omissions towards Her Majesty, being entirely ignorant how uneasy to her my frequent attendance must be, after what had happened between us. I explained some things which I had heard Her Majesty had taken amiss of me, and then with a fresh flood of tears, and a concern sufficient to move compassion, even where all love was absent, I begged to know what other particulars she had heard of me, that I might not be denied all power of justifying myself. But still the only return was, *you desired no answer, and you shall have none.* I then begged to know if Her Majesty would tell me some other time? *You desired no answer, and you shall have none.* I then appealed to Her Majesty again, if she did not herself know that I had often despised interest in comparison of serving her faithfully and doing right? And whether she did not know me to be of a temper uncapable of disowning any thing which I knew to be true? *You desired no answer, and you shall have none.* This usage was so severe, and these words, so often repeated, were so shocking (being an utter denial of common justice to one who had been a most faithful servant, and now asked nothing more) that I could not conquer myself, but said the most disrespectful thing I ever spoke to the Queen in my life, and yet, what such an occasion and such circumstances might well excuse, if not justify. And that was, that *I was confident* Her Majesty *would suffer for such an instance of inhumanity!* The Queen answered, *that will be to myself.* [She meant that that would be her own affair.] Thus ended this remarkable conversation, the last I ever had with Her Majesty. I shall make no comment upon it. The Queen always meant well, how much soever she might be blinded or misguided.'

That was clearly the end for Mrs. Freeman, for though the Duchess still held her posts, she retired from the court, kept state at Holywell, and never saw Mrs. Morley again. Nevertheless, she wrote to her when, in June, the Queen, pursuing a policy already begun of replacing Whigs by Tories, was said to be going to dismiss Sunderland. It is an amazingly good letter,[1] written with all the freedom of an equal, yet with respect, imploring the Queen to look where she was going before giving herself over into the hands of the other party. It is true that at this time, she says, 'I used to send my Lord Godolphin my letters to the Queen, before I sent them to her, to see if he would add or alter anything in them, after she came into hands that made it necessary to be cautious', but this letter he thoroughly approved. 'I think the copy you have sent me is very just and true,' he told her, 'and may do a great deal of good to everybody.'

It did no good from Godolphin's point of view, for Anne, feeling her strength, was determined to free herself from what she had come to look upon as a galling tyranny, which indeed it was. Sunderland was dismissed on the 14th of June, to the great alarm of holders of funds. That was bad enough; Marlborough felt he was tottering, and declared he would retire into private life as soon as the campaign was over. But worse was to come. Without any warning whatever, Anne sent a note to Godolphin, saying that to save him the humiliation of returning his staff of office, he might break it. He protested, but to no purpose; and in justifiable rage, for he had served the State honestly and well, he smashed it to bits, and threw the pieces in the grate. That was the end for the Whig party. Harley and St. John, or rather Harley and Mrs. Masham, were triumphant, and the old servants dismissed by one who had once written:

I will never forsake your dear self, dear Mr. Freeman, nor Mr. Montgomery, but be always your constant and faithful friend; and we must never part until death mows us down with his impartial hand.

[1] It is too long to quote, and too good to spoil by giving mere extracts. It may be found in *Private Correspondence*, I, 339.

Mrs. Freeman was also, of course, dismissed, though not at once; the Queen did not proceed to this step until she was quite sure either that the Duke would not resign, or that the country could get along without him. But during the autumn of 1710, it became clear to the Duke at least (through the agency of Shrewsbury, a cunning, powerful double-dealer, who had been made Lord Chamberlain without any of the Ministry being consulted), that the Queen would get rid of the Duchess as soon as possible. The latter hoped to force a reconciliation, but this was plainly beyond all question, and the Duke wrote to her:

> I am still of the opinion that the only good you can do is to be quiet, by which you will give them no handle to use you ill before my return.

So Lady Marlborough remained what she called quiet, that is, she did not actually go to worry the Queen. Instead she wrote her innumerable and interminable letters, long narratives of their past history together, tremendous screeds accompanied by papers and documents and heart-rending extracts from Anne's own effusions, which must have made poor, unfortunate, faithful Morley scream with vexation. She even went so far as to threaten to publish the Queen's letters, in a full, and no doubt annotated, edition. But out of this horrid squabble there emerged one pleasant, generous remark, made by the Queen. At the end of November 1710, Swift, in one of his *Examiners*, drew up *A Bill of Roman Gratitude* (£994 11s. 10d.), compared with *A Bill of British Ingratitude* (£540,000), an attack, of course, upon Marlborough. At the end it was suggested that the Duchess had purloined £22,000 a year in the execution of her offices. Sarah drew up a vindication, which she had sent with a copy of the libel, to Anne, who read it, and remarked, '*Every one knows that cheating is not the Duchess of Marlborough's fault.*'

The way the Duke was treated on his return was shameful. Parliament had already insulted him by not voting him the usual thanks; he could feel the Grand Alliance melting away from under his feet. If Sarah were dismissed, he would have to resign, but the matter could not be allowed to remain in suspense: he was ill; anxiety was killing him. On the 17th of January 1711, at what seemed a propitious moment, he carried Anne a humble letter from Sarah, which implored, for the Dukes'

sake, that all might be made right. For a long time the Queen
would not open the letter, and when in the end she read it, she
merely said, 'I cannot change my resolution.' For something
like an hour the Duke pleaded, but was at last told that the
Queen must have the gold key of Sarah's office within three
days. At this Marlborough threw himself on his knees. Let
them at least have ten days, so as to concert measures to soften
the blow. But whatever he said, Anne, in her maddening way,
reiterated that she must have the keys, reducing the time to two
days. When the Duke told his wife the outcome, and he still
stuck to his resolve to resign, rather than have it seem that his
resignation was due to her dismissal, she overrode his objec-
tions, and insisted on his taking the key back that evening. It
was a dignified action. Marlborough, in handing back the key,
once more asked for an explanation, but only obtained an
answer faltering and confused.

A little while afterwards Sarah sent in a statement of her
accounts, and added to them a request that a £2,000 a year she
had refused on her appointment to the post of Mistress of the
Stole might now be made up to her. Anne granted the request,
and passed the accounts without comment, though her friends
had kept them a fortnight in the hopes of finding a flaw. Indeed,
the Duchess had certainly done well as a servant, and saved the
Crown many thousands of pounds. Her daughters did not succeed
to her places. She still, however, kept the Rangership of
Windsor Park, since it had been granted her for life.

Marlborough did not resign after all. Whig and Tory alike
importuned him to stop on; he felt he could not fail Eugene,
nor the pensionary Heinsius. In the last resort he was loyal to
the Grand Alliance, and was great enough to pocket his personal
pride. Proceedings in Parliament at this date showed him that
in remaining he was only sacrificing himself, for whatever he
might do would be undermined by the secret correspondence
carried on between the new Ministry and the old enemy France.
There is no need to follow here the difficulties and glories of his
last campaign, nor the troubles consequent upon the death of
the Emperor, the factions at home, and the schisms within both
the Whig and Tory parties, nor the manoeuvres that led to the
Treaty of Utrecht. For a moment, in 1711 it seemed as though
the Whigs might once again prevail; but Mrs. Masham was too

strong. On the 31st of December, the Queen being present, the following entry was made in the books of the Council:

Being informed that an information against the Duke of Marlborough was laid before the House of Commons, by the commissioners of the public accounts, Her Majesty thought fit to dismiss him from all his employments, that the matter might undergo impartial investigation.

And the next day, in order disgracefully to carry out a separate peace by making certain of a majority in the Upper House, patents were issued for calling twelve new peers to that Chamber, one of the names being that of Mrs. Masham's husband. It was too late for the Whig pamphleteers to write:

> From a dozen of P[eers] made all at a start,
> To save H[arley] from Scaffold, and S. [John] from Cart
> *Libera nos domine.*

There is little more to be told of the great scene. Since her dismissal the Duchess had done her best to fight the social battle bravely, and now lived at Marlborough House, which had been built for her by Wren, and of which the site had been granted her some years before by the Queen. She let it be known that she would entertain brilliantly that season, and the dismissal of the Duke made no difference. But it was too late. Peter Wentworth, writing to his brother, says he agrees with a countryman who remarked of her lavish entertainment at St. Albans, that 'it was very noble and fine, and if she had lived so two or three years ago it might have signified something, but now it would signify nothing'. She worked her hardest, under pressure from the Duke, to get Blenheim finished, now constantly quarrelling with Vanbrugh, who wanted to construct a noble memorial and a great work of art, whereas all that John and Sarah now craved for was a place to lay their weary heads. There had already been so many lets and hindrances; what with Godolphin having been chary with funds in the early days, then there being trouble with material and hold-ups with the workmen, and of course trials with Vanbrugh, whose design she had never liked, preferring Wren's. The last year, also, there had been a check on account of money, the Queen refusing to sign Harley's (Lord Oxford's) demand for more credit (the original estimate had already been doubly exceeded), because of some sordid fishwives' squabble over the fittings, the brass door-knobs, in the rooms in St. James's the Duchess had been asked to vacate. And on June the 1st, 1712, the Queen gave orders for the work at Blenheim to be stopped.

It would seem that this was the time for the ageing couple to withdraw, and live quietly together, but it was now a grim world, full of calumny, derision, and low Grub Street attacks, such as *A Grand Enquiry* or *What's to be Done with Him*; they always cut the Duke to the quick. It was a world in which the Marlboroughs could wield no more power. When the preliminaries of the Treaty of Utrecht were made public, they believed they saw all their labours of ten years or more undone before their very eyes. Opposition was hopeless, one could but watch the betrayal of one's friends, and, while negotiations were in progress, the defeat of one's troops, which had never before suffered defeat. Then, in the summer, their best and oldest friend, Godolphin, died at their house near St. Albans, the Duchess recording the death in her bible as that of 'the best man that ever lived'. Harassed and weary, open to incessant attacks in both Houses, the Duke decided to go abroad, to live perhaps in peace in that Empire of which he was a Prince. He sailed from Dover at the end of November.

Nor was England any longer a place for his wife, especially as some of her old Whig friends were upbraiding her for having ruined their cause by her tyrannizing temper. As though the Whigs did not owe her all they had had! So the Duchess joined her husband early in the next year, after she had helped to settle the family affairs. She also had some things of her own to do. For one thing she wanted to get rid of a richly set miniature of the Queen. In Swift's words, 'she took off all the diamonds, and gave the picture to one Mrs. Higgins (an old intriguing woman, whom everybody knows), bidding her make the best of it she could'. The other important action she wished to carry out was to give away some mementos. Writing on the 9th of January 1713, Lord Berkeley of Stratton noted: 'The Duchess of Marlborough hath given great presents at her taking leave of her friends, several diamond rings and other jewels of great value, to Dr. Garth for one.' It is like a last valediction, as though the rings being given away were funeral ones, as though this voluntary exile might in itself be looked upon as the final act, and the Duke and Duchess of Marlborough be counted as dead.

III

The Long Epilogue

When, after certain advances had been made them, the Duke and Duchess of Marlborough came back to England, on the 1st of August 1714, they were met with a salvo of cannon, and the news that Queen Anne was dead. They meant to enter London privately, but they were formally received at the gates of the city, and were escorted to their house by two hundred gentlemen on horseback, numerous relations in coaches and six, besides a guard of City Volunteers, who fired a volley before leaving them. As they passed along, the people cried, 'Long live King George—long live the Duke of Marlborough!' It was something like old times. There was only a small flaw; the Duke had not been appointed one of the Regents to govern the country before the new King came over.

The Jacobite scare soon passed away, and the triumph of Whig policy was complete, even if it was the city rather than the politicians that had brought it about. The day after his arrival, the Duke was visited by foreign ministers, he was sworn of the Privy Council, and reappeared in the House of Lords. He then retired to Holywell, to get over his pique at not being one of the Regents, an omission for which the Hanoverian Minister came to apologize. While in seclusion the Duchess gave him advice. 'I begged the Duke of Marlborough upon my knees,' she recounted afterwards, 'that he would never accept any employment. I said, everybody that liked the Revolution and the security of the law, had a great esteem for him, that he had a greater fortune than he wanted, and that a man who had had such success, with such an estate, would be of more use to any court than they could be to him; that I would live civilly with them, if they were so to me, but would never put it into the power of any king to use me ill. He was entirely of this opinion, and determined to quit all, and serve them only when he could act honestly, and do his country service at the same time.'

5

Now was the moment to settle down and live quietly; yet it is nice to taste the sweets of power after a graceless exile. Moreover, when the King landed some weeks later, Marlborough was one of those who met him; and disgusted Tories noted 'that the acclamation *God save the Duke of Marlborough!* was more frequently repeated than *God save the King!*' So somehow the Duke once more found himself Captain-General, of importance in the new Whig Cabinet, while many of his family had exalted posts. Though he did not take the field against the Pretender in 1715, he organized the campaign, and foretold the exact spot, Preston, where the Stuart forces would be put to rout.

Nevertheless, the couple lived on the whole at Holywell, and attended to family affairs. Both were eager to get Blenheim finished, and after Parliament had granted a certain sum, they set the work forward at their own expense. The Duke took an especial interest in the laying out of the grounds, and the planting of trees and shrubs, while the Duchess harried Vanbrugh to get ready a place for them to live in. She was also eager to see her granddaughter, the Lady Harriott Godolphin, married, and had pitched upon Lord Clare, soon to be Duke of Newcastle, for the happy bridegroom. He was vastly rich, as well connected as could be, and seemed to her to be the sort of silly young man she could very well manage. She had begun the attack while abroad, and since Vanbrugh was on good terms with Lord Clare, being his architect, she had employed him as match-maker. But for the moment the affair fizzled out. Lord Clare had high ideals where marriage was concerned, and did not at all approve of the way young women were being brought up. Besides, Lady Harriott was not very good-looking; and though Vanbrugh declared that his wide experience taught him that she would soon have a most agreeable face, and would be very well liked (and had his lordship noticed her excellent figure?), Lord Clare would not at that time take the plunge.

Then, at the beginning of April 1716, the Duke and Duchess were hard hit by the death of their favourite daughter, Lady Sunderland. The blow was all the more severe as they had lost their next most loved child, Lady Bridgewater, while they were abroad. Lady Sunderland had been, perhaps, the only one of their daughters who really loved them: she understood her

mother, could cajole her, and often protected her father from
his wife's more virulent rages. In a letter she left for her
husband to read after her death, she asked him to hand over
her girls, and any sons too young to go to school, to the care
of her mother. The Duchess was much moved by the letter
when it was sent on to her, and at once gladly undertook the
charge, begging only for some little thing, such as a silver cup,
which her daughter had been in the habit of using, and for a
larger lock of her hair than she already had. The Duke was
still more sorrowful, and it was possibly owing to his grief
for her loss, that less than two months after her death, he was
prostrated by his first stroke.

It was a severe one; it paralysed him, and though until the
end of his life he continued in harness, he was never again the
same man. He partially recovered, but he always had an
impediment in his speech which prevented him from saying
certain words (unluckily not known), and always

From *Marlb'rough's* eyes the streams of dotage flow.

He passed the rest of his days a dignified, tall, but slightly bent
figure, in which could be seen, if not the irresistible person who
had charmed a dozen courts, at least the great warrior who had
never lost a battle. Yet his mind was not clouded, and whenever
he went to Council, as he sometimes did, what he said was sound
and to the point. But he cared little for public life, preferring
to wander about the grounds at Blenheim or Holywell, and
much happier seeing his grandchildren at their music lessons,
or acting *All for Love*, than he was when playing sixpenny
ombre at Bath.

From now, therefore, the whole weight of the family affairs
fell upon the Duchess, and very soon she had her hands full
over the marriage of Lady Harriott Godolphin, for Lord Clare,
or rather the Duke of Newcastle, was coming up to the scratch,
being determined to marry somewhere before the winter was
upon them. Now, however, the Duchess was inclined to haggle;
she wanted, as Vanbrugh said, in a grandson-in-law as in
everything else, to have an article good and cheap. But she was
getting tired of Vanbrugh. Instead of finishing the house, he was
idling about with walks and fruit trees at the old Manor,
Rosamond's Bower, which he had been ordered to pull down

ages ago; and building a fantastic bridge with a lot of silly
rooms in it, over a preposterous rivulet he was forced to
enlarge to suit the bridge. Now that the Duke, who liked
Vanbrugh, was out of the way, she would get rid of him. And
luckily for her plan, at this time she found a certain Mr. Walter
at Bath, who would act as a go-between in the hopeful marriage.
She played her cards unbeknown to Vanbrugh, who was
astounded to find himself dropped. But in Vanbrugh, for once
in her life, she found her match in free speech. He was a great
man in his own worlds, and knew it, and he was not going to
be played the fool with, even by the Duchess. He wrote to her:

. . . a Match-maker is a damned trade, and I was never fond of
meddling with other people's affairs. But as in this, on your own
motion, and your own desire, I had taken a good deal of hearty pains
to serve you, and I think with a good deal of hearty success, I cannot
but wonder (though not be sorry), you should not think it right to
continue your commands upon
Your obedient humble servant,
J. VANBRUGH

Her answer was bland and ingenuous in the extreme:

. . . if any third person (she wrote), will say that I have done
anything wrong to you . . . I shall be very sorry for it, and very ready
to ask your pardon; but at present I have the ease and satisfaction to
believe there is no sort of complaint against
Your most humble servant,
S. MARLBOROUGH

She never, of course, conceived it possible that she should be
found enough in the wrong to have to ask anybody's pardon.
She had always been ready to apologize if she erred, but then
she knew very well that she never did err. In the meantime she
covered some thirty sides of paper with accusations against
Vanbrugh as an architect, and saw to it that he should handle
the document. Sir John was really angry, and threw up his post
on the spot.

These papers, Madam (he wrote in November 1716), are so full
of far-fetched, laboured accusations, mistaken facts, wrong inferences,
groundless jealousies and strained constructions, that I should put a
very great affront upon your understanding if I supposed it possible
you could mean anything in earnest by them, but to put a stop to my
troubling you any more. You have your end, Madam, for I will
never trouble you more.

Thus she got rid of Vanbrugh. The marriage she had schemed took place, and she employed Hawksmore, Vanbrugh's lieutenant, to finish off Blenheim.

These were vexations, but they were minor troubles, as it were safety valves for her furious energies. What she was most concerned to do was to establish herself once more as an important personage in the public eye. She lived much in London, dragging the unfortunate Duke up to Marlborough House, to receive as much as he could, and to be a focus for the 'malcontent' Whigs. For the Duchess was not at all pleased with the conduct of the ministries at this time. They were Whig, but they were the wrong sort of Whig; there was too much of the influence of Walpole and Townshend about them. It was true that Sunderland, by means of personal intrigue with George I, became Secretary of State in 1717, and Lord Treasurer (Prime Minister) in 1718, temporarily excluding Walpole and Townshend, but by then she had quarrelled with Sunderland. Everybody found him an unbearable person, but so long as his wife had been alive, his behaviour to the Marlboroughs had been perfect. But in 1717 he had the effrontery to marry again, and to marry beneath him; and what was more, to make over to his new wife much of the money that should have gone to his children. The Duchess wrote stinging letters, but they served no purpose.

Yet the definite break with Sunderland did not occur until the end of 1720. At that time there were rumours floating about the court that the Duchess was not so loyal to the Hanoverians as she ought to be; but out of consideration for her husband, she kept this tattle from him. Then one day the Earl of Sunderland asked him to go and see him. The Duke came back from the interview so shattered, that his wife was alarmed at his appearance, and asked him what was the matter. 'I have been to Lord Sunderland,' he said, 'who accuses you of a plot to bring in the Pretender, and of furnishing him with a sum of money.' She was haughtily contemptuous, but hearing that the Duke also was implicated, she went to court to see how the land lay. Instead of being warmly received, as formerly, she was cold-shouldered; but to make sure there was no mistake, she went again. There could be no doubt as to the royal attitude. She therefore wrote a letter of refutation, which she had translated into French, not herself knowing the language which, besides bad Latin, was the means of communication at court, and arranged for a meeting with the Duchess of Kendal (Madam Schulemberg), the King's ungainly old mistress. The Duchess of Kendal took the letter in to the King, inviting Lady Marlborough to wait for an answer; but the latter refused, on the plea that she could not speak French, though really because she wanted an answer in writing. When it came, it was not satisfactory.

St. James, Dec. 17, 1720. Whatever I may have been told upon your account, I think I have shown on all occasions, the value I have for the services of the Duke, your husband; and I am always disposed to judge of him and you by the behaviour of each of you in regard to my service. Upon which, I pray God, my Lady Marlborough, to preserve you in all happiness.

GEORGE R.

A week later, imputing the trouble to Mr. Secretary Craggs, an old friend, with whom, however, she had been at feud since 1712 over the question of an anonymous letter she laid to his door, she wrote a stronger appeal to the Duchess of Kendal. She said she was 'injured beyond expression', and pointed out that since she and her husband had staked their all on the Hanoverian line, it would be sheer madness on their part to favour the Pretender. The only reply she got was a reference to the King's previous note. It was wildly aggravating. She thereupon threw herself into the arms of the anti-court party, headed by the Prince and Princess of Wales, who received her and the Duke with so much fuss that one would have thought it was the Churchills and not the Guelphs who were the royalties.

In 1721, there was further trouble over Blenheim, Some of the leading contractors who had not been paid, sued the Duke for arrears, and with his name coupled that of Vanbrugh, who had signed all the orders. It put the Duchess in a fume. The Government was really liable for these particular charges, but she tried to turn them all off on to Vanbrugh, declaring that the claims made were for unauthorized things. In a fever-heat she wrote a tremendous statement of her case, which she had printed and privately handed around. Vanbrugh, on his side, wrote the most amusing and racy of legal documents, called

A Justification of What He Depos'd in the Duke of Marlborough's Late Trial. When nearly through, Lady Marlborough's *Case* fell into his hands, and he let fly with a pen as blunt as her own, in which the Duke's guile in refusing ever to sign an order was shown up in a not very pretty light. The Marlboroughs lost the case in court and on appeal, and Vanbrugh in his turn sued for arrears of salary owing; but an injunction was brought against him. Lady Marlborough never forgave Vanbrugh, and when some four years later wished, with a party from Castle Howard, to visit the completed Blenheim, she gave orders that neither he nor his wife was to be allowed inside the gates. He had his revenge a little later, for he got his money through Walpole 'in spite of the hussy's teeth'.

It was lucky perhaps that at this time the Duchess was in control, for she was one of the very few people who kept their heads amid the seething excitement of the South Sea Bubble. She insisted upon selling out when the stock was very high, and realized a vast sum of money, although the Duke, and all her advisers, implored her to stay in. She was firm. She saw what it was leading to; she even realized the criminal folly of it; she was the loudest in the demands that the promoters, Sunderland among them, should be tried. But most of those implicated, Sunderland and her enemy Craggs, died with mysterious suddenness in the next year, 1722.

Soon afterwards, in June, the Duke relapsed into what was evidently his last illness, when staying at Windsor Lodge. The Duchess was frantic, sent for the local physician, swore at him roundly for being a fool, though the Bishop of Winchester was in the room; and, it is said, she wanted to follow the unlucky leech downstairs to pull off his wig. Other doctors were sent for, but it was clearly the end, and he died in the early morning of June the 16th. The body was embalmed, and taken to Marlborough House, where it lay in terrific state (admission by ticket), until August the 9th, when a procession of the utmost pomp bore it to Westminster Abbey. A funeral car had been especially built, which the Duchess preserved, and when in 1735 the Duchess of Buckingham wanted to borrow it for her son's funeral, she was told 'It carried my Lord Marlborough, and shall never be used for anybody else.'

Sarah Churchill survived her husband some twenty-two years,

but in spite of what seems a never-failing vigour, it is a tale of energy impotently spent, of futile bickerings and law suits, of dealings in property and scribbling of opinions. Yet, if even the things she did worthy of note are signs of a deep frustration, all the time we are aware of a distinct character, of something that would leave the world the emptier when she left it. She was a personality to the end, and though no longer to be taken account of in the political sphere, she was always somebody to be reckoned with in the social realm. So much was she so at first, that soon after her husband's death, in her sixty-third year, she received two offers of marriage. The first was made six weeks after the Duke's funeral, by the Earl of Coningsby, an old friend of the Marlborough's, who had fought side by side with William. But 'the best, the worthiest, the wisest of women' refused the old gentleman, who wrote in strains of calf-love. To the 'proud' Duke of Somerset, who had just lost a wife Lady Marlborough had hated, and who proposed to her immediately after the Earl's repulse, she said, that were she only thirty, 'she would not permit even the Emperor of the world to succeed in that heart which had been devoted to John Duke of Marlborough'. Instead, at his request, she found him another, more suitable bride.

Unfortunately, her Grace cared for neither of her surviving daughters. Lady Godolphin, who now became Duchess of Marlborough, she thought insufferably silly. She could not understand why she took up with, and mothered, poor old half-blind, gouty Congreve. When the poet died in 1729, the young Duchess gave him a splendid funeral, had a waxwork figure made of him, gout-bandages and all, to sit at table with her, and erected a monument in the Abbey, of which the inscription referred to the happiness and honour Henrietta, Duchess of Marlborough, had enjoyed in his company. 'I know not what happiness she might have had in his company,' her mother growled, 'but I am sure it was no honour.' Nor did she get on better with Anne, Duchess of Montagu, who had behaved badly to her parents ever since her marriage. 'Old Marlborough' seemed to visit upon her the contempt she had for the Duke—but after all, she had chosen him. He was extremely charitable, and did much good without babbling about it, yet his mother-in-law wrote in 1740:

All his talents lie in things only natural in boys of fifteen years old, and he is about two and fifty; to get people into his garden and wet them with squirts, and to invite people to his country houses, and put things into their beds to make them itch, and twenty such pretty fancies like these.

And if she did not care for her daughters, they did not pretend to lose any love over her. They said things about her, which forced her to write one of those innumerable justifications of her conduct an unjust world seemed to make needful. 'I am sure', she wrote to a friend,

. . . you cannot but have heard all the vile things that have been reported of me, which has forced me to collect a great many disagreeable things in order to vindicate myself to those that I value most, and as I have had reason to think you always my friend, I desire the favour of you ro read this long paper. You will see by it how long I have endeavoured to hide my misfortunes from the world, but now there is hardly a possibility of a reconcilement between me and my children, from the very injurious aspersions which they have publicly thrown upon me, I neither can nor I think ought to suffer any longer under it; and if I had not taken so much pains to conceal their faults, at the same time that they and their wretched friends were making all manner of false reports to me, I believe it had not been possible for them to prevail so much as they have done. I have known people of the most calm temper very much warmed upon account of their reputation, and having bore what I have done for so many years, rather than hurt my children, I hope nobody will blame me now for what I do, which I am forced to by them to prevent my being pointed at where ever I go.

Some of her grandchildren, however, she was fond of, especially those of the Spencer branch, the eldest son of which succeeded to the title on the death of Henrietta Godolphin in 1733. She especially liked Lady Diana Spencer, 'my Dy', as she used to call her, who seems to some extent to have returned the affection. In 1727 she plotted a brilliant marriage for her, with no less a person than the Prince of Wales (son of George II), to whom she offered a hundred thousand pounds with her granddaughter, a good bait for a penniless Prince. By that time 'old Marlborough', not being so well received at court as she felt she ought to be, had turned against George II and Queen Caroline, and she, as well as the Prince, thought it would be great fun to spite the King. The marriage was arranged to take place secretly at Windsor, but Walpole somehow got

wind of the affair, and put a stop to it, so 'the secret was buried
in silence'. In 1731, however, much to her grandmother's
delight, Lady Diana married Lord John Russell, afterwards
Duke of Bedford.

Other granddaughters were not so satisfactory. Lady Anne
Spencer, now Lady Anne Bateman, introduced her brother
Charles, who had become Duke of Marlborough, to the daughter
of Lord Trevor, whom he married; and as Lord Trevor had
been one of the great Duke's implacable enemies, Sarah was
frenzied. She banished her grandson from Windsor Lodge, where
he had been staying, and then, under the pretence that the new
Duchess had stripped the house, she had a puppet-show made,
in which eight Miss Trevors, cousins of the young Duchess,
were depicted as rooting up the shrubs in the garden, and her
granddaughter-in-law was shown as running off with the hen-
coop under her arm. She had another cause of anger against
Lady Anne Bateman, in that she had made her brother meet
Henry Fox; so that when the young Duke was captured by the
court party, she sarcastically remarked, 'that is the Fox that
has won over my goose'. Nor did she get on better with Lady
Anne Egerton, Lady Bridgewater's daughter. After continual
supposed offences, she procured her picture, and blackening the
face over, she wrote underneath, 'She is blacker within', and
hung the frame in her own sitting-room, to the huge delight
of all her visitors.[1]

Her real favourite was Jack Spencer, a naughty but engaging
young man, who somehow won his grandmother's heart, and
it was to 'her Torrismond', as she called him, that she left the
bulk of her fortune, on condition that he would never take any
employment under the Government, save the Rangership of
Windsor Park. With the young Duke she could not get on at
all, and on one occasion amused the great world by going into
court against him. The action was a so-called 'friendly' one
between him and his brother, for the division of certain property.
Charles claimed the sword of honour the Emperor had given the
great Duke. 'What!' the Duchess exclaimed, bursting with
righteous indignation, 'shall I suffer *that* sword, which *my* lord
would have carried to the gates of Paris, to be sent to the
pawnbroker's, to have the diamonds picked out one by one?'

[1] This story is also told of Lady Anne Bateman: I follow Thomson.

Her behaviour was not so unnatural as it seems, for as a matter of fact, Charles behaved extremely badly to his grandmother; he was always going to her to back his bills, and eventually raised money on a *post obit* against her death. His later history shows her to have been fully justified in keeping what she could of the family estates out of his hands.

Nor were her quarrels confined to her family. She was for ever finding reasons for fighting somebody: it was necessary to her. Pope's line in the character of Atossa, partly modelled on her, 'Finds all her life one warfare upon earth', need arouse no pity. She revelled in it; it kept the life in her body. Never of a contemplative nature, having passed her whole life in action, in forcing her will upon other people, how could she subside into an old age of vegetable tranquillity? She also had to go on in harness until she died. She had more lawsuits over buildings; she quarrelled with the court for allowing a certain person and not herself to drive through St. James's Park. She wrangled with the Duke of St. Albans over her privileges in Windsor Park. She squabbled over her money in the funds, and whenever she possibly could, she fought with Sir Robert Walpole. She did not mind his cynicism, she could tolerate his outspokenness, but she could not abide his boorishness, and what she thought was his overbearing manner. On one famous occasion, when he had laughed at her, she told him roundly that 'great men seldom heard the truth, because those who spoke to them generally wanted their favour; and when anybody told them the truth, they always thought that person mad'. She added that whenever he wanted to her the truth about himself, she would be happy to see him again.

In fact she became a little mad over Walpole. He became her bugbear, a dark and ominous monster who would ruin the nation. The older she grew the more she thought the country was going to the dogs, entirely on account of Walpole's folly, and the general corruption of humanity. She could not help remembering the reign of Anne, of whom she often spoke, and always with respect, without realizing that there had been giants in those days. From 1737 onwards the notes she jotted down grew more and more foreboding.

1737. I don't think anything good can happen, except by some accident that I cannot see into.

1737. Sir Robert . . . from the love of power, it is plain he has ruined England.

1737. God knows how soon this country may be made yet more miserable than it is.

1738. I think, whatever changes happen, there can be nothing now that is good, there being such a general corruption among all people.

1739. I compare our situation to a ship near sinking.

1740. When I press them [*patriots*] . . . all I can get is, that some accident may bring things about to be better.

She lived in constant dread that the National Debt would be cancelled, so whenever she could she bought land.

1738. From fear of a sponge I have sold my stocks low, and bought land dear, which I did because I thought *that* would hold longest.

1739. (In her eightieth year.) In the city to bid for Lord Yarmouth's estate, which I believe I shall have, and I do think it necessary to do it, because land will be the last thing that is taken from us, and I expect, a little sooner or later, a sponge, which will put an end to all stocks, and money lent to the government.

But indeed at this time she was very depressed, as can be seen from several entries.

1737. I am a perfect cripple, and cannot possibly hold out long: and as I have little enjoyment of my life, I am very indifferent about it.

1738. I think one can't leave the world in a better time than now, when there is no such thing as real friendships, truth, justice, honour, or indeed anything that is agreeable in life.

1739. As to my own particular, I have nothing to reproach myself with. . . . But, alas! there is such a change in the world since I knew it first, that, though one's natural pleasure is to love people, the generality of the world are in something or other so disagreeable that 'tis impossible to do it: and added to this, I am a cripple, lifted about like a child, and very seldom free from pain.

Yet we must not have a picture of a poor old woman, huddled in a chair wanting to die: we have to remember that this last note bears the same date as the one where she records going to the city to bid for more landed property. And she was always ready to set herself right in other people's eyes. A few years earlier the Bishop of Chichester had taken upon himself to reprove her for 'ill-grounded suspicions, violent passions, and a boundless liberty of expressing resentment of persons without distinction from the Prince downwards'. Seeing her reputation for waspishness, he was a little anxious as to how she would take it, but she was charmed. Quoting Montaigne on plain speaking between friends, she went on to say:

I beg of you never to have the least scruple in telling me anything you think, for I am not so partial to myself, as not to know I have many imperfections, but a great fault I will never have, that I know to be one.

Yes, it was the same as it had always been, with young John Churchill, with Queen Mary, with Queen Anne, with Sir John Vanbrugh—she was ever ready to apologize and reform if she could be proved in the wrong, but then she could invariably prove her behaviour perfect. So on this occasion she showed at enormous length how entirely in the right she was. But when she came to be over eighty, she thought it time to make a general statement, to proclaim to the world how absolutely blameless she had been from her first coming to court to the year 1710; and so, with the aid of a minor writer called Nathaniel Hooke, she compiled her famous *Conduct*. Nobody, of course, that mattered, cared a straw, except as a matter of gossip; but a few busybodies, of the sort always ready to argue about anything at any time, took the matter up and hotly replied. The Duchess was highly astonished, and outraged, and employed Henry Fielding to help her write her defence.

Yet life was not all black; there were still moments when charity was pleasant to distribute, and power was good to use. She founded alms-houses for decayed gentlewomen at St. Albans, and once she had the pleasure of making the Bank of England draw in its horns. It was at the moment pressing on Child's Bank, making it uncomfortable for that house, so one of that family came to her to explain the affair. Then—how good it must have been to be able to do it!—she gave the suppliant an order on the Bank of England for one hundred thousand pounds, thus putting a stop to the attack. Nor was she without friends and correspondents, especially Lord Marchmont, and, strangely enough, that out-and-out Tory, Pope. An odd friendship this, the old crippled Duchess, and the old twisted poet, united in a sardonic, disillusioned view of mankind. Pope read her his character of 'Atossa', telling her that it was meant for the Duchess of Buckingham, as it partly was: but she was not to be fooled; she told him she knew well enough whom it was meant for. She sent him a thousand pounds, thinking that by this means the 'character' would be quashed, but Pope saved for future ages one of the most brilliant of his portraits. She also had other amusements, for wherever she was, at Blenheim, Holywell, or, as was more usual, at Windsor Lodge, she would be wheeled about her garden, or would listen over and over again to the eight tunes played by a chamber organ she had bought for a thousand pounds, which she considered cheap, since it was 'an infinitely less sum than some bishopricks have been sold for', she explained. Sometimes she read a little, and highly relished the fourth part of *Gulliver's Travels*, the sound sense of which made up for the childishness of the first three. There was also the fun of making her will, of leaving £20,000 and a house to Pitt for standing up to Walpole, and £10,000 and a house to Lord Chesterfield, for being an honest man; besides the little remarks she could leave as legacies. And so she went on in a world from which all her real friends had departed, from which even the memorial to Queen Anne she had had erected had melted away into mud; but still active, still scribbling letters and notes, and sorting papers, full of an energy that seemed as if it would go on for ever.

But we are nearly at the end, and it is time to appraise that greatness that was certainly hers. Whatever else she may have done, she had for some years virtually been Queen of England, more free, more rich, and more powerful than her lawful ruler. That may have been largely chance, but what belongs to her own self is a rushing vitality always and everywhere directed to one end; a worldly end, a shallow one if you will, but one must be chary of judging other people's values. She left her mark upon history, and if that mark would not have been so plain had she had another husband, his would not have been so deep had he had another wife. For sheer work done, for crude horse-power, she has no equal of her sex in English history except Queen Elizabeth. She was an amazingly efficient machine, and if it is a pity that she had not a wiser head, no one can say that it was a muddled one. Though she met men on their own ground, using feminine methods, an unfeminine neglect of detail caused her failure; it was the feminine artifice of Mrs. Masham, pitted against her masculine bluffness, that brought about her fall.

With others who live to her age we are aware of a slowing

down, as though the engine were gradually tiring. But with her it is not the same: there is no feeling of petering out, of the works being worn. That particular bundle of nerve and tissue seems capable of going on and on, asserting itself when and where it can, to all appearance blind to events beyond its personal orbit. In 1740, it is true, she was ill, but we do not have a feeling of sickness; it is as though she merely had nothing to do. She lay on her bed for some days without speaking, but when she heard the voice of the doctor say above her, 'She must be blistered, or she will die', she spoke: 'I won't be blistered, and I won't die.' She was right; she was not blistered, and she went on for four years more, to the very end gathering together, and docketing, material for her husband's *Life*, which she engaged two distinguished poets, Glover and Mallet, to do for five hundred pounds a-piece, on condition that not a line of it should be in verse. But suddenly she came to a full stop, as far as one can see in mid-career: some accident happened to the machine, and Sarah Jennings died at Marlborough House on the 18th of October 1744, leaving behind none who loved her, but a very great deal of valuable property in land.

JOHN WESLEY
(1703–1791)

CONTENTS

JOHN WESLEY

PART I

THE SEEKER AFTER SALVATION

§ 1. THE SEARCH (1703–1735)

It is difficult to be humble. Even if you aim at humility, there is
no guarantee that when you have attained the state you will not
be proud of the feat. But not everybody considers it a virtue,
and as a small boy at Charterhouse, John Wesley had no great
opinion of it. On the contrary, he thought it well to dominate
the smaller fry, whom he would gather around him to exhort
and admonish; and when asked why he did not join the boys of
his own age, he answered, 'Better to rule in hell than serve in
heaven!' Pride is one stumbling-block to the Christian life;
another is too great a fondness for reasoning. Wesley would
accept nothing that his mind would not sanction, and from his
earliest days insisted upon passing every suggestion through
a fine sieve of thought. Even when asked if he would have some
more bread, he used to say, 'Thank you; I will think of it', a
precociously 'methodic' system (it is not too early to use the
word) which exasperated his father. 'I profess, sweetheart,'
he shot out tartly at Mrs. Wesley, 'I think our Jack would not
attend to the most pressing necessities of nature unless he could
give a reason for it.'

Such an attitude forebodes an intolerably dull man; but
luckily, to this rationalism Wesley added an intense curiosity in
whatever might be going on, and even at the end of his life
seized eagerly on anything new. Thus, as a fascinated old man,
he tried out in his own person the healing powers of electricity,
and discussed, if in a somewhat theological way, the then
budding theories of evolution. Nor did his enquiring mind stop
at those things which seem amenable to reason, and he always
found the supernatural delightfully seductive. This aspect of
existence was indeed forced upon him in his early youth, for

while he was at school his father's parsonage in Lincolnshire was the scene of the most astounding, if not very awesome, manifestations. There was a prank-loving being, a poltergeist (his sisters used to call it Old Jeffrey), which knocked mysteriously, opened doors, made noises as though money were being lavishly poured out or all the bottles under the stairs were being smashed. It gloried in rattling the warming-pans on the walls; sometimes it went so far as to push Mr. Wesley; and once it set a trencher spinning in a most intriguing manner. It appeared twice, the second time as a kind of bat-eared white rabbit, which evaded the tongs with which the manservant pursued it. Wesley's curiosity was never at rest about Old Jeffrey, who stimulated him to search out other mysteries, such as that of an apparition near Oxford, and another of a nearby, haunted house. His interest was vividly stimulated by the report of the Bishop of Raphoe, who told of a young man who levitated strangely out of the episcopal window to sup with the Devil. There were some problems, then, which resisted reason; and to the question why such things were permitted only a baffling answer could be returned; even his mother, so good a guide on knotty points, was of no help. All that one could be certain of was that the world of matter was interwoven with one of impalpable, rarely visible influences.

John was one of ten living children (nine others had died), being a few years junior to his brother Samuel, and only a little older than Charles, the remainder, sisters, some earnest, some not quite so grave, being scattered on either side of him. They were mostly reasoners, for they came of an arguing stock. Their parents also had liked to think things out for themselves, for, both born Dissenters, they had both returned to the Church as by law established. They knew their own minds, stubbornly. For instance, at the end of the seventeenth century, Mr. Wesley noticed that his wife was always silent when the King was prayed for, and thus discovering that she was a Jacobite, he declared that unless she became as good a Whig as he was, he would leave her. She stood firm, and leave her he did. Luckily William III soon died, and the couple was reconciled under Anne, the earliest fruit of their reunion being John, who inherited their wilfulness. The discipline of his education, entirely conducted by his mother, helped to encourage strength of character. At five years old the children were taught to read, one day only being allowed to learn the alphabet, and they were made to cry softly after being whipped, measures essential in a large, understaffed household. Mrs. Wesley's motto, 'Break the child's will', ultimately had the opposite effect; but she did succeed in breaking, or at least cracking, her husband's. She had the misfortune, she told her son, never to think like his father; but when any difference arose, for example as to whether she should hold a 'conventicle' at home when the rector was away, it was she who won. She ruled the house, except on extraordinary occasions, while old Samuel Wesley, stern, harsh, ambitious for his sons, worked out his commentaries on the Book of Job.

In 1720, John left Charterhouse, elected to a scholarship at Christ Church, Oxford, where he soon found the life of the average undergraduate was formless, and lacking in seriousness. He made up his mind to change that, for himself at least; and taking an old note-book of his grandfather's, headed it with the mysterious symbols:

2 f-n-r ·O r. l· .n 2 O ·q. .n. f L. f;

a cryptogram which in ever varying forms, later intermingled with shorthand, he used all his life for the diary he never ceased to keep, and which he enlarged into his voluminous *Journals*. Translated, the heading reads, 'A General Rule in All Actions of Life', an imaginative claim, which was followed by abstracts from a few of Jeremy Taylor's most inspiring paragraphs. There lay, in a sense, the germ of Methodism. But Wesley was not yet nineteen, and for the next few years he found it difficult to stick even moderately close to his rules. It was hard always 'to entertain awful apprehensions of the presence of God' on fine mornings when life smiled, to employ every spare hour in religion, to avoid curiosity as to all useless employments and knowledge, above all to resist the delights of conversation, which is the charm of university life. If there was one thing harder, it was to get up in the morning. For Wesley liked his bed, he was gregarious, lively and witty, he loved 'knowledge', however idle, and had a passion for logical argument, though he was always careful to argue on the right side, since he despised dialectical fireworks. Besides, frivolous reading was

so entrancing, not only the *Spectator*, which he would find at
the places where he went to drink coffee, but *Jane Shore*, or
still older plays, such as Ben Jonson's; and who could resist
Robinson Crusoe when it first came out?—a grave waste of time,
for in those days it was not yet plausible to regard that tale of
adventure as the spiritual autobiography of a godly man. So
while Wesley went about, chattered, read, played tennis, wrote
flippant letters to his brother Samuel enclosing verses on Cloe's
favourite flea or such like, he would sorrowfully enter up in his
diary, 'boasting, greedy of praise, intemperate sleep . . . heat in
arguing'. He lived, he declared, in the practice of 'known sins',
which made him very uneasy before his three times a year
participation in the Lord's Supper; but since he was not long
after to stigmatize dining in Hall on Friday as 'grossly sinful',
it is not likely that his delinquencies were very alarming.

Although, like the rest of his family, he was desperately
poor and always in debt, he managed to go about a little; and
towards the beginning of 1725 went with his friend Kirkham to
the latter's home, the rectory at Stanton in Worcestershire.
There he met the three Kirkham sisters: Mrs. Chapone (though
not the famous one), Damaris, and above all, Betty, known to
her familiar friends as Varanese. With the last he fell in love,
while she on her part, in a phrase at once religious and loyal,
told him that she 'loved him more than all mankind, save her
God and King'. But what is the good of a penniless man falling
in love? 'Whether or not you will be engaged before thirty, I
cannot determine', his sister Emilia wrote to him; 'if my advice
be worth listening to, never engage your affections before your
worldly affairs are in such a position that you may marry soon.'
However, there are higher planes on which twin souls can meet,
and if one may not talk love, one can talk religion; and since
this was a subject Varanese was happy in, the passionate
friendship prospered. Miss Kirkham induced Wesley to read
Thomas à Kempis, and, more studiously than before, Jeremy
Taylor. Having found 'a religious friend', and no doubt feeling
the stress of a hopeless love-affair, Wesley began to think about
religion more profoundly, He was led to consider taking orders.

His parents were delighted at this change of temper; apparently he had never before shown them his serious side; but
there were a great many things Wesley wished to clear up in his

own mind before taking this step, and it was to his mother, not to his father, that he applied for help. Old Wesley had had a scholar's ambitions for his son, but Susanna had more spiritual aspirations for him. What, after all, was learning? Wesley agreed, there was so much to be learnt that one could not learn it all; and besides, once one had learnt something, how could one know that it was not all a sheer waste of time? Take the good Bishop Berkeley. How easy it was to destroy his graceful, elaborate, philosophic structure! His mother always listened sympathetically, and it is not for nothing that, whereas Mr. Wesley is referred to as 'the father of the Wesleys', his wife is known as 'the mother of Methodism'.

Pride, and reason—those were the gnarled rocks upon which the ship of the soul might split: yet after all, we may ask, is it necessary for great religious leaders to be humble? Do we associate that quality with St. Paul, or Savonarola? But Thomas à Kempis was emphatic upon the point, and if Jeremy Taylor was not quite so decisive, he seemed to incline the same way. Yet to be humble is to deny the favours God has bestowed upon you. 'As to absolute humility,' Wesley told his mother, '. . . consisting of a mean opinion of ourselves considered simply, or with respect to God alone, I can readily join with his [Jeremy Taylor's] opinion. But I am more uncertain as to the comparative, if I may so term it; and think some plausible reasons may be alleged to show it is not in our power, and consequently not a virtue, to think ourselves the worst in every company.' How can one not believe one's self better than a freethinker? he went on to argue. To be humble in such company is to lack knowledge of your neighbours.

His mother does not seem to have determined the point, but on others she was more helpful. On reason, for instance. 'Faith is an assent on rational grounds', Wesley declared (it is the position we have come to call latitudinarian); 'Faith must necessarily at length be resolved into reason.' No, his mother told him, it is 'an assent to whatever God has revealed to us because He has revealed it'. There are some things it does not do to reason about. These points settled, the questions which next most concerned Wesley (they were the pivots of his future life) were, how to be certain of God's love to all; and in what way was one conscious of salvation? As to the first, Thomas à

Kempis was too Calvinistic. The idea that God had condemned some men before birth to the everlasting bonfire was repugnant to Wesley; he had no taste for Tophet flares. Yet, the question is a difficult one which has puzzled the astutest theologians— how reconcile God's knowledge of everything, past, present, and future, together with His omnipotence, with man's free will? Mrs. Wesley solved the problem; it was beautifully simple. God knows what will happen, but He does not cause it to happen, any more than our knowledge that the sun will rise tomorrow is the reason why it is actually so punctual. So much for Thomas à Kempis and the first problem: Jeremy Taylor on the second was more than a little frightening. One could not be sure that one's sins were forgiven, he said. What then! Wesley cried, Is grace so weak that its presence cannot be felt? Must men go about in perpetual fear and trembling? 'God deliver us from such a fearful expectation as this!' Thus Wesley set out on his search for a saving faith, the only solution; for justification by works is a Popish doctrine, and therefore not to be considered by a good son of the English Church, though, of course, works also are essential to salvation. Wesley decided to devote his life to these questions, feeling that the salvation of one's own soul is the most important problem life has to offer. He became ever more serious, then earnest. He began, it is a severe discipline, to keep his diary much more fully; and in September 1725 he became a deacon.

During the next six years a demon attendant upon John Wesley would have found himself at various times in the company of three very distinct personalities, all with much the same, but not identical, outward features, and bound within by a strong family likeness, but no less three curiously different persons. At Epworth, he was a dapper little country parson, helping his father both there and at Wroote, where for some time he was curate. He would visit the parishioners, take his sisters to whatever village fairs might be within reach, dance with them whenever he could, would swim, and go shooting plover. At Wroote, rather a pigsty of a place, with, according to some of the family, suitably porcine inhabitants, he set about improving the garden by making seats; and at Epworth he would discuss religion with his mother, or dutifully help his father transcribe his elucidation of Job—to be presented to

Queen Caroline. He was, perhaps, from his father's point of view, a little too filled with the sense of his mission, for he was not always there to do the copying, and once there was a sharp disagreement over the unfortunately beautiful Hetty Wesley. John thought his father's drastic action in marrying her off to a lout unduly harsh, and not only opposed him at home, but publicly denounced his severity in the pulpit at Wroote in a sermon on Christian Charity. There was a tearful reconciliation; the young curate was contrite and diligent, but then, for he would never give in, he preached an equally ruffling sermon, this time on Rash Judging. Old Mr. Wesley did not say anything to his Jacky; instead he complained bitterly to Charles. But somehow the profound jars in the Wesley family—everything in that family was profound, will-impelled—healed, at least outwardly; and this second misunderstanding, which occurred in 1726, was also smoothed over, for Wesley went back to help his father from 1727 to 1729.

Oxford saw a different Wesley, a brilliant young don (he was elected a Fellow of Lincoln early in 1726) who went about looking very grave—one could not think of him dancing or going to fairs—and who was not very companionable. He was a good classic, and a shattering logician, his brother Fellows conceded; but why would he not breakfast with them, or come to gossip and crack donnish jokes? and besides, why could he not get his hair cut like everybody else? And really, to communicate every Sunday was to take one's religion, or one's self, or something or other, far too seriously. They began to laugh at Wesley, a criticism which he hated. But, as his father said, it is a callow virtue that cannot bear being laughed at, to which his mother added that she was sure 'it is a strong and well-confirmed virtue that can stand the test of a brisk buffoonery'. So Wesley endured; he knew it was his 'calling to go through evil report and good report'. He was determined to take his religion earnestly; he was going to be a *real* not a *nominal* Christian, and all his energies were devoted to this end. As to not cutting his hair, he could not spare the two or three pounds a year (in wigs?) that it would cost him; even his mother's plea that short hair was conducive to health could not move him; it might improve his complexion, or give him a more genteel appearance, but only positive ill-health would induce him to shear his locks. And nothing would persuade him to waste his time in idle, so-called *harmless* talk with the other Fellows. Harmless! why every moment wasted was harm to the soul, damping all good resolutions to work hard, to sleep less, to avoid the lure of *Gulliver*, to combat unclean thoughts. Few of the people who so assiduously invited him to breakfast truly loved or feared God. 'I resolved', he was to write, 'to have no acquaintance by chance, but by choice; and to choose such only as would help me on my way to heaven.' There appeared to be singularly few of these in Oxford, so he tried to escape to a school in Yorkshire, the chief attraction of which was that it lay in such a ghastly hole that nobody would go near it; but he did not get the post.

The Wesley that the people of Oxford began to see after 1729, when he returned from Epworth (the authorities thought, not oddly, that the man appointed lecturer in the classics and moderator of the classes ought to reside in college), was the same man, but exaggerated; for he found that his brother Charles had, with one or two other young men, founded a sort of society to lead the religious life. This was a delightful surprise, for when Charles had first come to Oxford and John had remonstrated with him for his levity, he had answered, 'What, do you expect me to be a saint all at once!' Charles, spurred on by a young man called Morgan, had taken to doing good works, to living according to strict rule, to submitting his poetry to religious themes. Since in 1726 John had read Law's *Serious Call* and *Christian Perfection*, he also had come to think that priests should attend to the poor and sick rather than to points of grammar or the elucidation of Hebrew syntax. He joined his brother with enthusiasm, and at once sprang to the leadership of the group. Thus Oxford beheld with astonishment a tiny coterie taking Christian doctrine literally (it was to happen again a hundred years later), incessantly praying, rigorously observing fasts, living meagrely so as to give all they could to the poor, and preaching, yes, actually in jails! They would meet together several evenings in the week to read the Greek Testament; their hours were strictly allotted to various forms of work; they never took their ease. Thus inspired, John at last conquered his intemperate sleeping, by setting his alarm clock first at six, then at five, then at four. Life was all ardour and stringency; the group wept over their sins; it was said that they even opened veins to cool the intemperance of their blood. To mock at them became the thing; they were called the 'Super-erogation Men', their society was the 'Holy' or 'Godly Club', they were even dubbed in derision, reviving an old nickname, 'Methodists'. Such was the young don of Lincoln.

But at the same time there was another strangely different Wesley in Worcestershire and Gloucestershire, the Wesley admired, cherished, by Varanese and her friends the Granvilles. They on their part saw a High-Church parson, little, but neatly and compactly built, exceedingly active, with beautiful auburn hair, which, parted in the middle, fell to his shoulders in graceful curling locks, and defined a cameo-featured face set with most expressive eyes full of assured fire. There were two Granville sisters, Ann and a young widow, Mary, Mrs. Pendarves, whom Wesley had met in 1725 when he was first attached to Varanese. That was an attachment that had lasted, for in 1727, Martha Wesley had written to her brother complaining of not having heard from him—'When I knew that you were returned from Worcestershire, where I suppose you saw your Varanese, I then ceased to wonder at your silence, for the sight of such a woman, "so known, so loved", might well make you forget me.' Varanese, she knew, was 'so dear' to Wesley. But in about 1730 her attention began to be occupied by a certain Mr. Wilson, whom she afterwards married, and Wesley turned his to the Granville sisters. He fell ecstatically prostrate before first one, then the other; but it was Mary who fascinated him the most.

She was young, lovely, appealing, with a cultured and spirited mind which had been the delight of her uncle George Granville, first Lord Lansdowne, poet and Jacobite. She brought to Wesley the aroma of another world, the world of brilliance and fashion, and, above all, she led him into the realm of delicately fastidious personal relations. It dazzled him. Was he in love?—Yes; but with a vision. His love was begotten by despair upon impossibility. She on her part might have married him, since she cared nothing for worldly glamour, having refused Lord Baltimore, prince of Maryland, to succumb in 1743 to the protestations of Dr. Delany: but how could Wesley have married her? It was not only that he had no money—even his Fellowship would be lost on marrying—but how could he intimately approach so glowing, so ethereal a creature? And by now Wesley was wary of love; his experience with Varanese had taught him that it was 'an avenue for grief'. Mrs. Pendarves did her best to promote familiarity; both she and her sister were entranced by the diminutive clergyman, so full of earnestness, culture, and vitality; and they gave the brothers a clique name such as they all had. Mary was Aspasia, Ann was Selima, Mrs. Chapone became Sappho; thus Wesley was Cyrus, and Charles, gracious poet, was drawn into the charmed circle as Araspes. One can live an idyll even though haunted by religious fears.

A correspondence followed (Charles's letters are lost), on the surface suave, artificial, formal, yet seeming to heave underneath with all the agitations of suppressed passion. 'My dear Varanese' is mentioned again and again, but it is Aspasia who now makes Cyrus's heart-strings vibrate, as they did, with 'that soft emotion with which I glow even at the moment while I consider myself conversing with a kindred soul of my Varanese'. If he walked with Varanese, it was of Aspasia that he thought, of her gestures, of how she looked when she sat on that tree-trunk; even darkness could not shade that 'image of God'. Thus, deliciously, he instructed the sisters in the holy life (how much better a thing Selima would find existence if only she would get up at six every day, to give one hour to private, one hour to public prayer), while they on their part took upon themselves to cure 'those improprieties of behaviour which in my inexperience of the world so frequently betrays me': they initiated him, in short, into the subtle delights of feminine friendship, of intuitive reactions. And, amid all their iridescence, it was above everything their humility that made him wonder; humility! in people so brilliant, so refined, who, Selima especially, made such rapid progress in divinity. His own humility was, as usual, sadly lacking. 'For want of this I cannot follow you as I would', he wrote sadly to Aspasia; 'I must be left behind in the race of virtue. I am sick of pride, it quite weighs my spirits down. O preserve me that I may be healed!' So the delightful correspondence went on all through 1731; was it not pleasant to be consulted on matters of conscience, such as whether Aspasia should go to concerts on Sunday evenings, more than pleasant to be told that the beauty of holiness shone in one's face? Cyrus was distracted if Aspasia left him too long without a letter; what had he done to offend her? He counted the days till he should see her. And then, the dangers of the town! Cyrus grew ever more solicitous for Aspasia, for it seemed to him that she was wasting the inestimable gift of herself on the butterfly triflers of London society! Then, suddenly, Aspasia took alarm; a postscript to a letter ran ominously, 'I must insist upon your burning all my letters, and pray don't make use of any epithet before my name when you write to me. I have not time to tell my reasons.' Alas, she had not time to write again at all, for though Wesley answered the letter, no word broke the silence of the Dublin that had engulfed her. Was this the end? Had it all been an ineffable dream? Impossible that there should be nothing left, not even a few pages of writing! He burnt her letters; she had insisted; but— not till he had taken careful copies of them.

The disappointment seemed to unify the three John Wesleys; at least, two of them disappeared. He became one man, the earnest leader of the Holy Club. It was with renewed ardour that he plunged into the life of austerity, of self-denial, of diligent devotion, undertook the search for a saving faith. Method! that was the only way. There was no direct evidence that one had attained salvation—he at least could feel no assurance: but by acting according to rule, especially that of the primitive Church, one could not go far wrong. One could obey all the injunctions contained in the various rubrics, and thus live the holy life, for if a saving faith might be difficult to reach, there might be a saving method. Ever more method! The Holy Club redoubled its rigours (what did it matter if Morgan had starved himself into a consumption, and died mad?), fasted more, even on days which were not definitely laid down for fasting, prayed, practised rescue work, exorcised spirits from haunted houses, kept ever more aloof, courted the ridicule which had once made life so uneasy to John (for as John had been told on his ordination in 1728, a priest was one who bade defiance to all mankind), filled up every moment. 'Leisure and I have taken leave of one another', he had written to his elder brother some years earlier. Good heavens! he had not known what he was saying; the diligence of those days was mere idleness to this; now he made himself ill from zeal. The Club did indeed debate whether one could be righteous over-much; and though they decided that this was possible in three ways—by raising up one virtue to the detriment of another; by exalting grace to the neglect of law; or by laying too great burdens upon one's self—they came to the conclusion that they were in no danger. Yet Wesley felt that he was not renouncing the world as wholly as he should, not nearly so well as his mother had succeeded in doing. How was he to do this? he asked her. 'What is the surest and shortest way? Is it not to be humble? Surely this is a large step in the way. But the question recurs, How am I to do this? To own the necessity of it is not to be humble.'

Something was wrong, perhaps at the very basis. When he and Charles had walked to Epworth in 1731, discovering on the way that they could very well read as they walked, and so not waste precious time, they had found on their return that their converts had lapsed. The same thing happened in 1733: during an absence of Wesley's at home, the community of twenty-seven had dwindled to five, one of whom immediately after seceded from fear of singularity. There must be more method still. Every ritual was crammed into their devotions; they debated, and against John's judgment resorted to the dubious practice of ejaculatory prayer. It did not dawn on Wesley that it was his own magnetism that had attracted the group, and that without him all this rigour was meaningless.

Then, in 1734, his father, thinking himself failing, suggested that his second son should succeed him at Epworth. No, no, he must stay at Oxford, even if he became more and more outcast, even if he had fewer and fewer pupils, even if he made no converts. At all costs he would make sure of salvation; and when that year Aspasia made an advance, sending him a letter from Dublin, his answer was cold, final. How could she think that he could help her? 'I sincerely thank you for what is past.' The key was turned in the lock, unequivocally. Cyrus was dead. Thus, headed by Wesley, the remnant of the Club, reinforced by Whitfield, went deeper into the mysteries of the faith. Ought they not to mix water with the wine at the Lord's Supper? Clearly that had been an omission. Yet still Wesley felt he was getting no closer. He dabbled in the writings of the mystics; they were dangerously seductive, and nearly ship-wrecked his faith; but their 'noble descriptions of union with God', he found in the end, 'made everything else appear mean, flat, and insipid'—works, faith, everything. Mysticism! It abolished love—and, of course, though Wesley did not say this, made the mediation of God's Son unnecessary, Christianity superfluous. 'The Mystics are the most dangerous of its enemies', Wesley decided; 'they stab it in the vitals.' No; there was no release with them.

With whom then? The question became acute, for in 1735 his father pressed him, this time insistently, to apply to succeed to the living, and so make a home for his mother and sisters after the rector's death. The younger Samuel, snugly ensconced as headmaster of Blundell's school near Tiverton (where he was looked upon as something of a rigid prig), had stoutly refused the succession, and joined in urging his brother. At this renewed demand, John shrank aghast, and compiled a terrific screed to his father, in which, in twenty-six long argumentative sections, he proved that it was better for his soul, and therefore better for Christianity, that he should stay at Oxford. Surely he could do most good where he was most perfect. At Oxford he had every advantage—a few close friends to watch over his soul, freedom from half-Christians, freedom from care, which last St. Paul had said was essential: at Epworth he would relapse into the state of a mere ordinary parson, hated by his parishioners: for, once he had told them what he thought of them, all his present popularity with them would evaporate. Through all the letter one can feel Wesley writhing at the prospect that he, who, as Law had penetratingly told him, wanted to convert the whole world, should be cabined in a desolate parish. Old Mr. Wesley loyally tried his hardest to chew his son's indigestible logic; but he confessed that he did not understand it all, and very much doubted whether his son had arrived at any universal truths in his gigantic epistle. The young man's obvious duty was at Epworth. The younger Samuel thought so too. Not to undertake a cure of souls when offered was, he told his brother, to go back on the promises made at ordination. Wesley fiercely resisted this argument; he was under no necessity to undertake a cure of souls, and he wrote to the Bishop of Oxford to confirm him in this view, as was duly done: at the same time, how did Samuel know that he would not accept one of the College curacies? In fact, he probably would. Suddenly, however, for no revealed reason, he gave in. Nevertheless, when his father died the old man's dream was not fulfilled, and another man got the living. Perhaps the authorities had not liked the Jacobite sermon Wesley preached before the University in 1734; perhaps they did not approve of mixing water with the communion wine. At all events Wesley was allowed to struggle after salvation at Oxford.

Not for long, however: for a few weeks later it was suggested to him that he might go to Georgia, under Colonel Oglethorpe, founder of the colony. Wesley jumped at the offer. There, among the Indians whom he would convert (simple people, crying out for light, begging to be taught), he would be able to achieve holiness. Freed from temptations to eat or drink too much, away from women, except such as were, he felt, scarcely of the same species as himself, far from the lure of talk, in which the tongue might utter phrases not salted with the divine wisdom, surely he would become *fully* converted. Yes, he would go to Georgia; he would undertake vicarial duties temporarily at Savannah; then he would convert the Indians. But he made it quite clear that his dominant motive in going was to save his own desperately seeking soul.

§ 2. GEORGIA (1736–1737)

John Wesley, with his brother Charles, who was going out as Oglethorpe's Indian Secretary, settled down in a cabin partitioned off in the forecastle. There they would be able to dwell in seclusion, and gain strength for their operations against the devil, who, as Wesley said, hates aggressive warfare. It had been suggested to John that he might well begin his ministry among the passengers, a collection of very average 'adventuring' colonists leavened with the presence of a few Moravian Brethren, earnest, primitive Christians, and he leaped at the opportunity.

The brothers began with self-discipline, by seeing how little they could eat: no meat, no wine, only rice and biscuit—and immediately set out upon their task. Here was fruitful soil, not the scoffing indifference of a university; and, besides, they had the passengers at their mercy. Those destined for salvation could not escape as people could at Oxford; there was no getting away from the ship, nor from the Wesleys, who pervaded every corner of it in their tireless activity. Matters began well enough; the Wesleys succeeded in putting ashore a notoriously drunken servant-girl before they sailed; a man who objected to the only cabin being used for services left the ship at the first port out; and Oglethorpe got rid of the second mate, 'an oppressive, insolent, turbulent man . . . an unrighteous and wicked man'. There was a fair number of communicants, a child or two and some Quakers were presented for baptism, sickness induced a grateful seriousness in a woman and a sailor. The Wesleys, much encouraged, decided to give up suppers.

But then things did not go quite so well. Some people objected to so much, such continual, expounding and being read to; the woman who was serious when ill became less so when well. And soon the ship was rent by a dissension. A Mrs. Hawkins, 'a gay young woman', showed signs of repentance. Wesley, delighted, after long and frequent catechisings, admitted her to the communion table. This very much upset the other ladies, and their husbands, and even split the Methodists. Charles, more rigorous than John, who always leant towards charity, was 'perverse' on this point; Ingham and Delamotte, two members of the Holy Club, sided with Charles in thinking Mrs. Hawkins a hypocrite; Oglethorpe was unsound, and Wesley had to reprove him. The bickerings among the women grew ever fiercer, the tension among the men terrific. Wesley, harassed, decided that he must take no pleasure in food and drink, for the only times at which he was at all at peace were when he was learning German to be able to talk with the Moravians.

Then there were storms; seas burst into the cabin, and Wesley found to his horror that he was unwilling to die. He was therefore unfit. There were some, indeed, who, supported by the sailors, declared there had been no danger, but that merely showed that they were true cowards, who did not dare face even the idea of death. The only people who seemed unalarmed were the Moravians. 'In the midst of the psalm

7

wherewith their service began . . . the sea broke over, split the mainsail in pieces, covered the ship, and poured in between the decks, as if the great deep had already swallowed us up. A terrible screaming began among the English. The Germans looked up, and without intermission sang calmly on. I asked one of them afterwards, "Was you not afraid?" He answered, "I thank God, no." I asked, "But was not your women and children afraid?" He replied mildly, "No; our women and children are not afraid to die."' This gave Wesley courage to minister to his crying, trembling neighbours, and he was able to record, 'This was the most glorious day which I have hitherto seen.'

And so the voyage went on, with prayers and exhortations, tending the sick, writing sermons, learning German, which, however, proved an intractable language. Oglethorpe gave up his cabin to a woman who was ill, the Wesleys surrendered theirs to Oglethorpe, and slept where they could, in whatever beds happened to be vacant, or on boards. Towards the end of the journey, his bed being wet, John lay down on the floor, and slept soundly; 'and I believe', he wrote, 'I shall not find it needful to go to bed, as it is called, any more.' On the whole an exciting if confusing journey. Everything had not gone well, but now and again the Lord had opened broad paths.

On the 8th February 1736, three days after they reached land, Wesley had a peculiar experience. He asked the advice of Mr. Spangenberg, the Moravian pastor, with regard to his own conduct. 'Do you know yourself?' Spangenberg asked him; 'Have you the witness within yourself? Does the Spirit of God bear witness with your spirit that you are a child of God?' Wesley was surprised at this question from a man of his own age, and did not know what to answer. The good German noticed his confusion, and enquired, 'Do you know Jesus Christ?' A difficult point, and Wesley paused before he answered, 'I know He is the Saviour of the world.' 'True,' the Moravian replied, 'but do you know He has saved you?' This was not at all the procedure Wesley was accustomed to: it was usually he who asked the questions. He managed to bring out, 'I hope He has died to save me.' Spangenberg had little more to ask, since the answers did not seem satisfactory. He only enquired again, 'Do you know yourself?' to which Wesley hesitatingly returned, 'I do'. Yet he feared he had spoken nothing but vain words.

— This was the introduction to two years the record of which reads like the wildest fantasy, whether we regard Wesley simply from the inside, or see him merely as others saw him, externally; while if we consider the immense discrepancy between the two, and the utterly topsy-turvy results of the Wesleys' efforts, we feel that everybody in Georgia must have been a little mad. Wesley, except in one instance, was ruthlessly logical, methodical to an extreme, with a directed passion which seemed fanaticism to the mixed humanity, some riff-raff, some pietistic, of the infant colony, with its passions rough and ready, inclined at times to turbulence.

The moment Wesley landed, he began to display that astonishing activity which he never left off, and at the same time submitted himself to the rigid discipline, the strenuous reaching out after salvation, which gave him a sense of proportion so different from that of the average parson. The spirit within, known only to himself, drove the man, unflaggingly, relentlessly, to further ardours and endurances. Beginning the day at five, he would fill it with devotions, prayers, visits, secretarial work for Oglethorpe (Charles proving thoroughly inept), writing for long stretches punctuated every hour with a short spell for prayer, learning piety from the Moravians, teaching himself German, translating hymns from that language, acquiring Spanish so as to talk to the Jews, besides attending his English parishioners, conducting prayers in French, reading the Greek Testament, poring over devotional books, instructing, exhorting, baptising, marrying, burying, and for relaxation dipping into Plato (although he had renounced the classics), swimming in the river among the alligators, gardening, building, and, once, for half an hour, playing upon the flute— above all singing, singing when alone, singing when one man came to visit him, singing among the Moravians. Reading his diary, one gets the impression that he sung his way through his life in Georgia, often hymns of his own making. Method, method everywhere, in keeping his diary, looking after his books, in reading, in writing, in praying and fasting. Especially in fasting. During his first Lent, deciding that the ordinary fast was not enough, he would go the whole day without touching a morsel of food, ending it only with a little bread and butter at nine o'clock. Sleep? What did it matter where one slept?—in bed, or on boards, or out of doors in the drenching dews, from which one took no harm, unless a genteel education had led to despicable softness. Yet in spite of this mortification he enjoyed life—no sour Puritan here—enjoyed the little that he ate, delighted in swimming, revelled in the beauties of the countryside. And if his diary was dotted with the ejaculation Κύριε βοήθει (O Lord, come to the rescue!), it was only at periods of difficulty.

Oglethorpe found him invaluable, eager to help, untiring, a good secretary, a born organizer: but his parishioners did not find his organizing capacity so much to their taste. Schools, yes, he might institute them as much as he pleased, but his other arrangements were uncomfortable. Splitting up the service into two parts, with the part they most wanted to attend at five in the morning, might be according to the rules of the ancient Church, but it was inconvenient, as was the time in the afternoon he chose for his visits, a time when every decent, hard-working man would like to be tasting the joys of a siesta. And all this rigour, these rules about communion, this insistence upon plunging an infant three times into water when baptising it, this arrogancy with Dissenters, this refusal to bury good honest citizens because in life they had not had the exact religious colouring he himself displayed! The men did not like him. With the women, however, it was different. They warmed to the popular preacher side of him, especially as he always dilated upon the doctrine of love rather than that of fear, to his mixture of humility and pride, his eagerness to help, his spruce figure, and his 'Adonis locks of auburn hair, which he took care to have in the most exact order'. Women; there was a possible snare: they were weak creatures that had to be helped, but was it wise to have too much to do with them? He had asked Spangenberg's advice when he arrived, especially about Mrs. Hawkins, and the worthy Moravian had answered in the words of Thomas à Kempis: 'Have little to do with good women; but commend them to God'; which dictum Wesley amended to 'Have little to do with women'. 'I stand in jeopardy every hour', he wrote to his brother in discreet Greek: 'Two or three [of my parishioners] are women, younger, refined, God-fearing. Pray that I know none of them after the flesh.'

For Charles had gone a hundred miles south to Frederica, with Oglethorpe, and at once got into difficulties. As a secretary he was useless, as a pastor he was unendurably strict. What with early prayers, objecting to shooting on Sunday, and trine immersion for infants brought to baptism, he was soon thoroughly unpopular. Besides, Mrs. Hawkins was there, whose husband, given to a little Sunday shooting, was surgeon at Frederica. Mrs. Hawkins, young and gay, we remember, and her friend Mrs. Welch, believed that life was meant to be physically enjoyed; and both seemed to feel that the best person to enjoy it with would be Oglethorpe. They went to Charles Wesley and confessed that they had committed adultery with Oglethorpe; they then went to Oglethorpe and told him that his secretary was spreading this libel about him. The astounded governor was furious, after the manner of a man of action; he would be seized, as men of action so often are, with ill-disciplined spasms of religion, now hot, now cold, flying into rages, then brimming over with honeyed love. When the perturbing Mrs. Hawkins came to him with her story, he turned against Charles, ordered his people to provide him with nothing, not even boards to lie on, and forbade them to touch his laundry. Charles's life grew intolerable; he was shot at, he fell ill, he believed that his enemies were possessed of devils (whence, possibly, his brother's extreme fasting), and John came to the rescue, being nearly drowned on the journey. While there he seemed to make a little progress with Mrs. Hawkins; but then she grew angry, and Mrs. Welch swooned. 'God will reveal all', Wesley noted down; 'Open my eyes.' As to Oglethorpe, his mood varied, and in sum Wesley found Frederica an evil spot, where he had to talk to his brother in Greek in lonely places, and where their lives were in danger. He took Charles away, and both the brothers were glad to escape. Charles made one more attempt to live at Frederica, but on a second failure soon went back to England.

John found Savannah better than Frederica. The people there submitted more willingly to organization; they were 'affected' at what was said to them. And if attendance at church fell off after the first occasion—the people of Savannah might be allowed their share of natural curiosity—there were some stout believers and some remarkable returns of sinners to righteousness. Small religious societies were formed, which compensated Wesley a little for not being able to visit the Indians, the 'main design' of his going out. But soon Wesley had to go back to Frederica, to wrestle with Mrs. Hawkins, who, however, grew very angry, and Wesley 'got no good'. There were, indeed, some bright symptoms even there; Wesley was heartened by an exemplary death, and Oglethorpe forbade shooting on Sundays. On the other hand, one of his parishioners, Horton, told him, 'I like nothing you do. All your sermons are satires upon particular persons, therefore I will never hear you more; and all the people are of my mind, for we won't hear ourselves abused. Besides, they say they are Protestants. But as for you, they cannot tell what religion you are of. They never heard of such a religion before. They do not know what to make of it. And then, your private behaviour—all the quarrels that have been since you came have been 'long of you.' But then, as Wesley was to remark, it was his business to talk, to tell home-truths; he was not for the 'accursed principle', as he called it, of 'He that hath ears let him hear'. It was precisely the people who seemed to have no ears that he was determined to make listen. Even Mrs. Hawkins. Back again in Savannah he wrote her a letter, a painful task, relieved by interludes of song. Nevertheless Wesley began to be troubled; his will was aroused, a desire appeared in him to force, to dominate; these people should, they must, do as he told them; thus he drenched them, in Southey's phrase, with the physic of an intolerant (and therefore intolerable) discipline. Yet he loved his flock, he was passionately eager to save them, and spared no pains, instructing them privately in religion, but still he felt that things were not going as they ought. A visit to Charleston freshened him to make another attack upon Frederica.

He sallied forth straightway upon Mrs. Hawkins. She greeted him with a demand to know what two Greek words meant in a letter Charles had written him, and which had been intercepted. Wesley's answer was evasive; he did not translate the words, but said that only she and Mrs. Welch were pointed at in them. Her husband came in and raged, and Wesley, exhausted ('no sleep; fleas', is a diary entry of the time), burst into tears.

The amiable couple then threatened that they would have both the brothers unfrocked. After that there were scenes with Oglethorpe, scenes with Horton, and the next day a terrible scene with Mrs. Welch, who publicly heaped scurrilous abuse upon him. Worse was to follow on the third day. Mrs. Hawkins sent for him. She threatened him with a double-barrelled pistol, and when he struck her hand up, rushed at him with a pair of scissors, threw him down on the bed, and cried that she must have either his life-blood or his hair. A servant girl came in, and Mrs. Hawkins shrieked for a knife; menservants came, and at last a constable and another, who began to take hold of the demented woman. But at that moment Hawkins, coming in, forbade anyone to touch his wife and demanded what that scoundrel Wesley was doing in his house. What Wesley was doing at that moment was to grip Mrs. Hawkins's wrists securely, so she seized his cassock with her teeth, tearing both his sleeves, and bit his arm. Degrading scene; and afterwards Oglethorpe was of little help.

So Wesley, after a perilous journey, getting lost, sleeping in the open, and encountering a storm at sea, returned to Savannah, where he found to his horror that his *locum tenens*, an Independent, had broken the rules about baptism and was only haphazardly publishing banns before marriage. 'Oh discipline! Where art thou to be found?' Wesley cried; 'Not in England, nor (as yet) in America.' The 'as yet' is significant; and he settled down ever more fiercely to organize, to visit, to exhort, to methodize his own life. And then, since Frederica was a part of his parish, he, after a while (we are now in October 1736), went back there, though without much hope of doing good.

But there was one parishioner to whom he thought he might bring comfort, one who had been much under his particular care for some time, Sophy Hopkey, niece of the wife of Causton, chief magistrate of Savannah, who had surrendered her to Wesley's discretion. She was eighteen, and sunk in the despondency of a broken love-affair with a dubious character called Mellichamp, who wildly threatened bloodshed if she married anyone else. From the first she had interested Wesley, and, dressed in white since she had discovered that his preference lay that way, had daily had recourse to him for spiritual aid;

moreover she had nursed him through a fever due to his having taken a little meat and a dash of wine at Oglethorpe's request, who was afraid that his abstention might be misconstrued. Miserable at the Caustons', she had fled to Frederica, and Wesley found to his sorrow that in that ignoble spot her religious notions had vanished. She 'was scarce a shadow of what she was. . . . Harmless company [that dread snare] had stole away all her strength.' She panted to go back to England, and not all Wesley's readings from the *Serious Call* and Ephrem Syrus could move her; only when he pressed her hand did she dissolve into tears and confess that her determination to go home began to stagger. Clearly she was in a dangerous condition. What was Wesley to do?

He went to the fort to consult Oglethorpe; no one was there except Horton, who was waiting for the governor; but, when the latter came back he ignored Wesley and rushed to kiss Horton. The action was full of meaning; Wesley's influence had sunk! Oglethorpe, busied with the affairs of the infant colony, could not be bothered with the problem the parson put to him. Send the girl back to Savannah, he said, a decision which prostrated her in a passion of weeping. Very well, Wesley agreed, but how? Why, in Wesley's boat.

It is dangerous for a susceptible man to travel for a week alone in the company of a charming girl, ten times more so if she is a damsel in distress, appealing to all that is generous and warm-hearted in a man eager to save her soul. Wesley hoped that he would emerge free, buoyed up as he was by the belief that she would hold firm by her repeated desire and design to live single. Through storms, in which she expressed her indifference to life, in calms, and encamped on romantically uninhabited islands, he studiously read to her Bishop Patrick's *Prayers* and Fleury's *History of the Church*, but he could not always keep clear of personal issues. How far was she engaged to Mellichamp? He was constrained to ask. 'I have promised to marry him or none at all', she answered. Then, in spite of himself, the words bubbled out of Wesley's mouth: 'Miss Sophy, I should think myself very happy if I was to spend my life with you.' 'I am every way unhappy', she wailed in a flood of tears; 'I won't have Tommy for he is a bad man. And I can have no one else. Oh sir! You don't know the danger you are in.' Thus, although the conversation ended with a psalm, it was two very overstrung, nerve-racked mortals that finally arrived at Savannah.

How marvellous she was! So still when he expounded, so unweariedly active at other times. Wesley adorned her with every perfection, every virtue, every grace. She could live on bread and water, was 'patient of labour, of cold, heat, wet, badness of food or of want; and of pain to an eminent degree. . . .' Neat, she despised the fripperies of dress; thoughtful, she loved retirement; her quick understanding 'reached the highest things and the lowest'. 'As her humility was, so was her meekness. She seemed to have been born without anger. . . .'

But no! No! The thought of marriage was as distressing as the thought of not marrying Sophy. Wesley trembled at the notion that he would not be able to keep his celibate resolves. 'Naked to follow the naked Christ' was his ideal, not connubial happiness; he knew that if he married he would not be able to resist the temptations of the state, the snug fireside. His friends, whom he consulted, gave ambiguous answers, as did the Bible from which he sought guidance by chance reference. So she continued to come to his house, where, immediately after breakfast, they would join in Hickes's *Devotions*, to be followed by a French lesson, and that again by prayers. In the evening they would ponder Ephrem Syrus, and afterwards Dean Young's or Mr. Reeve's *Sermons*, or, dullest of dull Puritans, Dr. Owen. Strange Galeottos, but Galeottos none the less, and Wesley began to waver. In vain he drained devotional works of their virtue, imbibed anatomy and medicine, struggled with German grammar, plunged into Spanish, sought refuge in Hebrew, took boat and cut down trees, prayed with Delamotte, sang, wrote letters, and ever more rigidly trampled bare the paths of parochial duty—he drew fatefully nearer the precipice. Would it not be better to flee from Georgia? But escape was not so easy; the better parishioners implored him to stay until his place could be filled: he could not abandon them.

Physical adventure, absence from Savannah, seem to have a little distracted Wesley's thoughts from the enticing Sophy, whose name does not appear for some time in the *Journal*, except when he advised her to sup earlier and not go to bed immediately after. He would tramp the woods with Delamotte, wading breast-high through swamps, sleeping out and getting his clothes frozen as hard as the trees against which he rested. He made a dash to Frederica, where he stayed three weeks, though his life was in danger, and he utterly despaired of doing any good there. But the abnegation did not last, and when he came back he rushed off instantly to rescue the docile Sophy from company he thought would not improve her. Then a month of torture followed (February 1737); celibacy tugged him, Sophy tugged him; he was in a 'great strait'. He still thought he would remain single, but a quasi-proposal, impulsive as his former one, escaped him without the consent of his mind; centred in himself, he harried the luckless Sophy into distraction: if he had wished, he could not have driven her into a neurotic state with more fiendish skill.

Sophy's half-hearted repelling of that second half-minded offer seemed to him a 'narrow escape'. The bewildered saviour of his own soul ran for strength to a Moravian pastor, who alarmingly told him that he saw no reason why Wesley should not marry. Luckily Ingham and Delamotte, always watchful over Wesley's spiritual welfare, were made of sterner stuff and unequivocally disapproved of the idea. Ingham doubted the girl's religion and sincerity, and as for her determination not to marry, upon which Wesley seemed to count, he had better not put it to the test. But still Sophy came for French lessons, and still the barricade of Hickes's *Devotions* was not enough. He fled to the woods, scribbling a hasty note, 'I find, Miss Sophy, I can't take fire into my bosom, and not be burnt.' He cut down trees, studied, sang, had recourse to the long-abandoned ejaculatory prayers, examined himself. Sometimes he was cheerful, but sometimes God hid His face, and Wesley's heart sank like a stone. To leave Sophy was like a sentence of death; nevertheless, when he went back he told her that he would not marry until he had been among the Indians. 'Private prayer, uneasy', the diary for that day records; and later, 'More uneasy. κύριε βοήθει.' The next day the wretched Sophy told him that people marvelled what she did so long at his house, and added, 'I don't think it signifies for me to learn French any longer.' He made no protest, and it is small wonder that when next he saw her she was 'sharp, fretful, disputatious'.

Ah, but she would never marry, she had said so. Time and again she as good as proposed to Wesley, but he cheated himself with her outspoken negative. The atmosphere grew ever more hideously tense. One day was 'indeed an hour of trial. Her words, her eyes, her air, her every motion and gesture, were full of such softness and sweetness', Wesley confessed, 'I know not what might have been the consequence had I but touched her hand. And how I avoided it, I know not. Surely God is over all!' The next day he did touch her hand— but no, she would never marry, it was no use proposing. Still, it would be better not to touch her any more—ever.

Delamotte, who lived in Wesley's house, saw it all through the tears which gushed from him at the thought that he would have to live away from his adored leader. Wesley assured him he would never marry, but Delamotte told him that he did not know his own heart. Perhaps not; then he would tame it, by furious bouts of logic, by learning Italian, by singing, by being more thankful in eating; but even these exercises produced no cure; he was just as undecided. An appeal to God through lots would settle the question. He and Dalamotte put into a hat three pieces of paper on which were written the injunctions 'Marry'; 'Think not of it this year'; 'Think of it no more', and with a sigh of thankful relief Delamotte found that he had drawn the last. Another trial by sortilege brought the answer from the Searcher of hearts, 'Converse with her only in the presence of Mr. Delamotte.' So, it was decided; there could be no doubt now what God wanted. Wesley felt relieved.

But the worst agony, for both the lovers, was yet to come. Four days later, on March 8th, Sophy told Wesley that she had entirely cast Mellichamp out of her heart, but that Mr. Williamson was paying her his addresses. Williamson! a person, Wesley declared, 'not remarkable for handsomeness, neither for greatness, or knowledge, or sense, and least of all for religion!' But, Sophy assured the lover who would not see, she would never do anything without first consulting him. He was in the toils; even if he saw her only in company, he admitted, he would love her more and more. It was beyond his strength to break it off. He went into the house and found Mrs. Causton in a rage at a letter from Mellichamp to Sophy which she had intercepted. She rated the helpless girl, shouting at her,

'Get you out of my house; I will be plagued with you no more. Mr. Wesley, I wish you would take her, take her away with you.' Wesley, controlled, answered that Sophy was welcome to a room in his house—or she might go to the Moravians. This was too much for Sophy; she burst into tears.

The next day Wesley went back to them. Mrs. Causton said that both she and Sophy were most grateful for all he had done, and—would he publish the banns of her niece's marriage with Williamson the next Sunday! Wesley thought he was dreaming. Was this a trick to entice him? He put the suspicion away as unworthy. He asked if Sophy were willing. Yes, he was assured by Williamson and by both the Caustons, unless he had any objection. It started into his mind 'What if she means, unless you will marry me?' But he checked the thought with, 'Miss Sophy is so sincere; if she meant to she would say so.' She had indeed said so, again and again, but Wesley had been deaf. What could the poor girl do more? Desperate to escape Mellichamp, still more desperate to get away from the Caustons, she had to marry somewhere, and she wanted to marry Wesley. But he had hung off. When he saw her she once more told him, in answer to his reproach, that he had not consulted her, that she had only agreed if he had nothing to object. But Wesley's desire to save his soul was stronger than his desire to marry Miss Hopkey: he ignored the offered opportunity.

Nevertheless when he went home he walked up and down in agony. He had never felt such pain, never known such an hour. 'To see her no more; that thought was as the piercings of a sword.' He was weary of the world, weary of light. He sought God, but God forsook him. Then Causton appeared; he did not at all approve of this match. What exactly had passed between Sophy and Wesley? Wesley innocently told it all. 'If you loved her,' the astounded Causton burst out, 'how could you possibly be so overseen as not to press her when she was so much moved?' Well, he concluded, Wesley might make sure that the girl really knew her own mind. So Wesley went to her again, and asking her if she was decided, accepted her assurance that she was; and yet, when that evening he read to the family out of Bishop Hall's *Meditations*, Sophy fixed her eyes alternately on him and Williamson, steadily, as though reading them both. Williamson was alive to the meaning of that scrutiny, and wisely carried her off three days later and incontinently married her. 'On March 4th,' Wesley was to say in reference to the day of the lot drawing, 'God commanded me to pull out my right eye; and by His Grace I determined to do so: but being slack in the execution, on Saturday March 12th, God being very merciful to me, my friend performed what I could not.' The dedicated soul was saved; reason supporting pride had won the battle against love; but that the real casualty had been the unfortunate Sophy does not seem to have occurred to the man striving after salvation.

A violent emotional storm such as the one Wesley had passed through does not at once leave a man in peace; nor did the people concerned do so. Williamson was angry and forbade his wife to see Wesley; it unsettled her, and besides, he might make her too strict for his comfort. Wesley himself was in some doubt as to Sophy's integrity. Had she dealt quite openly with him? She professed that she had, so he was able to admit her to Holy Communion. Then further doubts arose; Wesley heard things, he even enquired about things—Sophy had never really broken with Mellichamp until her marriage, and had been toying with Williamson for weeks. What did it count that she did tell Wesley that if he had pressed her at any time, she would have accepted him? He could not forgive (it never entered his head that he was entirely to blame); he was very worried; the 'case', as he came to refer to it briefly, was the subject of frequent discussion with his friends. And then she became wearied in well-doing; she grew lax in fasting, she neglected half the services, she did not come to communion— and, worst of all, she never declared herself penitent for her duplicity with Wesley! He would have to take disciplinary action. When at last, on August 7th, after a long interval, she presented herself to partake in the Lord's Supper, he repelled her from the table.

There was an immediate uproar. Williamson, without hesitation, had a warrant made out for Wesley's arrest for defamation of his wife's character and for refusing to administer her the sacrament, by which Williamson declared himself in-jured to the tune of a thousand pounds. On the 9th Wesley was apprehended. He denied the first charge, and stated that the court was not competent to judge the second, and was ordered to stand his trial. Williamson demanded a bail of £50, but the clerk interposed, 'Sir, Mr. Wesley's word is sufficient.' Then Causton grew busy, and on the ground that Wesley's action was an insult to his family, entered zestfully into a glorious period of suborning witnesses, in which, since he was store-keeper as well as chief magistrate of Savannah, his efforts were crowned with success. A terrific Grand Jury was empanelled consisting of forty-four people—nearly the whole adult male population of Savannah. The result as regards Wesley was prejudged; but there was another, a curious one, unforeseen by Causton; being unpopular, his own character was enquired into (he was in consequence ultimately dismissed his post); and though the jury found against Wesley, a minority signed a statement exonerating him and ascribing the whole of the accusations to Causton's malice.

Wesley was in a strong position; nine of the ten counts against him were on purely ecclesiastical grounds—he had not buried, baptised, conducted services, properly, and so on. These he ignored. As to the tenth, defaming Mrs. Williamson, he was prepared to answer it. Yet, strangely enough, though he appeared at five or six courts as they sat, he was never called upon to do so.

But it was quite plain to Wesley that he had better leave Savannah. He was doing no good; people did not care for his ministrations. He had given his heart, his mind, his body, to their redemption; they replied that he was some kind of Papist, that they had been happy enough until he came, but that since then there had been nothing but quarrels, that his visitations were inquisitions—in short, that they did not at all like his sort of Christianity. Perhaps they felt that he was too con-cerned to become a saint. Wesley felt no obligation to stay. He had, indeed, been appointed pastor of Savannah, but against his will, and only as a stop-gap: he had come to convert the Indians. But he was not allowed to go to them, on account of the danger; and besides, even if he went, the prospects of success did not seem very encouraging. The Indians were not, after all, the noble savages he had hoped; they were degraded drunkards, lechers, murderers, they were eaten up with idleness. He had met some of them when they came to Savannah; and to the chiefs he always appeared in full canonicals. They had said, indeed, that they would not mind having it explained to them what Christianity was about, but they did not want to be made into Christians, as their fellows were in Spanish-American lands, without this simple preliminary being gone through. Christians? What were they? Were they the people who lived at Frederica and Savannah? If so, after observing their behaviour, they would rather retain their own religion.

So Wesley, after consulting his friends, decided to leave Georgia; and on November 22nd, 1737, went to tell Causton that since the latter had called him a hinderer of the peace, he proposed to depart immediately. He then posted up a notice to that effect. He made preparations to go on December 2nd; but on that day Causton sent for him and told him that he could not leave unless he gave security to appear before the court and gave bail as to Williamson's charge. Wesley answered that he would give neither bond nor bail at all. Thereupon the magistrate published an order forbidding anyone help Wesley to go. So Wesley decided to make a bolt for it, and that evening slipped away in company with three others, who, for reasons less commendable than his own, also wanted to leave Savannah. They made their way out of Georgia, getting lost, nearly dying for want of the water which Wesley discovered by poking his stick into the ground, and which they then dug down to with their hands, and finally arrived at Charleston. There Wesley expected worse trials than contempt and hunger, which are easy to be borne, namely respect and fullness of bread: however, he just managed to survive these crosses, though his spirit was drained by ease and harmless conversation, and on Saturday 24th he left America hoping, if it pleased God, some day to return.

§ 3. SALVATION (1738–1740)

Wesley never at any time lacked moral courage, even to battle against himself, which is the hardest of all struggles; for pride or mere pugnacity will enable a man to defy vulgar opinion. If on a given day he would have to register failure in his diary— that he had wasted a few minutes, or had been inattentive, that he had done no good, or been 'lost'—five o'clock the next morning would find him sparking for the fight, optimistic, brave. But on the voyage home he lost his resilience. He was profoundly depressed, seized by a vague fear of he knew not what danger, from which crying to God brought only passing relief. He tried to hold forth, to exhort, to create a flock, but found that he was utterly unwilling to speak; and even though he was easier after beginning to instruct the cabin-boy, he was once more a prey to inhibition. Was it God's will that he should be silent, he wondered, or was it a temptation from nature, or the Devil?

The voyage went on, mainly in storms—once it blew 'a proper hurricane'—and Wesley found to his dismay that he was still afraid of dying. Quoting Donne he cried:

> I have a sin of fear, that when I've spun
> My last thread, I shall perish on the shore,

for though he could usually say, 'Verily, if the Gospel be true, I am safe', in a storm he would think, 'What if the Gospel be not true?' Suppose he had surrendered all—ease, friends, repute, country, life—for a mere dream, 'a cunningly devised fable!' 'I have a fair summer religion', he wrote in bitter self-contempt, and in the fullness of his heart convicted himself 'of unbelief . . . of pride . . . of gross irrecollection . . . of levity and luxuriancy of spirit'. There were indeed moments when, from preaching, or from making good resolutions, his spirits revived, but continual self-examination bogged him in despondency. Yet how difficult it was to know what was right, when, as he saw, he had for many years been tossed by various winds of doctrine. In the reaction from the Popish error of justification by works, he had nearly fallen into the mistake of magnifying faith to too amazing a size: and if English divines had rescued him from well-meaning but wrong-headed Germans, the English divines themselves cut the rock from under his feet by interpreting the scriptures in various ways. He had been in a sense too zealous, he found, had applied the local rules of Provincial Synods as though they were universally applicable, and committed other blunders of the same sort; he remembered with horror his flirtings with the mystics. His faith! What was his faith? Even devils have faith—of a sort. His pride was abased. 'Oh!' he groaned in despair, 'I went to America to convert the Indians; but who shall convert me?'

When such a cry issues from a mood of intense depression, the answer is usually not long in coming, and it came to Wesley exactly four months later than the prayer torn from his heart, through the mouth of Peter Böhler, whom Wesley met soon after getting back to London. This Moravian, nine years younger than Wesley (who was now thirty-five), had come across with a group of other Germans; and Wesley, on meeting them, being always drawn towards Moravians and irresistibly attracted by Böhler, found them lodgings near his own. He needed just then to have by his side someone who was calm, at once warm and placid in the faith, for his outer as well as his inner life was troubled: there were unpleasant interviews with the Trustees of Georgia, and already he was finding that his ministrations were not liked, for preaching in London on February 5th, 1738, he was immediately told that many of the best of the parish were so offended that he was not to preach there again. He had enlarged on the text, 'If any man be in Christ, he is a new creature', and something in his fervour, perhaps a suggestion that his hearers had a good deal too much of the old Adam about them, had upset their content in their genteel, self-flattering faith. On the next Sunday, after holding forth in another church on Charity—'Oh hard sayings! Who can bear them?' he was told that there also he was not to preach any more. He went off to Oxford with Peter Böhler.

The Moravian was exciting; there was something about him ordinary Christians, even good ones, had not got. His words, even in the Latin they conversed in, were suggestive, if not always understandable. What did he mean, for instance, when he said to Wesley, 'My brother, my brother, that philosophy of yours must be purged away'? Reason! Surely reason must not be abandoned? Wesley went back restlessly to London, where he preached two or three times, deciding that that sermon was the best which had given the most offence. No more fair summer religions for other people; religion was to be a flail, a scourge, or, as Mr. Chesterton has expressed it, 'a terror, a splendour, a necessity, and a nuisance'. He rushed about, first to Salisbury to see his mother, who was staying with one of her married daughters; and he was about to go to Tiverton to see Samuel, when a message was brought to him that his brother Charles was dying at Oxford. He started off at once, resolving

8

on the way to be absolutely open and unreserved with all he met (that is, to preach at them without delay), to labour after seriousness, and never to laugh—'no, not for a moment'; never to speak a word that did not 'tend to the glory of God, not to talk of worldly things'. The stormy path was the only one; his old doctrine of cheerful Christianity was forgotten.

Charles was recovering from his pleurisy by the time John got to Oxford, where he found Peter Böhler, who talked, talked to such purpose that the next day the Moravian clearly convinced the elder of the brothers of unbelief, of want of that faith 'whereby alone we are saved'. Unbelief! At once it struck Wesley that he must stop preaching. How could he who had no faith dare to exhort? 'By no means', Böhler said; 'Preach faith till you have it; and then, *because* you have it, you *will* preach faith.' Thus two days later Wesley began to impart this strange new doctrine of justifying faith, though his soul started back from the work. Justifying faith! What was this faith? He could not say, he had not himself got it: he was only certain that it was essential to have it. The first man to whom he preached, a criminal under sentence of death, was converted. Happy omen!

Perhaps, as Böhler said, if he preached enough what he did not believe, he would come to believe it. At all events, when a few days later he took a journey north with a friend, they lost no opportunity of declaring the truth, on the roadside, or at inns where the good people who wanted to eat their suppers in peace were apt to be resentful; but the laggards were soon brought to a better mind. Indeed, if the two friends did not open, God would reprove them for their negligence by sending a stinging downpour of hail. So at Altrincham they tackled a Quaker, who was 'well skilled in, and therefore sufficiently fond of, controversy', and, after arguing for an hour, Wesley somewhat inconsistently advised him to dispute as little as possible; and once when a man overtook them on the road, whom they found more inclined to speak than to hear, 'We', Wesley records, 'spoke and spared not.' Others again were cautioned against talkativeness and vanity, and these experiences stirred Wesley so greatly, that when he got back to Oxford, he abandoned formal prayers, finding that those he invented gave him greater relief.

On March 23rd he met Böhler again, and was more and

more amazed at the accounts he heard of the fruits of living
faith, holiness and happiness. But, after preaching a little more,
and finding no miraculous change in himself, he decided to wait
in silence and retirement in the country. Böhler, however, called
imperiously to him, and on April 22nd Wesley went to meet
the Moravian again. Now he agreed to all that Böhler said, but
yet he could not understand what he meant by 'instantaneous
work'. How could faith be given in a moment, how could a man
be turned *at once* from darkness to light, from sin and misery to
righteousness and joy? 'Look at the Bible', Böhler said; and to
his astonishment Wesley found that nearly all the conversions
recorded there were instantaneous. Still he resisted. That was all
very well, but those events had taken place in the first days of
Christianity, and things were altogether different now. Böhler
unhesitatingly produced several people who had had the
experience in their own persons. Wesley could only cry, 'Lord
help Thou my unbelief!' These proofs convicted him of being
too dilatory; really he ought not to preach any more; but his
mentor told him that he must on no account hide his talent in
the earth. So Wesley promptly declared his new belief in this
faith which struck, at the house of old Mr. Delamotte, to a
company which included his brother Charles. They were all
profoundly shocked. Charles especially was horrified at what
he called his brother's 'worse than unedifying discourse', while
Mrs. Delamotte was so overcome that she abruptly left the
room. How scandalous of Wesley to say that he had not faith!

But Charles soon veered round. A recurrence of pleurisy
brought Böhler to his bedside, who at last made him see that
only grace, not a so-called 'belief', could save. In the meantime,
while waiting for this faith to come, the brothers and a few more,
on the advice of and under the guidance of the compelling
Moravian, who was about to leave them for America, formed
a society which met in Fetter Lane. It was not strictly a
Moravian society, and not yet Methodist, but it differed from
other societies, which the Wesleys, among many more, had
founded both at Oxford and in Georgia, in that it was not
merely a gathering for religious talk, but involved a discipline,
a division into bands, and a mutual confession of temptations
and faults. Then John preached more vigorously than ever in
the churches, so vigorously as to be forbidden the use of three

more pulpits. But he was by no means always cheerful. From May 10th to 13th he was sorrowful and very heavy; he could not read, nor meditate, nor sing, nor pray. A letter from Böhler refreshed him a little. The next day, being a Sunday, he again preached at church, and was again told he was to preach there no more, and realised more fully than ever how intolerable the doctrine of faith was to men, especially to religious men. In some bitterness he wrote to Law, reproaching him for not having opened his eyes to the doctrine of grace; but Law got the better of a short controversy, remarking shrewdly that Wesley must not think he had changed his faith because he had changed his expressions. The week after, Charles had another relapse, and on the Sunday suddenly received the light and was as suddenly cured of his pleurisy. 'Who is so great a God as our God?' Wesley demanded.

But the three days following were days of unbearable gloom: Monday, Tuesday, and Wednesday, he felt continual sorrow and heaviness in his heart. Yet Wednesday, 24th, seemed to begin with some hope. At five o'clock he opened the Greek Testament and read, 'There are given unto us exceeding great and precious promises, even that ye should be partakers of the divine nature.' But how could he partake? He wrote agitatedly to a friend, 'How am I fallen from the glory of God! I feel that I am sold under sin. . . . Does "His spirit bear witness with our spirit that we are the children of God?"' Alas! with mine he does not.' He was desperate; but, opening his Bible again before he went out, he read, 'Thou art not far from the kingdom of God.' Perhaps there was promise there, a promise that seemed to be strengthened when he went to St. Paul's in the afternoon and heard Purcell's music ascending the glorious dome, bearing upwards the words, 'Out of the deep have I called unto Thee O Lord; Lord, hear my voice!' He was profoundly moved. Under the influence of these words, and of beauties to which he was always susceptible, it was with reluctance that he allowed himself to be dragged that evening to seek, surely a gloomier God, with a society in Aldersgate Street. A layman was reading aloud Luther's preface to the *Epistle to the Romans*; and then, at about a quarter to nine, while the voice was describing the change which God works in the heart through faith in Christ, Wesley felt his own 'strangely warmed'. All at once he was sure that he did trust in Christ, Christ alone, for salvation; and an assurance was given him that the Son of God had taken away *his* sins, *his*, and saved *him* from the law of sin and death. Ah yes, he had believed before, but with the faith of a servant, not that of a son. Then, faith had been an assent, even if an assent to what God had revealed because He had revealed it; but this, now, was a sensation, a warming of the heart; it felt like a physical embrace. At last!

But still, not safety. That very evening, in the solitude of his room, he was much buffeted with temptations, and ever and anon during the next few days hideous doubts, varied temptations, shadowed his happiness with gloom. Although the texts at which he opened his Bible were always encouraging, 'Yet the enemy injected a fear, "If thou dost believe, why is there not a more sensible change?"' A Moravian told him that he must not fight with temptations, but flee from them the moment they appeared, and take shelter in the wounds of Jesus. Gradually he felt himself stronger. On the Sunday after his conversion, he declared, at the house of Hutton, a God-seeking bookseller with whom he had lodged, that until the 24th he had not been a Christian! The scandal was terrific. He was attacked as an 'enthusiast', a seducer, a setter-forth of new doctrines. The Huttons, in terror for their children, thought he had gone mad, and told him that if he had not been a Christian five days before, then he must be a consummate hypocrite. Wesley, however, was confident and calm: he had not been a Christian, not in the way that he now was; he had been a mere nominal Christian, a poor simulacrum, so why not say so?

But Mrs. Hutton could not let the matter rest there, and she wrote to Samuel imploring him either to confine or to convert his brother when he went to see him, 'For after his behaviour on Sunday 28th, when you hear it, you will think he is not quite a right man.' Strange delusion, wild-fire, rank fanaticism, such are the words that occur in her letter. Samuel, correct, uninspired, orthodox, was horrified and remonstrated vigorously, while old Mrs. Wesley, hearing the Huttons' account, was equally perturbed, until John, in his own fascinating person, made it all clear to her. These things probably did not much shake Wesley, it was his own experiences that continued to do so, for he found that he had not altogether got dominion over

sin, was not always triumphant over temptation. One day at
Oxford, for instance, he spoke with sharpness instead of with
tender love, of one that was not sound in the faith. Immediately
God hid His face, and he was troubled. Still finding 'a kind of
soreness' in his heart, he decided to go to Germany to see the
Moravians and their leader Count Zinzendorf; accordingly, he
sailed for the Continent on June 13th, in company with Ingham.

Holland was delightfully clean, Germany picturesque, the
Moravians charming, and Herrnhut, 'the place where the
Christians lived', of overwhelming interest. Wesley noted
every detail of the organization, how the sexes lived separately,
and even within the sexes were again separated by ages
('according to growth, like cabbages', Southey comments),
being even buried in different parts of the cemetery. He observed
how they were schooled, how they worshipped, how they sang
in processions, were split up in hierarchic bands, with monitors
public and secret, and how, when the time came, the young
men and maidens were paired off by order or by lot. He was
entranced; they were attractive people, holy, devout, who could
give enthralling accounts of their religious experience, and
Count Zinzendorf himself was the most Christian of men, if a
little dictatorial. It was with regret that he tore himself away
from them; they were perfect people; and yet, and yet—when
the glow had cooled—were they, after all? Doubts grew, and in
September 1738 he began a letter to them: Did they not
neglect joint fasting? Were they serious enough, utterly innocent of levity? and were they busy enough? Further, were
they not too reserved, apt to use guile, and inclined to magnify
their own Church too much? Finally, most significant question
of any, 'Is not the Count all in all? Are not the rest mere
shadows, calling him Rabbi . . . ?' Wesley did not send that
questionnaire, but after a time for consideration he did write
them a letter, in precisely the same vein. From that time
Wesley knew in his bones, however much his heart might
mislead him, that he could never become a Moravian; his will
would have clashed with Zinzendorf's, and it was Wesley who
must guide, Wesley who must lead.

But the Moravians in Germany counted for little in the
tremendous excitement, the nervous exaltation, of the next
few months. Wesley lived in a state of extravagant strain, his

intense emotionalism exacerbated by his asceticism and his wretched allowance of sleep. It was his will alone, one would think, that made it possible for him to survive, a will to dominate, first himself, then others—a will almost, it would seem, to dominate God! At least he would wrest from God the faith that he wanted, for even in the strenuous weeks which followed, and in which so much happened that seemed directive, if not directed, Wesley was still not in possession of *assurance*, of certain faith, of a sense of forgiveness of sins, of dominion over temptation. The almost intolerable rapture of what was nearly miraculous sank sometimes, even now, into a trough of despondency; he would feel dead, not only in heart but almost in body, until the same stimulus—preaching, or a conversion, or some manifestation—would have the same tonic result.

The account of these two years in his *Journal*, or in that of others, in his diary, in the lives by his biographers, read like a whirling dream, a vortex of unbelievably many physical and spiritual events. Coming back from Germany in an elated mood, singing, it would appear from his diary, more than usual, he found work to do. There was preaching in the churches, from more and more of which both he and Charles were being excluded, preaching in other places, exhorting the Fetter Lane Society, helping Charles in his newly discovered work of converting condemned criminals, interviewing the dismayed Bishop of London, and collecting and publishing not only abridged editions of edifying works, but manifestoes, and collections of hymns written by himself and Charles or translated from foreign tongues. But even so he never ceased to examine himself; he was still his own chief interest, and when he went down to Oxford in October, he found that though he was 'new' in many things, as a convert should be, new in holiness, in designs, in desires, in conversation and in actions, he still could not find in himself the love of God or of Christ; he had no settled, lasting joy in the Holy Ghost. Still, he thought he had a measure of faith; his warming of the heart had not been meaningless. But then, on a second visit to Oxford, he met his old friend Delamotte, who administered a severe, astringent dose. 'You are better than you were at Savannah,' Delamotte told him (so much had thought eroded his devotion), 'but you are not right yet. You know that you were then blind, but you do not see now. . . . You have a simplicity,' he went on, 'but it is a simplicity of your own: it is not the simplicity of Christ. You think you do not trust in your own works, but you do trust in your own works. You do not believe in Christ.'

Pride! Was he never to be rid of pride? Consulting the Bible by lots brought some relief, and on January 4th, 1739, he humbled himself again by writing: 'I affirm I am not a Christian now . . . I have not any love of God. I do not love either the Father or the Son. . . . Again, joy in the Holy Ghost I have not . . . I have not the peace of God!' Ultimately he did attain the full sense of forgiveness of sin, with all its attendant joys, but it was when he had ceased to think so perpetually of himself. The tremendous struggle was in the end resolved—when Wesley was merged in his calling.

What this calling was soon became apparent. It was, in fact, as callings so often are, the fulfilment of his ambition, which was, as Law had so clearly seen many years before, to convert the whole world. The time seemed ripe, the moment waiting for the man. There were strange manifestations of the power of God in Scotland, and on a wholesale scale in New England. Nor were encouraging symptoms lacking in London. One woman had seen Christ in a vision at her bedside; another had met Him in her garden, had talked with Him, drunk of His blood and, embracing Him, had been washed in it. A prophetess had uttered in Wesley's presence, and he could not ascribe the performance either to hysterics or to artifice. Wesley grew ever more inspired—at the love-feasts of the society in Fetter Lane, at sermons where crowds listened entranced, and at private meetings where people would fall to the ground in an agony of conversion. Lunatics were cured. He preached 'a new way', direct experience, a new birth, and, in Moravian language, the 'indwellings', the 'getting into Christ', which so enraged his brother Samuel. He went to Oxford again, and there a woman who had opposed this 'new way' suddenly 'fell in an extreme agony, both of body and soul', and was converted. And in the midst of these excitements, he was called upon to go to Bristol.

The call came from Whitefield, who had come back from Georgia (he had sailed from England on the day that Wesley returned) and was soon to go back there as Vicar of Savannah.

He had been preaching at Bristol, inaugurating his evangelistic
career with striking success. He was extraordinarily eloquent;
his zeal, his sincerity, his love for his fellow-creatures, and his
gift for oratory at vast open-air meetings, moved even the
notoriously brutal miners, till their faces, black with coal-dust,
were furrowed white with tears. He had always been emotional.
As a servitor at Oxford he had adored the Wesleys from afar,
and had become worthy to belong to the Holy Club by starving
himself into collapse: and now this appeal to thousands, the
bringing of them gloriously to God, satisfied his rapturous needs.
Or nearly. What was still lacking was martyrdom; he wished
to reach Christ through a sea of blood; he longed to wear the
martyr's crown; at least he was sure he would be imprisoned.
But as no one would imprison him, he could only hope that he
would some day be a good enough Christian to deserve incarceration. Meanwhile, Bristol was being converted, but
Whitefield had to leave Bristol to come to London and then
go back to Savannah. Would Wesley come to carry on the
glorious work?

Wesley did not want to go, the more so as he found himself
fully employed in London, even though there was by now
hardly a church in which he was allowed to preach. He resorted
once more to the *Sortes Biblicæ*, and found that he was to go—
and die there. The society was consulted, Charles was fiercely
against his brother's going, and the discussion went on for hours.
Again the Bible was referred to by the method of chance, and
again and again the message was, expressed in different ways,
Go—and die there! There was no help for it: Wesley must go,
and he went, convinced that he was journeying to his death.
Charles was wild with grief. 'He left a blessing behind him',
he wrote of his brother in his diary: 'I desired to die with him.'

Death was mysteriously withheld, as was Whitefield's
martyrdom, and Wesley plunged into the work. At first he
professed himself much perturbed at 'this strange new way of
preaching in the fields'. All his life, he said, till quite lately,
he had been very tenacious of every point relating to decency
and order, and would have thought the saving of souls almost
a sin if it had not been done in a church. But since he had already
considered the possibility in London, on finding that the
churches would not hold the enormous congregations he

attracted, two days after reaching Bristol, which was the day on which Whitefield left, he 'submitted to be more vile', and preached to about three thousand people from a little knoll. Methodism, in his own phrase, was 'beginning to begin'.

To the Church, Bristol, with its degraded colliers at Kingswood, its Dissenters (largely Quaker), and its atheists, seemed barren ground; to Wesley it appeared white for harvest. The people flocked to hear him, crowding rooms so that the floors gave in, driving him to stand on tables in streets, to preach in natural amphitheatres; his fame grew, and he was invited to Bath. And then, on the day before Easter 1739, there was the earliest of those manifestations which were his wonder and (at first) his supreme joy. A young man listening to him was seized with a violent trembling and collapsed; but on the congregation calling upon God, he found 'peace and joy in the Holy Ghost'. The signal instances of God's mercy increased in number, in violence, in strangeness. Sometimes the people on either side of Wesley were mown down in swathes; at others, individuals fell in paroxysms of bodily anguish, shrieked, fought, foamed at the mouth, the attacks sometimes continuing for days. They were being born again, born of God, but it was they who suffered the indescribable pains of child-bearing. Wesley's imagery again and again expresses this, even when the event was not quite successful, as once when they had grieved the jealous God by questioning his work. 'The children came to the birth,' he recorded, 'but there was not strength to bring forth.' But failures were rare. Strong resisters, even Quakers, were struck to the ground; mothers followed the example of their daughters and fell into fits; many would roar in the disquietude of their spirits, and sometimes the whole floor of a room would be covered with writhing figures calling upon God, filling the air with their moans.

Nor were the agonies entirely due to being born; they were often caused by the expulsion of the Devil. Sometimes his satanic presence was only to be inferred, as in the case of the girl who had to be held down for three days; at others he declared himself to be there. Once, when Wesley was summoned through a drenching shower to see a girl, and arrived 'cold and dead, fitter for sleep than for prayer', on seeing him, the devil in the girl 'burst out into horrid laughter and said, "No power,

no power; no faith, no faith. She is mine; her soul is mine, I
have her, and will not let her go!"' Still worse was the girl of
nineteen who had to be held down by three people. Wesley
blandly gives the account.

'It was a terrible sight. Anguish, horror, and despair, above
all description, appeared in her pale face. The thousand distor-
tions of her whole body showed how the dogs of hell were
gnawing her heart. The shrieks intermixed were scarce to be
endured. But her stony eyes could not weep. She screamed
out . . . I am damned, damned; lost for ever. Six days ago you
might have helped me. But it is past. I am the devil's now. I
have given myself to him. His I am. Him I must serve. With
him I must go to hell. I will be his. I will serve him. I will go
with him to hell. I cannot be saved. I must not be saved. I must,
I will, I will be damned. . . . She then fixed her eyes on the
corner of the ceiling, and said, "There he is; aye, there he is.
Come good devil, come. Take me away. You said you would
dash my brains out; come, do it quickly. I am yours. I will be
yours. Come just now. Take me away."' What could be a
clearer, more gratifying proof, of the reality of demoniac
possession?

The curious thing is that these manifestations were only
permitted when John Wesley was the preacher; they never
happened with Charles, with Whitefield, or, definitely, with
any others of the group. It was the more striking when Whitefield, who had been ministering in London for some days, asked
Wesley to go with him to a gathering, and then invited him
to preach. At his own sermons nothing untoward occurred; but
the moment John opened his mouth, people were struck to the
ground. It was amazing. It was not that he was a very eloquent
preacher; he spoke in short, economical phrases; he could not
hold a candle to Whitefield as an orator, but his sentences
seemed to clutch at men's hearts and drag them out. Brushing
his hair back with his hand, the face he presented to his hearers
would fill them with awe, and he used his eyes in such a way
that each felt that they pierced *him* alone, that his words were
meant especially for *him*. He seems to have exercised a sort of
hypnotic influence on his audiences. Perhaps he was conscious
of this power, and liked to use it, for God had given it him to
convert with, and convert he would. For though he might

speak the words of humility as much as he liked, the spirit of pride was there, pride that he had been chosen to do this work. And perhaps also the hysterical displays satisfied his hungry emotionalism, cheated by his failure to love and to be loved humanly, a longing he professed to have eradicated. And above all he could rule, rule in hell while serving in heaven. His doubts vanished, his fist of unhappiness disappeared.

Not that all was smooth, even inside the circle. Charles was not at all comfortable about these noisy and not very exalting signs of grace. Though he was not blind to psychological possibilities, for once he and his brother had been overtaken by insane laughter when about to pray together, yet he suspected fraud, and one or two cases being discovered, he induced his brother to discourage them, though not to forgo them altogether. Whitefield, again, began to show a regrettable tendency towards the doctrine of predestination; Wesley refused to discuss it, the first sign he showed of realizing that there were things more important than doctrine. Let Whitefield, let anybody, believe what they would, so long as they believed the supreme thing, the assurance of faith. Thus he refused to allow an aspirant to join the Fetter Lane Society, not because he was a Calvinist, but because he would insist on discussing his doctrines publicly. Nor was the society itself going altogether smoothly. At meetings the young men would show, to the detriment of prayer, that they were interested in the young women, and the difficulty was to separate the sexes without hinting at the insulting reason why. Further, there was a slight difference of opinion as to whether secret monitors should be appointed, on the Moravian pattern, a suggestion which Wesley scotched. If he was to be admonished, let it be openly. But on the whole there was no cause for anxiety; the brethren were united, and Wesley continued his ministrations at Bristol.

Outside, of course, there was terrific opposition. Most of the clergy thought Wesley out of his wits and refused him their pulpits. Bishop Butler, of *Analogy* fame, thinking that 'pretending to extraordinary revelations and gifts of the Holy Ghost' was 'a horrid thing, a very horrid thing', haled Wesley before him. Saying coldly that the accounts of the conversions he heard, and which Wesley joyfully confirmed, were 'very extraordinary indeed', he asked him by what authority he preached in his diocese. The general authority of ordination that Wesley claimed was not enough for Butler, who forbade him to continue. That did not stop Wesley, but the Bishop took no action. Samuel Wesley grew ever more aghast at his brothers, and implored them to return to sanity. When he heard of John's interview with Butler, he warned them lest they should, not be excommunicated from the Church (he deplored the feebleness of its discipline), but themselves excommunicate the Church, a prophesy which fell on deaf ears, and which, since he died in November 1739, he did not live to see justified. Old Mrs. Wesley was at first averse to this new faith; then, one day, at Holy Communion, she felt that at last all her sins were really forgiven her, and her criticism ceased. Lay opposition was more furious still. Wesley could triumphantly floor such a miserable antagonist as Beau Nash with a witty retort; for when Nash scornfully told him that he judged from common report that Wesley's preaching frightened people out of their wits, Wesley told him that he did not dare judge *him* by common report. Other attacks, however, in papers and magazines, in prose and verse, by word of mouth and in preposterously large pamphlets, full of defamation and misrepresentation, were not so easy to answer. In fact, Wesley at this time did not answer them, even that most galling one which spattered him with the muddy name of Papist. Fools! As though he had not again and again abjured justification by works! So he went on through the storm, acquiring and building a meeting house at Bristol, the cost of which, though penniless, he took upon his own shoulders. God, he did not know how, would provide. He also took over a ruined building in London, near Finsbury Square, called the Foundery.

At the beginning of November 1739, Wesley went back to London, and then the state of affairs he found there was far from encouraging, for the Fetter Lane Society was woefully at odds within itself; there was sullenness, quarrelling, variance over fundamentals. It was the fault of Charles. He was more original than John (a comparison of their poems shows it)—it was he who had started the Holy Club, it was he who had first been converted, but he had not a tithe of his brother's driving power, his will to mould things as he wanted them to be; he had none of his ambition, being altogether a simpler man. In some ways he was as extreme as his brother, certainly in his addiction to the more picturesque portions of obsolete ritual, but he was at this stage of his development more gentle to others, more able to see their point of view. He dreaded the roughnesses in which his brother rejoiced, crying ha! ha! amid the trumpets, and so had let the society be invaded by a grievous heresy.

It was a form of quietism, of 'stillness', as the Moravians who expounded it called it. There would have been no harm in it in a general way—Wesley himself had taken to heart the text 'Be still, and know that I am God'—but as applied by the members who embraced it, it had two serious consequences. First, it denied that there could be degrees of faith; either you had full assurance, or you had nothing. Then, secondly, if you had nothing, it was no use to do anything but wait—no prayer, no Bible-reading, no good works, no fasting, could avail you anything; to partake of the Lord's Supper was meaningless. Wesley could accept neither of these propositions: he knew that there were degrees of justifying faith; he had felt them in himself, had seen it operate in others. You should wait for Christ and be still, but at the same time use all means of grace. Not to do the latter was to deny all the ordinances of the Church; it meant schism, and the idea of separating from the Church of England was one which Wesley would not harbour for a moment. The meetings were ominous; there were none of those glorious gatherings which went on with prayer and singing till one, till two, till three o'clock in the morning. Either the brethren sat grimly silent over their tea and bread, or there were acrid disputes. It became clear that the true believers would have to separate from the Moravians, with whom, except for a trifling variance over the question of episcopal succession, they had been almost identified. The issue swayed in the balance for weeks; it was with dismay that Wesley saw most of the society becoming engulfed in this dark mysticism, far above *him*, he declared, and hankering after French prophets. If there was to be a prophet, he would not be a Camisard! At last, on Sunday, July 30th, 1740, he decided to act. He went to a meeting in Fetter Lane, at the end of which, having been silent till then, he read a paper stating the Quietist view, refuted it, and then asked those who agreed with him to follow him out.

Many started after him, but they did not all go far, because one of the Moravians, guessing what was coming, had hidden Wesley's hat under those of all the others; and Wesley's search for his own under the tumbled pile at the end of the room so delayed him that the Moravian leader had time to dissuade some of his followers from deserting. Nevertheless eighteen or nineteen out of the sixty-odd went with Wesley; and when they met at the Foundery on the Wednesday, they saw their numbers swelled by sixteen men and most of the women. The Wesleyan Society of Methodists was clearly and distinctly established as a new and separate organization.

PART II

THE EVANGELICAL REVIVALIST

§ 1. THE FIRST LEAPS (1741–1743)

And now a new Wesley, the real Wesley, emerged, the man of action, indomitable, full of explosive energy. The prig-Wesley of Oxford, together with the smoothly fashionable parson; the rigid authoritarian of Savannah, together with the egotistic saviour of his own soul; the torn and riven Wesley, the almost fanatical theolept of the recent months, gradually disappeared, to give way to the man who—the phrase is famous—transformed the countryside of England. To say that in his great leadership, in his organizing which amounted to genius, in his passionate and untiring work of regeneration, he at last found himself, is in a sense true; to say that he at last lost himself is truer still.

Wesley had made his port, but the society had yet to squeeze through perilous straits, only just scraping between the rock of predestinarianism on the one hand, and the maelstrom of Moravianism on the other. For, cogitating in America, Whitefield had decided that he must fly the colours of Calvin. Not, he explained, that he had read anything of Calvin's; no, the doctrine of election had been imparted to him more simply by the agency of Christ and His apostles; indeed, he had had it direct from God, who had singled him out. Thus authorized, he implored Wesley, whose feet he repeatedly said he was ready to wash, to read and to think, and to rid himself of his pestilential notions of 'universal redemption', of 'free grace', of possible 'sinless perfection' in this life. Why must Wesley dispute? he asked fretfully, who, after all, had disqualified himself from judging the question by admitting that he had not the witness of the spirit within himself. He, Whitefield, daily felt Christ's blessed Spirit filling his soul and body as plain as he felt the air which he breathed or the food which he ate. 'I hope', he wrote, 'at this time I feel something of the meekness and humility of Christ.' There seemed to be more hope than fact in the statement, and Wesley was not the man to submit to such arrogance. Let Whitefield plead as much as he liked that a division in their ranks would injure the cause, that it was likely to rob them of a satisfactory martyrdom; he would never for a moment, for any reason, confess adherence to a doctrine of predestination. Why, it made God out to be worse than the Devil! He believed in universal redemption (which is not the same thing as universal salvation), and that if there were some elected to do special work (as he knew there were, feeling himself to be one), most men deserved hell, from which they were only saved by the righteousness of Christ being imputed to them. Whitefield did not relieve the tension by bidding Wesley be more cautious in discovering God's will by lot, and reminding him that the method had told Wesley that White-field ought not to go to America, where he had glamorously spread the light. Either Wesley must abandon sortilege, or suppose that God might be wrong.

The astonishing lucubrations from Whitefield, in which he begged Wesley not to dispute, and himself disputed, in which he swore he would never leave Wesley, yet left him as he did so, were private and far away; they called for no immediate action. But Wesley had to contend with a centre of disaffection nearer at hand, and public. The Kingswood school for colliers' children, of which Whitefield had laid the foundation, and which Wesley had completed, was under a layman, ignorant but holy, called Cennick, who was devoted to Whitefield, and now embraced the stimulating doctrines of election and reprobation. In continual visits to Bristol, Wesley fought the heresy which at one time sadly depleted his own meetings. Cennick wrote orgulously to Whitefield: 'I sit solitary, like Eli, waiting what will become of the ark.' Once, he sighed, but with spiritual pride behind the sigh, the Gospel had seemed to flourish gloriously at Kings-wood; but now 'with universal redemption Brother Charles pleases the world. Brother John follows him in everything.' The letter, with all its sting, fell into Wesley's hands; he saw he must be prompt—Cennick was about to found a rival society.

Wesley therefore called a general meeting, at which he accused Cennick of plotting behind his back, and produced the letter, which Cennick unrepentantly avowed; whereupon the

9

gathering warmed to recriminations both theological and
personal. Wesley adjourned the meeting for a week—not,
however, to resume the discussion: for, born to command, he
was about to show that he was. After letting the Calvinists
babble for awhile, he read a short statement, which concluded
that he, John Wesley, with the approbation of the Kingswood
faithful, declared the predestinarians expelled from the society,
not for what they might think, but because of their 'tale-
bearing, backbiting, and evil-speaking, for their dissembling,
lying, and slandering'.

The reasons he gave were excuse enough, but the real point
at issue, however much he might gloze it over, was the doctrinal
one. This was made clear enough by Whitefield, when he came
over from America in the spring of 1741, to renew body to
body the contest of which the long-range preliminaries had
already made some noise in London. For, on February 1st,
those who went to the Foundery were mysteriously given
printed copies of one of Whitefield's most controversial, we
might say most insubordinate, letters to his leader. Wesley,
holding out one of the papers, had explained that it was an
underhand production, printed without authority, and saying:
'I will do just what I believe Mr. Whitefield would do were he
here', he tore it in pieces, an example universally followed, so
that in two minutes there was not one whole copy left. 'Ah,
poor Achitophel!' Wesley commented in his *Journal*. The evil
moment was shelved, but only shelved. When Whitefield
indeed arrived, he protested that he would never, never preach
against the Wesleys, he would rather die; but a week later he
declared with equal vehemence that he must attack the brothers.
It would be sinful not to do so. Wesley did his utmost to avert
the rift; he pleaded that the subject of election might not be
discussed at all; he drew as close as he dared to the predestin-
arian point of view: but it was all in vain. Whitefield set up
his own tabernacle; the Countess of Huntingdon, hitherto an
ardent follower of the Wesleys, founded her 'Connexion', and
the Wesleys were alone.

But by now Wesley had reached the stage where a doctrinal
difference, within limits, could not separate him from a man
whom he liked, and who had the spirit of regeneration in him.
Dissenters, even Quakers, his *bêtes noires*, were admitted to the

society. He was acquiring charity. Though Whitefield for some time attacked him, he himself never riposted, and when asked why he did not answer one of his former disciple's pamphlets, he replied, 'You may read Whitefield against Wesley, but you will never read Wesley against Whitefield.' It was not only because he felt controversy futile, but because he saw that a public difference put a weapon in the hands of their common enemies. In two years the leaders were friends again; and as a proof of how little Wesley felt resentment, he would consult Lady Huntingdon on the publication of his *Journals*.

Then Moravianism. There, it was not divergence but likeness that was the danger, for both the Wesleys were ineluctably drawn to the Moravians, John so much so that when he again met Peter Böhler, in April 1741, he exclaimed, 'I wonder how I refrain from joining these men! I long to be with them: and yet I am kept from them.' Charles was even more attracted; in fact, for a short time nothing did keep him from them. John made no complaint, for Charles was always completely open with him; he merely explained why he himself could not join them, although they were in many ways exemplary. They were too mystic; they sometimes acted with guile—the thing in the world Wesley most hated—they were inclined to exalt their own Church too high; they despised, actually scoffed at, self-denial. 'O my brother,' he cried out, 'my soul is grieved for you: fair words have stolen away your heart.' John saw himself about to be completely isolated, but Charles's loyalty to his brother, his intense reverence and love for him, dragged him back from the gulf, and the two were from then on inseverably united.

But two men, or three or four, cannot officer an army, and who was to help the Wesleys? Not the scandalized pastors of the Church of England, or at most one or two of the less easily frightened souls among them. Pastors of some sort there had to be, for without them the flocks relapsed from zeal, or slipped on the uncertain paths of theology. Wesley therefore appointed, to act as expounders, a few ardent souls who loved to explain: but what is the use of explaining if you are not anxious for a result? If you are, your explanation will insensibly merge into exhortation, and then, all unaware, you are preaching. Lay preachers!—then unknown to Mother Church. What would this

lead to? The expounders could not be reined in, all the less so
that they were unpolished men, unused to making nice distinc-
tions between their thoughts and their emotions. Maxfield, for
instance. During Wesley's absence at Bristol, he had taken
wing, and from expounding had risen to preaching, till even
Lady Huntingdon, the most exalted expert, had been deeply
impressed. Wesley rushed up to London to stop this ir-
regularity; but his mother, in her room beside the Foundery,
which she occupied until her death in July 1742, uttered the
words, 'John, take care what you do with respect to that young
man; for Thomas Maxfield is as much called to preach the
Gospel as ever you were!' Wesley hesitated, heard him preach,
and gave in. 'It is the Lord,' he declared; 'let Him do what
seems to Him good.' He excused the step to the reluctant
Charles: 'I am not clear that Brother Maxfield should not
expound in Greyhound Lane; nor can I as yet do without him.
Nor can I as yet do without him—that was the crux. What
was a mere Church ordinance compared with the work, Wesley's
work—so far had he already got from his worship of every
rubric he could lay his hands on. Before another four years had
passed he had irrefutably convinced himself that lay preachers
were scriptural, for necessity knows no law, not even the law of
logic. Not all the scribes who preached had been of the tribe of
Levi, he concluded; 'and if we come to modern times', he
added, 'was Mr. Calvin ordained?' Apparently not. Further,
in Germany, neophytes had to prove themselves preachers
before they could be ordained at all: and even in the English
Church parish clerks often read prayers, witness 'that singing
man' at Christ Church who murdered with his excrutiating
chant every lesson he read. Who had ordained him? Wesley
triumphantly asked. Why, there was not even a hint of separation from the Church in appointing—no, not 'appointing',
'allowing'—lay preachers.

But indeed, every haphazard event, every necessity of the
moment, seemed to conduce to the fated end, the founding of a
separate Church, with whatever abhorrence John Wesley might
cast the idea out of his mind. The general organization itself
of the society came into being through a mere practical need
of money; for Wesley's appeal for funds for his Bristol buildings
having failed to produce more than a fraction of the sum

required, it was suggested that every member of the society should subscribe a penny a week. A vague organization indeed; but when it was pointed out that some of the members could not afford this, one of the richer ones said that he would be responsible for eleven other brethren, and would make up from his own purse what pennies were lacking. This was a system with a form, and since it was universally adopted, the society was split up into classes of twelve, and these soon became, not only the financial unit, but the disciplinary one as well. The overseer became responsible, not only for the material harvest of his class, but also for its spiritual one. And it was Wesley, the master, who chose him, with extreme care as to his religious fitness. The class leader would make house-to-house visits, until these were found both impracticable and unsatisfactory; impracticable because mistresses did not always find it convenient for their cooks to be taken away from their work to indulge in religious exercises, unsatisfactory because, if there were internecine squabbles, it was better for the parties to meet face to face. In this way was the weekly meeting established.

Thus it was easy to watch jealously over the membership of the classes, and of the society; there were frequent and salutary purgings of backsliders, of disorderly walkers, of insincere members; the precious were sifted from the vile. Further, 'bands' were formed, of chosen folk, separated according to sex to stimulate each other by the recital of their religious experiences, of their temptations, of their relapses into sin—with consequences that were not always happy, because to admit a temptation sometimes seemed to imply yielding to it, and the result was a scandal. Tickets for the society, a form of passport, were issued, signed as often as not by one of the Wesleys, renewable at stated intervals; and these, sometimes plain, sometimes adorned with texts, mottoes, pictures of cherubim blowing trumpets, or whatever design seemed at the moment suitably allegorical, served as further checks. No longer need Wesley cry, 'O Discipline! Where art thou to be found?'

The next step was obvious enough—the provision of buildings, for open-air preaching is not convenient in all weathers: and besides, since many parsons refused communion to Methodists, it was necessary to have somewhere

where the Wesleys could officiate. Today these buildings dot the countryside with models of inspired dreariness, but comely or not, they marked a definite stage; for once a religious society has an organization of its own—and this was made clearer still when the first Annual Conference was called in 1744, and the society became the United Society of Methodists—its own preachers, and its own buildings, there is little use pretending that it is still within the fold of the Established Church. Nevertheless Wesley passionately repudiated dissent: far from being Dissenters, he declared, the Methodists were the sound part of the English Church.

Methodism, then, was being put on a solid basis, but no more in an outer atmosphere of calm, than, within, deliberately and with foreknowledge of the end. All the time there was the feverish excitement of night-watches, where sometimes they would sing and shout for joy till morning, of conversions, of schisms, of hectic opposition from outside. Still people would be struck down when Wesley preached, or, seized with fits, would come to the knowledge that their sins were blotted out; still there would be startling general conversions, as when at an all-night meeting Wesley descended to find a roomful of people groaning and crying out at the strength of the Lord, expelling their demons, and coming to the birth; still there were seceders to the Calvinists and to the Moravians, and occasional drastic purgings of the classes or the bands. Soon also the bitter paper attacks began to give place to physical violence. There had, indeed, in the early Bristol days been noisy interruptions, but the faithful had been able to sing louder than the intruding roughs had bawled; now, however, in London and elsewhere, the opposers became more brutal, and began to wrestle, to throw wildfire and crackers, to use cudgels, to hurl mud and stones; while in Wales, Seward, the first Methodist martyr, was killed with bludgeons. Wesley warmed to the fight, became more absorbed in the glorious work, was ever more active for every moment of his eighteen-hour day, feeling that ten minutes once lost were lost for ever, preaching, privately exhorting, making raids, as Charles also did, into Wales and into Cornwall, editing works of edification, to compose *The Christian Library* (once getting into trouble over copyright), and printing his own sermons, hymns, journals.

Even a severe fever hardly checked him in his course, that of the born organizer who was also a born evangelist; it was indeed the evangelist in him that brought the organizer into play.

But what, precisely, was his mission? To found a new Church? God forbid! To rescue the vast mass of the poor from a state of hopelessness, accomplishing, in fact, a social reform of unlimited dimensions? No. To revivify a drowsy Church then? If asked, he would probably have answered that he was merely carrying out his duties as a priest of the Establishment. What he was doing primarily was to satisfy his nature by engaging in works justified by faith, for if works without faith are meaningless, even impious, when grace is present they are the flower of faith. But apart from any conscious reasoning, almost one might say, unaware of what he was after, he was really impelled by an uncontrollable intent to impart the revelation that had been renewed in him. Woe unto all possessors of the truth who do not tell it! His faith before his conversion had been a reasoned approval, however hard to give, of God and his decrees; now it was a surrender, a surrender which made it urgent for him, not to save his own soul, but those of others. Not that he had yielded up reason—that philosophy of his was never purged away—and when an opponent stated that it was a fundamental principle in the Methodist school that all who came into it must renounce their reason, he retorted sweepingly, 'Sir, are you awake? Unless you are talking in your sleep, how can you utter so gross an untruth? It is a fundamental principle with us that to renounce reason is to renounce religion: that religion and reason go hand in hand, and that all irrational religion is false religion.'

Yet, though he refrained from saying so, the reason he meant was not that to be found in books, nor, exactly, the unaided reason of the mind. What had made his 'rational religion' significant to him, and precious, what indeed had been essential to his receiving it, had been a personal contact, a living connection—it was this that Peter Böhler had been to him—as though the torch must be passed on from hand to hand, in an actual apostolic succession. The torch! Wesley thought in terms of flame, of fire, heavenly fire, not that of hell, though he always felt that his rescue at the age of six from the blazing Epworth parsonage was symbolic of his being a brand plucked from the burning. Flame and fire were the words that came to his lips whenever he wanted to image the inner truth, the divine reality. Had not his heart been 'strangely warmed' at his conversion? 'There are twelve of you,' he told the Methodists of Carlisle, 'and all professing to have hearts on fire with the love of God.' At Woodhouse, when he preached, 'a flame', he said, 'is suddenly broken out'. Fire, the pure devouring element: Christ had said He came 'to throw fire upon the earth'. And, ever since Charles had written in a hymn:

> Oh that in me the sacred fire
> Might now begin to glow,

Wesley had loved to chant it as he rode about the country on his endless itinerancy; 'Spirit of burning, come!' he would sing; 'Refining fire go through my heart!' And at the end, when very old, he would still recur to the idea of the torch, saying—again the words are his brother's:

> Jesus, confirm my heart's desire
> To work, and speak, and think for Thee,
> Still let me guard the holy fire,
> And still stir up Thy gift in me.

Guarding the holy fire; that was what he was doing.[1] He was himself a flame going up and down the land, lighting candles such as, by God's grace, would never be put out; and as one reads the colossal *Journal* one gets the impression of this flame, never waning, never smoky, darting from point to point, lighting up the whole kingdom, till at last in due course it burnt out the body it inhabited.

§ 2. THE GLORIOUS BATTLE (1744–1769)

A noble monotony! Not to the man who lived those fifty years of whirling incident, of hard work, of tense excitement and danger. He flashed up, down, and across the three kingdoms, organizing, purging, preaching, every year riding at least four thousand five hundred miles, undaunted by weather, uncowed by mobs, indefatigably scheming, and bringing not only hope

---

[1] This, from Eayrs's *Wesley*, requires separate acknowledgment.

and happiness to degraded thousands, but clothes, food, health.
Not alone, however; for besides one or another companion that
he took with him, he felt that an angel was ever by his side,
while again and again it was clear that a special dispensation
was granted him. Storms would obscure the landscape all
around him when on the road, but where he travelled it was
fine; the ships on either side of him when he went to Ireland
(which he did twenty-one times) might lie becalmed, but his
own was bowled along by a spanking breeze. If he was so
placed at a preaching that the sun dazzled him, God would
gently interpose a cloud, or if He did not, would give his eyes
strength to withstand the glare. Calling on Christ would not
only instantaneously drive away lingering fevers, but would
also cure persistent lameness in his horse. 'Cannot God heal
either man or beast, by any means, or without any?' Wesley
asked. It was clear that He could, and did. 'What I aver here
is the naked fact', Wesley would write in recording some such
incident; 'Let every man account for it as he sees good.' On the
other hand, alas, Satan was sometimes dominant; and then he
would stir up contrary winds, though it was not always certain
that these should not be ascribed to God wishing Wesley to
stay a little longer in a place to do more good; and on one
occasion the Prince of Darkness inspired Wesley's horse with
so stubborn a reluctance to leave his stable that it was with
great difficulty that he was got on to the road, after much
jibbing and backing into gates. Influences not of the earth were
constantly operating—had Wesley not known this ever since
the days of Old Jeffrey?—even to the point of bringing back to
life men who were virtually dead. 'It is not the work of man that
hath lately appeared,' Wesley declared; 'all who calmly
observe it must say: "This is the Lord's doing, and it is
marvellous in our eyes."'

More marvellous, however, in eyes such as ours, removed
from these manifestations, is Wesley's own gallant hardihood.
If ever a spirit refused to be shackled by that inert thing the
flesh, it was that which drove, or carried, John Wesley's body
over hundreds of thousands of miles, through storms at sea,
through blizzards on land, torrents in rivers, and which in 1753
caused him to survive, unimpaired, an attack of consumption
so severe that, to prevent, as he said, 'wild panegyric', he

composed his own epitaph. Accidents, what did they matter? An
since he used to read as he rode, his reins slack on his horse'
neck, over the roughest of paths and fells, tumbles wer
frequent enough: but then, treacle and brown paper wer
easily got, and they provided a sovran cure for bruises. If ir
hospitably treated, as he was at first in Cornwall, he could fee
on blackberries; if there was no bed to lie on, well, he woul
lie on boards. Once, after about three weeks of such sleeping
he turned round in the night to his companion, and clappin
him on the side, said: 'Brother Nelson, let us be of good cheer
I have one whole side yet, for the skin is off but one side
Rain, snow, roads slippery with ice, these were nothing to hir
From his youth he had inured himself to weather, wearin
both by day and by night as few clothes as was possible, an
he had proved his toughness in Georgia. Besides, what h
willed, he willed.

Extract from the ' Journal ', February 1747.

Sunday, 15*th.* I was very weak and faint; but on *Monday* the 16t
I rose soon after three, lively and strong. . . . The wind was turne
full north, and blew so exceedingly hard and keen that when we cam
to Hatfield neither my companions nor I had much use of our hand
or feet. After resting an hour, we bore up again, through the wind an
snow which drove full in our faces. But this was only a squall. I
Baldock Field the storm began in earnest. The large hail drove s
vehemently in our faces that we could not see, nor hardly breathe
However, before two o'clock we reached Baldock, where one met an
conducted us safe to Potton. About six I preached to a seriou
congregation.

Tuesday, 17th. We set out as soon as it was well light; but it wa
really hard work to get forward, for the frost would not well bear o
break; and the untracked snow covering all the roads, we had muc
ado to keep our horses on their feet. Meantime the wind rose highe
and higher, till it was ready to overturn both man and beast. However
after a short bait at Buckden, we pushed on, and were met in th
middle of an open field with so violent a storm of rain and hail as w
had not yet had before. It drove through our coats, great and small
boots and everything, and yet froze as it fell, even upon our eyebrows
so that we had scarce either strength or motion left when we came t
our inn at Stilton.

We now gave up hopes of reaching Grantham, the snow fallin
faster and faster. However, we took advantage of a fair blast to se
out, and made the best of our way to Stamford Heath. But here a nev
difficulty arose, from the snow lying in large drifts. Sometimes hors

ld man were wellnigh swallowed up. Yet in less than an hour we
ere brought safe to Stamford. Being willing to get as far as we
ould, we made but a short stop here, and about sunset came, cold
ld weary, to a little town called Brig Casterton.

Wednesday, 18th. Our servant came up and said: 'Sir, there is no
avelling today. Such a quantity of snow has fallen in the night that
le roads are quite filled up.' I told him: 'At least we can walk
venty miles a day, with our horses in our hands.' So in the name of
od we set out. The north-east wind was piercing as a sword, and had
riven the snow into such uneven heaps that the main road was
npassable. However, we kept on, afoot or on horseback, till we came
) the White Lion at Grantham.

Some from Grimsby had appointed to meet us here, but not hearing
lything of them . . . after an hour's rest we set out straight for
.pworth.

That was stout enough work in all conscience; but what
trikes us with still more amazement and admiration is Wesley's
ehaviour when assaulted by mobs, his astounding escapes, his
tterly fearless outfacing of human brute-beasts in the riots
vhich distinguished the Methodist crusade. Wesley never
linched or quailed; not once would he hide or slink away. If
ifuriated gangs of hulking ruffians murderously battered down
oors to get at him, he would face them serenely, and so
errific was the spell he cast, that when this man, less than five
oot six inches tall, looked the burliest drunken hero in the eye,
t was the latter who recoiled. Or Wesley would start talking
1 his calm voice against a howling fury, and gradually the
umult would subside; and often the rabble that had come to
ljure him would disperse blessing him. If he had to walk
hrough a ravening mob, he would uncover his head so that
hey might see his face, and then the surging mass would give
vay before him. His favourite method was to go up to the ring-
:ader and take him by the hand; and then, time and again, the
ian who had come to incite others to homicidal wrath would
·ecome his protector. It seemed as though his life were charmed.
\lthough occasionally he would be struck to the ground, or be
it by stones, times without number he emerged unharmed
vhen missiles were hurled at him, blows aimed at him, walls on
vhich he stood to preach pushed down from under him. He
ells as an instance of 'how God overrules even the minutest
ircumstances', that when preaching at the Cross at Bolton,

'one man was bawling at my ear, when a stone struck him on the chest, and he was still. A second was forcing his way down to me, till another stone hit him in the forehead: it bounded back, the blood ran down, and he came no farther. A third, being got close to me, stretched out his hand, and in the instant a sharp stone came upon the joints of his fingers. He shook his hand and was very quiet till I had concluded my discourse and went away.' Again and again mud and stones were thrown into his coach when driving away from meetings, but he was always miraculously preserved, if once not so miraculously thanks to the protection afforded by a very large lady who sat in his lap to shield him.

The most amazing example was at Wednesbury. He was preaching there one afternoon, when a mob from Darlaston assailed the house. Dispersed once by prayer, the rioters came back at about five, and cried: 'Bring out the minister; we will have the minister.' Two or three of the ringleaders, brought into the house, and ready to swallow the ground with rage, were turned from lions into lambs after a few words with Wesley, who then went out to address the mob. Standing up on a chair, he asked: 'What do you want with me?' 'We want you to go with us to the Justice.' 'With all my heart.' The mob cried out with might and main: 'The gentleman is an honest gentleman, and we will spill our blood in his defence.' Nevertheless they insisted on dragging him that night to the justice, two miles through pouring rain. The magistrate, however, was wary. 'What have I to do with Mr. Wesley?' he asked. 'Go and carry him back again.' The silly mob then decided to go to another justice at Walsall, where they arrived at seven, to be met with the answer that the magistrate was in bed. Well, there was nothing for it but to go back, and fifty or so undertook to convey Wesley home. But just then a huge rush of excited Walsall men poured in like a flood, and overwhelmed the Darlaston convoy, battering them hideously. Wesley tried to speak, but 'the noise on every side was like the roaring of the sea'. The mob-leader, when he could make himself heard in the din, turned and said: 'Sir, I will spend my life for you; follow me, and not one soul here shall touch a hair of your head.' Vain boast. For three mortal hours the possessed rabble impelled Wesley up and down the streets, and across the river, shouting 'Knock his brains out! Down with him! Kill him at once! Drown him! Hang him on the next tree!' and even 'Crucify him!' Somehow he survived with no further damage than a flap of his waistcoat being torn off, mercifully not the one with papers and money in it. When he tried to slip in to the door of a house that he saw stand open, they dragged him out by the hair. He was hit twice, but both blows were as nothing, 'for though one man struck me on the breast with all his might, and the other on the mouth with such a force that the blood gushed out immediately, I felt no more pain from either of the blows than if they had touched me with a straw'. Going down a slippery hill, many tried to push him over, but he knew that if he fell he would never get up again, so he did not even stumble. Angels, Charles recorded, held him up. A lusty man behind him struck at him several times with an oak cudgel, a knock from which would have meant death, but every time the blow was turned aside; how, Wesley did not know. Another man came rushing at him through the press, and raising his arm to strike, suddenly let it drop gently, and stroked Wesley's head, saying: 'What soft hair he has!' The scene is typical of many which went on through years, down to the final act of the magistrates who had refused to see Wesley: they issued a warrant for his arrest on the charge of raising routs and riots!

And why, we ask, all this violence? This mob-fury? It seems inexplicable till we remember that the eighteenth-century populace dearly loved a riot. Anything was an excuse for this diversion—the Gin Act, an alteration at Drury Lane, Wilkes's Westminster elections—the frenzy culminating in the supreme orgy of the Gordon Riots, which nearly burnt London for a second time. But why the Methodist riots especially? That is a question that needs several answers. First, men are apt to resent being told they are sinful; they revolt against the idea of having to make an effort to be saved; and then, if one or two of a family of sinners repent, life becomes extremely uncomfortable for the rest. Why should anyone interfere with their cock-fighting, their drinking, their lust? This sort of thing must be put a stop to. Other incitements, happily invented, were not lacking. Wesley was in Spanish pay, plotting for the invasion of England; he was one of the Pretender's agents, for he was certainly a Papist in disguise; he had been punished for illegally

selling gin; he had tried to hang himself, but had been cut dow
at the last moment. Of course such a mad dog must be hunted
And then, a public speaker is always fair game, or seems so t
half-witted elements, and the Methodists deliberately wer
amongst the most degraded of the people. Go not only to thos
who need you, Wesley told his helpers, but to those who nee
you most. Again, the mob was egged on by the self-style
gentlemen, who were very well content with their placid religior
and who, not without just cause, dreaded enthusiasm, knowing
well from the history of the last century what it might lead to
And why disturb the submerged tenth in this way? Wesley fel
instinctively that the educated Christians were his wors
enemies, with their indifference (worst of insults), thei
security in their faith, and it was for them that he reserved hi
sermons on hell-fire and the wrath to come, preaching the lov
of God to the poor. As for the magistrates, apart from sharing
the feelings of their class, they could not help seeing tha
though the Methodists might not incite to riot, it was or
account of them that riots took place. And besides, some o
Wesley's preachers were crude men, arrogantly making much
of their own sanctity, without the innate good manners of the
Wesleys themselves; they did undoubtedly stir up passions un-
necessarily. Some, such as Nelson, best of men and mos
devoted of followers, were pressed into military service, and
attempts were made to take Wesley himself; but the man who
twice tried to do so grew so ashamed of his task that he le
Wesley depart quietly. But from day to day no Methodis
preacher knew what might be in store for him.

But if it was Wesley's magnetism, his personal charm, his
apparent humility that saved him, it was his unswerving
determination, his almost ferocious will-power, that enabled
him to carry out the work, with its complicated structure, its
wheels within wheels of which he was in complete and sole
control, and its ever-growing finance. His will! Even strangers
grew aware of that. One day he found himself riding with a
serious man; naturally they spoke of religion, and as naturally
disagreed, till finally the stranger, who got warmer and
warmer, told Wesley he was rotten at heart, and supposed that
he must be one of John Wesley's followers. When he discovered
whom he was talking to, he was filled with horror, as though

e had met the Devil, and spurred his horse on to get away. But,' Wesley relates, 'being the better mounted of the two, I ept close to his side, and endeavoured to show him his heart ntil we came into the street of Northampton.' Only *force majeure* could prevent Wesley talking, as when on the day of 1e snowstorm we have seen him battle with, he fell in with a lergyman; but alas, toothache quite stopped his mouth. Those 'ho had business dealings with him soon found what sort of 1an they had to do with. 'Sir,' he wrote to a landowner at 1ewcastle, 'I am surprised. You give it under your hand that ou will put me in possession of a piece of ground, specified in 1 article between us, in fifteen days time. Three months have assed, and that article is not fulfilled. And now you say you an't conceive what I mean by troubling you. I mean to have hat article fulfilled. I think my meaning is very plain. I am, ir, Your humble servant.' He got the piece of ground.

The building, the Orphan House, for which he wanted the 1nd, was one of the corner-stones of his structure, the apex f a triangle of which London and Bristol were the base points. Ie had first gone to Newcastle at the suggestion of Lady Iuntingdon, the St. Theresa of the Methodists, as Horace Walpole called her. Immediately his heart went out to the wild, staring, loving society', for it was always enlarged owards the desperately poor, even if in the north he sometimes ad to speak 'strong, rough words'. The land, however, was nly a beginning; how put up a building which would cost even hundred pounds? He had not a penny, he struggled along s best he could himself, and there was nothing for it but to uild on in faith. Luckily it had got about that he was rich, and o the Orphan House went up on his credit and trifling sub-criptions from the society. Eventually he did become rich, unawares' as he said, by the sale of his books; but at this early ime it really seemed that it was only by the grace of God that he building went up at all.

Usually the societies met in private houses, or rented uildings, which were occupied by the lay preachers, who now ormed a considerable band, They were, it need hardly be said, hosen by Wesley himself, who exacted from them promises f unquestioning obedience; they were to go where he wanted hem to, and when he wanted; he might dismiss them when he wished. No preacher was allowed to remain long in the same circuit—they were all itinerant preachers within that circuit, as the Wesleys were over the whole country—for a man would be apt to lose his fire, would go dead, if there were not something new constantly to be dared and done. And the excitement must never be allowed to cool to dimness, for the Methodist movement fed on excitement: the singing, the night watches, the spectacular conversions, trances, demoniac possessions, the thrice-yearly love-feasts (though materially of only cake and water), the fervid emotional appeal and the searching examinations, all contributed to keep the movement at an exalted tension. Wesley deliberately whipped it up in others, as he did in himself by every day renewing his experience of miraculous aid. It is not surprising that there were frequent fallings away, purgings by fifties and hundreds; even his preachers could not all maintain themselves on the dizzy peaks, and retired into private life. It really needed the continual impregnation by Wesley himself to keep the movement quick, whence his extreme jealousy to keep all the appointments in his own hands, his great reluctance to hand over buildings to trustees, his insistence that even when given up, the right to name preachers to chapels and masters to schools should be vested in himself and his brother during their lifetime. Trustees! If they appointed preachers, they would take care that none should preach against their patrons. The rule was peremptory: everybody should be responsible to Wesley; he was the fountain head, the oracle, the Pythoness herself. Ambition? Not quite, at least not in the ordinary sense; but the passion of the organizer, the will to power of a man determined to carry out some special work, the indestructible, burning need to rule. He had made this thing; he and no one else could be suffered to touch it.

And then, 1748, across these scenes of effort and strife, of dust and turmoil, of ceaseless journeyings, amid the tense concentration of constructive work, there floated into Wesley's vision the beckoning figure of Grace Murray, promising succour. She was a charming widow of thirty-two (she had recently refused an offer of marriage), and though she had risen to emotional heights and taken downward plunges, had been converted and counter-converted, she was now reconverted

and happily in part-charge of the Orphan House at Newcastle;
and she was so refreshing as a nurse, that if the itinerant
preachers fell sick, they did so more often at Newcastle than
anywhere else. Wesley himself was slightly ill there in this
year and, considering his nurse—so good a worker, so cheerful,
so neat—he thought that she would be the very wife for him:
he did not know that she was almost engaged to one of his
preachers called Bennet. He proposed, and she, dazzled at the
prospect of marrying the man who was by far the greatest in
her sphere, and in apprehension so like a god, blurted out that
'it was too great a blessing', and that 'she couldn't tell how to
believe it'. Then, for eighteen months, there was played out
the most amazing and wrily farcical series of scenes. First
Mrs. Murray said that she could not bear the idea of ever being
parted from Wesley; in less than a month she protested that
Bennet was her only love. Sometimes she travelled with one,
and sometimes with the other; then for some time Wesley
thought she was engaged to him, and then it would appear that
she was promised to Bennet, who for his part did not seem to
know which of them she was engaged to. In the summer of
1749 indeed, in Dublin, she went through a contract of marriage
de præsenti with Wesley; but in September, at Epworth, she
sobbingly agreed, before Wesley, to marry Bennet, who
claimed her as his by right; yet, by the end of the month Wesley
had once more made a *de præsenti* contract with her at White-
haven, after he had written a reproachful letter to Bennet, in
which he accused him of trying to snatch the widow from him—
'such a person as I had sought in vain for many years, and then
determined never to part with'. This seemed to settle the
question; the marriage would take place in a few days. But then,
suddenly, a fiercely angry, red-hot whirlwind blustered up from
the south—Charles Wesley. He stormed and fumed at his
brother. If this marriage took place the whole of Methodism
would be wrecked; the woman was of no standing, she was
engaged to Bennet, Wesley would be looked upon as a seducer.
Since Wesley was immovable, Charles, still raging, rushed off
to meet the vacillating woman at Hindley Hill. He flung himself
at her and embracing her cried, 'Grace Murray, you have broke
my heart', and then, by sheer impetuosity, he carried her off to
Newcastle, summoned Whitefield, summoned Bennet, hurled

the latter and Mrs. Murray through the marriage ceremony and went back to John. 'I renounce all intercourse with you,' he shouted, 'but what I would have with a heathen man or a publican.' He was beside himself.

Wesley had been in agony for some days, but calm and resigned, in spite of nights restless with fever: he had known what was happening, the desire of his eyes was being taken from him at a stroke. And here was Charles, the devoted, beloved brother, reviling him. But he felt numbed; 'it was only adding a drop of water to a drowning man', his capacity for emotion was exhausted. Whitefield prayed, Nelson prayed, they both burst into tears, the room was full of anguish—and then, infinitely relieving, Wesley's abounding charity overcame everything, and he and his brother fell speechless on each other's necks. John Bennet came in; neither of them could speak; they kissed each other and wept. . . . And the next day Wesley preached at five in the morning as usual.

But marriage called to him; he wanted to get married. For years he had declared against it for priests, in Georgia he had renounced it, at conferences he had intimated that preachers should be as eunuchs for the Lord's sake—even if he had for a long time sought in vain for such a helpmeet as Grace Murray. But now he was sure that he would be more useful married, that God wanted him to get married; he had felt this order with especial clearness when looking at Grace Murray: and in 1751 he felt it again when looking at Mrs. Vazeille, a widow of forty, staid, well-ordered, and of a good disposition. And why should he not marry? Charles had married in 1748, and Whitefield in 1741—though indeed the latter had declared when proposing that he was 'free from the foolish passion that the world calls love'—and it had made no difference to their ministrations. So, on the understanding that he would preach not one sermon the fewer, nor travel one mile the less, he married Mrs. Vazeille—but this time he did not tell Charles about it; indeed his brother was one of the last to hear of the sad event. And alas, the event did prove sad: for twenty years Mrs. Wesley, who appears to have verged on dementia, harried the life out of her husband. At first she did her best, but she could not bear the constant travelling, the hideous discomfort, the occasional mobbing, and besides, she was seasick when they

went to Ireland. But why, it may be asked, need she cling to
him so burr-like? The fact was that Wesley was inordinately
attractive to women: and, it must be admitted in extenuation
of his wife's behaviour, that he wrote incredibly foolish letters
full of warmth—purely Christian warmth, no doubt, but it is
difficult to distinguish—to many of his tenderer converts. His
wife became insanely jealous; she watched all his goings out
and his comings in, she rifled his pockets, broke open the
drawers of his desk, accused him of making Charles's wife his
mistress, would travel a hundred miles to see who was sharing
his coach with him, and even, it was reported, pulled him about
by his greying hair. 'My brother', Charles wrote pungently,
'has married a ferret', a phrase echoed by Berridge of Everton.
John bore it all with exemplary patience, was unfailing in his
care for her; but even he sometimes complained—to one of his
female penitents moreover—that he could not bear 'the being
continually watched over for evil, the having every word I spoke
every action I did, small and great, watched over with no
friendly eye; the hearing of a thousand little, but unkind
reflections in return for the kindest words I could advise'.
When she left him in 1771, never to return she said (not quite
accurately), he wrote: *Non eam reliqui, non dimisi: non revocabo.*
No, he would not call her back. And after all, he decided, God
had provided such a wife out of His wisdom: for since the
temptations of a calm hearth had not been offered him, he had
not been interfered with in his divine calling: he had not, as
could be seen, preached one sermon the fewer, nor travelled
one mile the less.

But whatever troubles and trials there might be in his public
or in his private life, there were two offshoots of his work
which gave him great joy. The first was his dispensary, which
he opened in 1746 for the poor of London. For many years he
had 'made anatomy and physic the diversion of his leisure
hours', and now, taking an apothecary as assistant, he set about
putting the means of health at the disposal of the poor, even
prescribing for simple ailments, amid the splutterings of the
outraged Faculty. He did not care. Must a man in imminent
danger of death wait for Dr. Mead to come in his chariot—and
die before he came? 'And when the doctor was come, where
was his fee? What! He cannot live upon nothing! So, instead

of an orderly cure, the patient dies!' The dispensary proved an enormous success, of continual benefit to the poverty-stricken; and another one was opened at Bristol. Further, in 1748, to reach those in out of the way places, he wrote a little book of medicine, *Primitive Physic, or An Easy and Natural Method of Curing Most Diseases*, admirable as far as general principles go (it is excellent that people should shave and wash their feet frequently), but perhaps a little wild in details. It might, for instance, be inadvisable to swallow three pounds of quicksilver ounce by ounce as a cure for twisted guts; and whether to wear leaves of celandine under and upon the feet will cure jaundice, is still, we may think, very conjectural. However, the booklet, easily slipped into the pocket, was immensely popular, reaching its twenty-first edition in 1785; and lest it should be objected that a man concerned with spiritual things should let the bodily ones alone, the epigraph it bore was *Homo sum; humani nihil a me alienum puto*. Two hundred and eighty-eight ailments are treated of, from infantile rickets to old age (though death is the only certain cure for that), running through serious diseases such as cancer, cholera morbus, and consumption, to such comparatively trivial ones as baldness, canine hunger, and stings: its perusal will teach you how to cure madness, or how to destroy fleas and bugs. Some of the eight hundred and twenty-four remedies involve the most enticing concoctions of herbs and drugs, but Wesley pinned his faith most to cold baths, and electricity, which he regarded as a species of fire. The handy little *vade mecum* of medicine might be obtained at any of his chapels.

Of less immediate success was the school at Kingswood which Wesley opened in 1748 to train up preachers, and which is not to be confused with the school for colliers' children. In the first few years the purgings of the unworthy had to be so frequent and so wholesale, that the numbers dwindled alarmingly, a result all the more disappointing in that everything was done to make the boys wholly perfect, by moulding them in their impressionable years, none being admitted after twelve years old. They got up at five, spent two hours in prayer, were sparingly fed, were every minute kept under the eye of a master, were put through a strenuous course of learning such as would not disgrace the Sorbonne, and were never on any account allowed to play, or, of course, allowed to be idle for a second. As a relaxation, however, they were occasionally permitted to see a corpse. At last, in 1768, Wesley had his reward. 'God', one of the masters wrote him, 'broke in upon our boys in a surprising manner . . . the power of God came upon them, even like a mighty rushing wind, which made them cry aloud for mercy. . . . While I am writing, the cries of the boys, from their several apartments, are sounding in my ears.' Nor did it stop, for every hour more children—their ages ran from eight to fourteen—found peace, for they had been lying at the pool waiting to be put in! The house rang with praise, to the high gratification of all who heard, or heard of it. Could there be a clearer justification of Wesley's educational system? No wonder he despised Rousseau's *Émile*! Some might avert their eyes from a painful scene of juvenile hysteria, but Wesley felt it as a return for all his struggles as the founder of a school, as direct evidence of the approval of God, and as a triumph for methodic discipline.

Discipline! The salt of religion: it sometimes appeared, indeed, that discipline was religion. At all events without it religion was like wine which lacked a vessel; spilt on the ground it became mysticism, enthusiasm, or sank dully out of sight. From being 'a politician of God', Wesley, himself so disobedient, so defiant of the Church while professing humility, seemed at times to become the mere drill-sergeant, as when he expelled two hundred of his Norwich members for slackness in attending class meetings. Discipline, in short, meant doing, and saying, exactly as Wesley ordered. It is not surprising that sometimes there were revolts.

That one or two people should break away was natural; Bennet's defection, and his becoming an anti-Wesley agitator eight months after his marriage with Grace Murray, had nothing significant in it. But the case of Maxfield was different. A man of no education, he had, we remember, been one of Wesley's first lay preachers. Ordained later as a priest of the Church of England by the Bishop of Londonderry, 'to assist that good man [Wesley] that he may not work himself to death', he had flourished exceedingly, and had married a rich wife. Feeling the importance of his mission, in 1762 he began to think that he might improve on the religion he had preached so long, especially on Wesley's doctrine of Perfection. The theological point is a little confusing to the layman, and Wesley's earlier utterances, not to mention Charles's poems, may easily lead one astray; but the issue seems to have been that whereas Wesley's Perfection meant a whole-hearted love of God and one's neighbour, which, by the constant help of Christ, kept ever-present sin in abeyance, for Maxfield Perfection meant that sin had been killed at the root; it was the difference between Perfection in Christ (the Arminian position) and Perfection outside Christ. Those who had attained the latter, as Maxfield had, were on a level with the angels, they needed no preachings, no sacraments, and they were beyond learning anything except from those equally sinless. Thus Wesley, who had no illusions about sin, was not fit to teach them. Then, to increase the ardour, Maxfield was joined by an ex-corporal of the Guards, named Bell, who, discovering from Revelation that he and his group would never die, announced that the end of the world would come fairly soon, in fact on February 28th, 1763. What Wesley objected to most, however, was not only these heresies and absurdities, and the excessive addiction of their people to meetings, but the behaviour of these in chapel, their 'irreverent expressions in prayer; their extolling themselves rather than God, and telling Him what they were, not what they wanted; their using poor, flat, bald hymns; their never kneeling at prayer, and using postures and gestures highly indecent.' Besides, they had little love to their brethren, no meekness, and they hated being contradicted. Worst of all, the preachers screamed, making what they said in their sermons unintelligible, and Wesley hated screaming. Their prophecies and ravings made some public stir and caused reflections to be made on Methodism; and while Wesley, as he said, gladly suffered the opprobrium of Christ, he had no mind to suffer that of enthusiasm. He was surprisingly patient with Maxfield, while the latter, on the other hand, intrigued against him, and invented improbable stories. Wesley bore certain resignations unperturbed, and even the declaration of some of the society that they would not be browbeat any more by him; but in the end a break was forced on him, and Maxfield left the society, taking some two hundred members with him. His explanation of the schism was that Wesley had said to him: 'Dear Tommy,

I will tell the people you are the greatest Gospel preacher in England, and you shall tell them I am the greatest', and that on his refusal Wesley had expelled him. Such was the ingenuity of Thomas Maxfield.

The break, however, was serious in that it deprived Wesley of one of the very few of his people who could administer the Sacrament. Whitefield, though Wesley in a sense worked with him as being a labourer in the same field, was not of his society; Charles had practically retired and lived at Bristol; the few clergymen who were Methodists, such as 'Mad' Grimshaw, Berridge of Everton, who was hardly less mad, and Fletcher of Madeley, were tied to their country cures. What was to be done? No English bishop would ordain Methodists. Luckily, just at the right moment, towards the end of the year there appeared in London the incongruous figure of Erasmus, a a Greek bishop. Any bishop would do for Wesley, as long as he was a real bishop. But was he? Wesley made careful enquiries. Yes, Erasmus was a bona-fide bishop—of Arcadia; of Arcadia in Crete, however. Wesley approached him: would he 'set apart' Mr. Jones? He would, and did. But the matter did not rest there, in spite of Charles's vehement protests. For when other lay preachers saw Jones exalted, they wanted to know why they also should not wear white bands, why they also, who performed so many priestly duties, should not share the privilege, for which they had long been pining, of administering the Lord's Supper? The complaisant Bishop of Arcadia gratified a number of them, but when some of them demanded to be consecrated bishops, he said he could not go as far as that. The experiment, however, was not altogether successful. Jones left the society, another was stopped from performing priestly functions, and a third made a schism in Sheffield. Nevertheless it was a finger post which showed the way (horrible thought!) to separation from the Church of England which Wesley loved.

§ 3. THE END CROWNS ALL (1770–1791)

'I can hardly believe', Wesley wrote on June 28th (N.S.), 1770, 'that I am this day entered into the sixty-eighth year of my age. How marvellous are the ways of God! . . . I am now

healthier than I was forty years ago. This hath God wrought!'
He seemed, indeed, to have eternal youth; and though at the
instance of friends he had exchanged his horse for a carriage,
he could still be seen, year in, year out, 'hurrying on, still
hurrying, hurrying onward', plying his anxious visitation
throughout the country, the only active survivor of the Holy
Club.

He was not much given to looking back, the present was
enough for him, the future would take care of itself; but still, if
he wished, he might glance behind to forty years of pilgrimage.
The Holy Club, Varanese, Aspasia; Georgia and Sophy Hopkey
—years of struggle against something resistant even to his will;
and then Peter Böhler, and his conversion, followed by thirty
years of the evangelical revival which had flowered ever since
he became a 'Gospel preacher'. There had been stirring scenes,
glorious manifestations of God's power; and even now, occasionally, repentant sinners would roar aloud or be struck to
the ground when they heard him. It was a long time since that
glorious triumph in 1742, when, forbidden by the new Rector
of Epworth to preach from the pulpit, he had held forth in the
evenings, standing on his father's tombstone, to congregations
larger than had ever filled the church, and so movingly that many
had dropped down as dead; when his brother-in-law, Whitelambe,
incumbent of Wroote, had told him that his presence inspired
awe. But the work had gone on, steadily increasing; the flame
had spread over the whole country; thousands of the most
degraded people had been rescued from misery and, better
still, had got rid of the terror of death. The organization had
grown, till now he had a hundred and twenty-three preachers
serving fifty circuits, alive with nearly thirty thousand members
of the society. If acrid hostility spat as formidably as ever in
papers and in pamphlets, the violence of mobs had largely died
down; magistrates were becoming more reasonable, people in
general less averse to the movement. It was being accepted.
And all the reins were firmly in his own hand—the preachers,
the stewards of the funds, the trustees of the buildings, the class
leaders: there was no item he did not know, no thread he did
not direct. Even the professional musicians had been brought to
heel when they had wanted to improve his hymn tunes in
preparing them for the press: the tunes should be pricked as

his people sang them, he insisted, effectively. His will! it was adamant still, his power unassailable, his energy unchecked by any brake. There was no diminution in his outpourings of sermons, letters, controversial pamphlets; he still kept his diary, published his *Journal*, edited the *Christian Library*, and through it all allowed no relaxation whatever in his incessant travelling. 'I am still a wonder to myself. My voice and strength are the same as at nine and twenty.' Such was the jotting as he entered his sixty-ninth year.

There was need for him yet as the inviolable guardian of the holy fire, for in 1771 the Calvinists once more tried to undermine him. Whitefield was dead; his plump figure, shaken by asthma, had worn itself out as he had wished it should: but he had left behind him a college at Trevacca in Wales, a seminary largely financed by Lady Huntingdon, impetuous, independent, proud. Wesley had preached there, and Fletcher of Madeley was the visiting superintendent. Now, however, released from the authority of its founder, its fledgling prophets wished to shake themselves altogether free of Wesley and his benign doctrine. Their opportunity arose when, in 1770, Wesley, himself liberated, since Whitefield was dead, from any restraint in openly expressing his sense of predestination, directed his Conference to declare in its minutes that Methodism had of late steered much too close to Calvinism. Lady Huntingdon took violent umbrage, and issued an edict to her rejoicing college that all must renounce these minutes or leave the seminary for ever—which Fletcher promptly did. The jubilant youths of Trevacca, styled by Wesley 'pert, ignorant young men, vulgarly called students', swelled with self-conceit, decided to attack Wesley at the Bristol Conference of 1771. Their leader, the Hon. Walter Shirley (of Lady Huntingdon's family), shot out an encyclical calling upon all men of his own sound faith to rally at Bristol for the Conference: they would gather together in their hordes, they would march upon the stronghold, they would force Wesley to expunge the obnoxious minutes. Alas, only about ten people answered this stirring trumpet-call, and Shirley found himself reduced to crawling humbly to Wesley, saying that he had not meant this and had not meant that, and would Wesley receive a deputation to discuss the question? Patient as ever (he could afford to be),

Wesley agreed, and a satisfactory document was signed to pour balm on the theological sore: but oddly enough, when this healing paper is examined, it is seen to contain nothing about election, but to deal entirely with refutation of the doctrine of justification by works! The real battle took place outside. Calvinists flew to the rescue, championed by the Rev. Augustus Toplady, known to fame as the author of 'Rock of Ages', who by pamphlet after pamphlet of adept scurrility, of theological Billingsgate, and accusations of bad faith, drew from Wesley the retort that he did not bandy words with chimney-sweeps, those notoriously dirty persons. The controversy was, however, raised to a dignified level by Fletcher, in his *Checks to Anti-nomianism*, which remains the classic on the subject. As far as Wesley was concerned, the result was the utter severance from Lady Huntingdon's Connexion, and the complete washing of Wesleyan Methodism from the least taint of the deadly doctrine of reprobation.

This attack, however, was from the outside and so feeble that it could never have seriously injured Methodism. Far more grave was the threat to Wesley's domination which arose within the society in 1779, in the form of restiveness among the lay preachers. Charles was really at the bottom of it. As he got older and less powerful in the ministry, he became bitterly suspicious of his lay coadjutors. He had never liked them. They were un-educated, arrogant; they usurped functions they had no right to; and if John did not take great care, they would drive him, or carry him, out of the fold. 'The preachers do not love the Church of England. When we are gone, a separation is in-evitable.' They, on their part, had no liking for Charles. In 1768 he had come to live in London, and now that the new chapel had been built in the City Road and was ousting the Foundery as the centre of Methodism, he insisted on preaching there twice every Sunday, to the exclusion, the excluded ones considered, of better men than himself. And besides not being so fiery in preaching as they were, he was most lamentably allowing his sons to take up careers as musicians (Charles was sure that this was God's will, but John knew better), which seemed to involve giving concerts in his house to the fashionable and the noble, no doubt excellent people in their way but devoid of justifying faith. There was a tussle, which the lay preachers looked upon as one between themselves and preachers in orders; but Wesley upheld his brother.

The crisis, however, was only delayed, and it soon exploded at Bath. M'Nab, the preacher Wesley had appointed there, was able to affect the Bath Society in a most edifying manner; but an Irish preacher named Smyth had recently so impressed Wesley that the latter had ordered him to preach at Bath every Sunday evening until he went back to Ireland. M'Nab furiously resented this, and such was the tumult in the Bath Society that Wesley set off for that place towards the end of November. Charles was at his elbow, egging him on to be firm, to deal strongly with these upstarts, to show none of that deplorable weakness and tendency to hedge that he had observed in him lately. The truth was that Charles in his old age was becoming panic-stricken; his behaviour indicated not strength but ossification, whereas Wesley himself was strong enough to be able to yield when it suited his purposes; he did not dote upon consistency. On this occasion, however, he fulfilled all his brother's expectations. He took the highest possible line and read the rebels a paper which declared his absolute right to rule without question, to exact obedience to the last movement of a man's little finger. That was 'the fundamental rule of Methodism', he stated, and we do not wonder that Toplady dubbed him 'Pope John'. The preachers had indeed one inalienable right, yes; that to leave the society if they wished. He made his meaning plain enough. Further, it appeared, from a letter he wrote soon after this, that he found it necessary to correct a little error into which some of his society had fallen in their view of the Conferences. These were not at all the parliamentary institutions many had seemed to suppose. They were merely meetings to which he called a few preachers together, to advise him, by no means to control him. In short, he made it perfectly clear that Methodism was Wesley. But then, he had no belief in democracy; administrators rarely have: in fact, it was plainly a fallacy, as he proved when Wilkes arose with his contention that power resided in the people. What nonsense! If this was true, why then everybody would have a vote. But since comparatively few people had votes, it was obvious that power did not reside in the people and was not meant to. He agreed with Charles that the society must be ruled by some head, who would be, while he was alive, and as far as possible after he was dead, himself. 'I chose to exercise the power which God had given me in this manner. . . .' 'Which God had given me': 'I chose'—the fiat had gone forth; and, though there was muttering and even protest among his helpers, the rebellion was crushed, and Wesley ruled supreme.

Yet at this stage it was not will-power alone which made Wesley dominant; mere strength could not have done it. There was something else—the devotion he inspired in his followers. They adored him, called him Rabbi, because there was a quality in him they would all have shared if they could—his infinite charity. It might seem, perhaps, that he loved only those who obeyed him; but those he loved so well, so whole-heartedly and forgivingly, offering himself to them so utterly, that they could not but surrender. He never spared himself. All the time he gave, gave everywhere, of the spirit that was in him. And it was abundant. Certainly there was in him the desire to rule; it was an instinct which shared the honour of possessing him with the desire to give, but then the end for which he wished to rule was selfless. Or at least, since Wesley was Methodism, and Methodism was Wesley; since his pride was transmuted into identification of himself with the thing he had made; since the morbid preoccupation with himself which had marked his early years had taken an outward direction—his actions had precisely the same effect as though he had been selfless. Without his intense egotism he would never have accomplished what he did. That it was as robust as ever is plain from his printing his *Journals*, an act which assumes that everybody will find their writer as interesting as he does himself, for, candidly, they are self-glorification from end to end. Even the *Arminian Magazine*, which he founded as a counterblast to the chief thorn in his flesh, the Calvinistic *Gospel Magazine*, deals largely with himself, though some of the first numbers were devoted to a discussion of the friend of his childhood, Old Jeffrey, and contained verse such as Prior's 'Henry and Emma', the inclusion of which love-poem scandalized those who were most stern for truth. Nevertheless, because giving was a part of his egotism, he came to be the best-loved man in England and Ireland.

In Scotland it was different; there he was only respected. He became chaplain to the Countess Dowager of Buchan, he was presented with the freedom of Perth, his congregations were crowded and attentive: but the Scotch, nurtured on theological discussion, would not receive justifying faith, the assurance of grace, and the possibility of sinless perfection (in Christ); 'they knew too much,' Wesley commented, 'therefore they could learn nothing.' They obstinately refused to fall down as though dead. Distinguished visitors were no compensation for this failure to strike fire, even if they included Boswell, armed with a letter from Dr. Johnson on the score that 'worthy and religious men should be acquainted with each other', for Johnson liked Wesley and his conversation, complaining only that the dog always had to be off somewhere and would never stay to fold his legs and talk. The acquaintance, however, did not develop: Boswell could not be convinced by Wesley's proofs of the existence of a ghost which was then making some stir.

This, indeed, was to get Wesley on the raw, for the common attitude towards ghosts was disappointing. The scepticism of most men was such that they would not accept them, though what was worse was the sad growth of disbelief in witches, in spite of the evidence for their existence being so irrefutable. There were other trifling set-backs. For instance, Dr. Madan, whose work as a preacher had once been so much blessed, flourishingly produced a treatise in favour of polygamy, a philosophy which Wesley's brother-in-law, Westley Hall, had practised. Also there was a period when the discipline at Kingswood School grew so lax that some of the boys actually turned against religion (that was because they had been allowed to play), and the staff had to be changed. Petty disagreements here and there were only to be expected, for, to quote one of Wesley's favourite texts, 'it must be that offences will come'.

But these minor rubs were of no real importance, for in spite of everything the society was spreading. In the ten years between 1770 and 1780 the circuits were increased by fourteen, the preachers by forty-eight, and the membership of the society by more than fourteen thousand. Moreover, there were the followers in America, over eight thousand, and rapidly increasing, served by forty-two preachers in twenty circuits. The difficulty there was that nobody was capable of administering the Sacrament. In 1780, Wesley implored the Bishop of London to ordain one of his preachers for the purpose, a man filled with God; but instead the bishop had sent out two men stuffed only with Greek and Latin, and what was the good of that? Well, there was only one thing left to do—Wesley must himself ordain. And why not? Many years ago he had been convinced by a book of Lord King's that bishops and presbyters were of the same order, a belief strengthened by a study of Stillingfleet's *Irenicon*: therefore, since he was a presbyter, and a presbyter was a bishop, he had a right to ordain. He would ordain. The only thing he must be careful in was to keep it very secret from Charles, who would most certainly object in no measured terms; so it was swiftly and discreetly that Wesley consecrated three priests for America. This was separation; Lord Mansfield, Chief Justice, had said, 'ordination is separation'. Charles was, as Wesley had foreseen, appalled: he agreed with Mansfield: Methodists were now Dissenters. The end he had so dreaded had come, the issue which had been raised, combated, and defeated at more than one Conference had finally triumphed. Samuel had been right; John had excommunicated the Church! However, he could not bring himself to quarrel with his brother; but he wrote to him: 'I believe God left you to yourself in that matter, as he left Hezekiah, to show you the secret pride that was in your heart.' Pride! it sounds like an echo from the very early years; but Wesley might argue that if he was still tainted with this sin, it had at least served a very useful turn. Wesley, however, stubbornly refused to admit that anything crucial had happened; he rested securely on Lord King. Nevertheless the immediate consequences were alarming. One of the men he had ordained, Coke, applied Wesley's argument that bishops and presbyters were of the same order and concluded that, since he was a presbyter, he was therefore a bishop as well. He and Asbury, whom Wesley had appointed 'superintendent' in America, called themselves bishops, and it appeared likely that Coke would take upon himself to ordain priests. They had forgotten 'the fundamental rule of Methodism', of which Wesley was forced to remind them, namely that Wesley alone could appoint a preacher, and that therefore Wesley alone could consecrate one. But even this symptom would not persuade Wesley that he, or any of his members, had left the Church;

he instantly forgot that one of his reasons for ordaining had been that priests consecrated by English bishops would 'expect to govern' the American Methodists—'and how grievously would this entangle us!' But no; Wesley's heart was perfectly clear upon the point (it is best not to enquire what his head was doing); he was to say till the hour of his death, what he had again and again said before, 'Separate from the Church of England, and you separate from me.' But he must have seen what was happening, what had happened; he had founded a new Church. He was not a very logical thinker, but in this, surely, he deliberately deluded himself. So he went on happily exercising the functions of a bishop, in all ordaining twenty-six priests, for overseas, for Scotland, and finally for England.

The fated end had come, but for a few more years the small, spare figure could be seen driving about the country in his chaise as tirelessly as ever, his wide, bright eyes glowing beneath the still abundant but now snow-white hair, his whole face mellowed by the years, shining with the beauty of holiness. Twice a day his yet active figure, extremely neat, extremely simple, without buckle or ruffle (no Methodist was allowed to wear a ruffle), the uniform black relieved only by the white bands of a Church of England parson, would mount the pulpit and exhort in a scarcely failing voice, sometimes for three hours on end, for if he found the people loving he would not know how to stop, and would begin over and over again. And visible upon his face, no longer quite so awesome, there dwelt an all-pervading serenity: for he had done his work, had provided for the further governance of the society, by, in 1784, drawing up a Deed of Declaration, forming a 'Conference of the People called Methodists'. Looking back upon all that he had done, he saw that it was good. 'I never fret', he wrote to, of all people, his wife, who died, little grieved for, in 1781. The only danger was that he might become too serene. 'Many years ago,' he wrote in 1785, 'I was saying, "I cannot imagine how Mr. Whitefield can keep his soul alive, as he is not now going through honour and dishonour, evil and good report, having nothing but honour and good report attending him wherever he goes." It is now my own case . . . I am become, I know not how, an honourable man. The scandal of the cross is ceased.' His early troubles, distractions, periods of deep depression, faded out of his memory so completely that he declared that he had never felt more than a quarter of an hour's low spirits. He never felt them for a moment now: he had passed into the calm of accomplishment.

But old age will not be denied for ever. Charles, much lamented, had died in 1788, and himself, in 1789, when on a pastoral tour in Ireland, was forced to record, on entering his eighty-sixth year, 'I now find that I grow old.' He could no longer walk as briskly as he used to do, and small print bothered him unless the light was very good. On New Year's Day, 1790, he wrote: 'I am now an old man, decayed from head to foot. My eyes are dim. . . . However, blessed be God, I do not slack my labour. I can preach and write still.' But he could not read, worst of deprivations for a man who had read every spare moment of his days, on horseback, in his chaise, everywhere—and everything—theology, history, poetry, the classics; Barclay's *Apology* (which he thought a feeble book), Hume, Milton, Tasso, Plato. However, he could still travel and preach. The poet Crabbe went, at Lowestoft, 'to hear the venerable John Wesley on one of the last of his peregrinations. He was exceedingly old and infirm, and was attended and almost supported in the pulpit by a young minister on each side. The chapel was crowded to suffocation. In the course of his sermon he repeated, a little inaccurately, though with an application of his own, Cowley's

> Oft I am by women told,
> Poor Anacreon! thou grow'st old;
> See, thine hairs are falling all,
> Poor Anacreon! How they fall!
> Whether I grow old or no,
> By these signs I do not know;
> But this I need not to be told,
> 'Tis time to *live*, if I grow old'

which he declaimed 'with a beautiful cadence'.

And he was still *living*, thriftless of his energy, when at the age of eighty-eight, on March 2nd, 1791, death overtook him hard by his chapel in the City Road, to which he had just returned after preaching his last sermon at Leatherhead. He knew he was dying and gave directions that he should be buried in nothing but woollens. On his death-bed he still sang hymns, cheerfully, until he was too weak and could only murmur phrases. 'Farewell, farewell', he whispered to those who came to say good-bye, the only one among them unmoved, happy. 'Now we have done,' he murmured, 'let us all go.' The last evening, 'finding his friends could not understand what he said, he paused, and with all his remaining strength cried out, "The best of all is, God is with us." Then, lifting up his dying arm in token of victory, and raising his feeble voice with a holy triumph,' he again repeated the words, 'The best of all is, God is with us.' That night, 'I'll praise, I'll praise', was all he could utter. The next morning, at about ten o'clock, he passed quietly away, without a groan; and his friends, standing around his bed, sang together a valedictory hymn.

Each of the hundreds who gathered to the funeral was presented with an effigy of John Wesley, arrayed in canonicals, adorned with a halo and a crown, the whole beautifully stamped on a biscuit and handed them in an envelope of paper.

GIACOMO CASANOVA
CHEVALIER DE SEINGALT
(1725-1798)

CONTENTS

GIACOMO CASANOVA

I

The Education of an Adventurer

(*1725–1746*)

Casanova has no standing as a historical personage, but he has the magnitude of a great character in fiction. He exists, not by virtue of any effect he had on his time, but because he is the hero of a long, episodic, often lubric, and sometimes libellous novel. His autobiography is a romance which is sure to amuse whenever it is picked up; but its unique quality will appeal with its whole force only to those who can free themselves from prejudice, or whose interest in mankind is so lively as to overcome any repugnance they may feel at intimacy with a man completely devoid of suppressions. You must not blush when you read Casanova, or at most, like the Prince de Ligne, must blush only at finding that you are not doing so. For it is safe to say that Casanova had no complexes, not even that commonplace affair an inferiority-complex (unless the writing of his memoirs is tell-tale), and no shame. How could he have? loving as he did the life which he lived intensely as perhaps only a poet can live it, for an adventurer of his kind is a minor poet as well as a man of action, and lives by the imagination as much as by the body.

He is valuable as a character in fiction for exactly the same reason that these persons have value; he is a distillation of something that exists in every one of us, not merely in his eminence as a procreative animal (for to attain that involves devotion to an activity that can easily pall, even in fancy), but rather of that something in us which bids us be free, to scoff at the restraints of society, to revolt against the maxim of 'safety first', and against our own continual care of ourselves—that something which makes us wish that we were fairies, to come and go as we please, and whose actions can have little effect on anybody.

Perhaps Casanova really was a fairy. Certainly, unless he is
largely regarded as one he becomes preposterous, unbelievable
an offence against common sense. Otherwise he had no right
to enjoy life so much, without remorse, and for so long. One
of his earliest mentors had told him that *Sequere Deum* was the
rule of life, by which he meant, 'Go wherever your impulse
leads you; take whatever Fate offers, unless you feel a strong
dislike for the gift', and this advice Casanova followed to the
end; it was almost his only principle; and since he was blessed
with a superabundant vitality, it led him into curious, exciting
and unholy places. He has, besides, that other necessary quality
of the hero of a picaresque romance, he is likable, if not
admirable. Moreover in life he had this winning quality, for
whenever he told the truth about an adventure of his, not glozing
over his own faults, he always found sympathizers, and made
friends: and if this result was partly due to his grace in telling
the tale, his skill survives in his artfully artless narrative
Infamous scoundrel! we will no doubt feel compelled to say
but then, as Volpone did to Mosca, we will cry out, 'My witty
mischief, let me embrace thee!' There was so much more in his
make-up than the rogue.

Giacoma Casanova was the eldest son of a Venetian actor of
Spanish descent, who died when his first-born was eight years
old, leaving him with two brothers, and a third to follow
besides two smaller sisters. Casanova the elder had established
his wife as an actress, in spite of vowing that he would not, a
profession which, with its prolonged absences in various
capitals, gave her every opportunity for neglecting her family
The eldest of her brood began the life which he was to turn
into a fantasy on April 2nd, 1725, but for his first few years he
was a sickly infant, half-idiot, suffering, he leads us to suppose
from over-richness of blood, an inconvenience which time was to
teach him how to allay, but which for the moment was eased
first by the incantations of a cat-attended sorceress to whom he
was led by his maternal grandmother, and then by the visitation
of a fairy who came down the chimney. His infancy was a blur
in his mind, from which he could dredge up only an anecdote of
how he managed with precocious skill to divert to one of his
brothers a punishment due to himself. The child was father to
the man. But then we have as an excuse that his reasoning

faculty was dormant until the age of eight years and four months, when it suddenly awoke to reveal the complete natural philosopher. It was when his mother, with the family protector, the patrician Abbé Grimani, and Giorgio Baffo, famed for his erotic verses (was not his name derived from the island of Paphos, the land of Venus?), were taking him to be boarded out at a sort of primary school at Padua, in the hope of bettering his health. Travelling by river, Giacomo awoke in the morning to feel no motion, but to see the trees passing by the cabin window. 'Why!' he cried, 'the trees are moving!' 'You silly child,' he was told; 'it's not the trees, but the boat.' He thought a moment, and said, 'Perhaps, then, the sun does not move either; it is the earth turning from west to east which makes it seem as though it did.' His mother and the priest mocked him for a dolt, but Baffo, embracing him, exclaimed delightedly, 'You are right, my child; the sun does not move. Pluck up your spirits, use your reason, and let people laugh as much as they like.' Casanova was eternally grateful to Baffo; but for him, he declared, his mind would have been blighted for ever; he would always have crouched under the yoke of a shameful credulity, whereas he now entered into possession of a faculty which, he confessed, had not taken him very far, but to which he owed all the happiness he enjoyed when he was so unlucky as to be lonely. Certainly his mind was never idle throughout his life; all through the *Mémoires* it peeps out as a sceptical and above all an inquisitive tenant of a boisterous body; it was an enquiring rather than a constructive mind, but extremely agile, and not altogether superficial. It was just the mind for a vehemently joyful, devil-may-care adventurer, a mind ever alert, speculative, able at once to wander in unchartered seas, and to turn its discoveries to practical uses. Casanova was half a philosopher, no empty-headed, rascally parasite and libertine; he was always eager to know things, especially himself. *Nequidquam sapit qui sibi non sapit*, 'his wisdom's vain who for himself's not wise', so he prefaced his *Mémoires*: and if, not being extravagantly introspective, he never attained a very profound knowledge of himself, at least he cleared his mind of cant.

The boy who had so unexpectedly discovered that he could think was put to board with a Slavonian woman at an establishment which he hated, where the provender was so meagre that,

his mind not being of the kind that acts as a check, he learned
to filch from the larder. For lessons he went to a Dr. Gozzi,
who, since he found his pupil intelligent, took him into his own
house, and, while imparting a somewhat narrow religious
doctrine, gave him a smattering of the sciences. There, in due
course, Giacomo's education was developed in other ways by
the doctor's young sister Bettina, a girl of thirteen, who
instructed her charge in one of the more obvious branches of
physiology, her teaching, however, going only so far as to
excite his appetite for more knowledge without completing it.
Nevertheless she succeeded in giving him the experience of
jealousy (one of his elder comrades was bolder than he was),
and also gave him the opportunity of witnessing several
attempts at exorcism, for she became possessed of devils, of
eleven thousand to be exact, owing to the machinations of a
sorceress. These somewhat complicated the amiable Bettina's
intrigues, and Casanova had profound suspicions of the demons,
especially as they seemed amenable to treatment only by a very
good-looking young priest. However, in 1737, her nervous
trouble was replaced by smallpox, of which she very nearly
died; every one of the household was kept from her, except
Casanova, who having already had the illness, tended her
devotedly. As a result he caught the disease again, which,
though mild, all the same left three marks upon his face.

Other sides of his education proceeded swiftly; already at
eleven years old he had astonished the company and delighted
Baffo by answering in a hexameter a Latin distich which, even
veiled in the decency of a dead tongue, it is not decorous to
repeat. He was destined for the law, though he wished to
become a doctor; and very probably he would have made an
admirable one, for not only would the profession have gratified
his scientific turn, but, as he was to say later, the practice of
medicine offers more scope for charlatanism than any other
accepted way of life. But if he worked, as he seems to have
done, he also played, falling in with a raffish set which taught
him to gamble and to fight, and would have taught him to
wench, but that he avoided the pitfall. According to his account,
the students of Padua were an intolerable set of ne'er-do-well
swashbucklers, continually at odds with the police; and Casanova, flourishing pistols and a carbine, banded himself with

them. In this way he first began to read the book of life for himself, a thing which it is essential to do, for mere theories of morals are like the table of contents of a book, which will tell you what the book is about, but will not save you from the necessity of reading the volume. Sermons and precepts are all very well, but 'man is an animal who can learn only by his own experience', he found; also he must test the warnings of the moralists to see whether they are valid. Thus once he was old enough to be let out alone he made the most of his opportunities; and some of the warnings did turn out to be true, for he was fleeced of his money, gambled on credit, and finally in 1739 had to apply to his grandmother for funds. She did not answer his appeal; with admirable promptitude, she came and huddled him back to Venice.

Then began what is, perhaps, the most incongruous phase of Casanova's life: he became, of all unlikely things, an abbé, duly submitting to the tonsure, and receiving the three minor orders. No solemn or ascetic abbé, indeed, but a happy, idle, dandified abbé of fifteen, his hair lightly powdered and scented with jasmine, which, though once cut off in his sleep by a severer churchman, was made all the more gracious by an expert barber sent by Senator Malipiero, who had taken the youth under his protection because he habitually ate as much as two people, and thus stimulated the appetite of the aged patrician. It was a fruitful protection, for though Casanova continued his normal education, getting Horace by heart, acquiring more than a veneer of Greek and a sound knowledge of other writers of antiquity (especially those who appeal most to curious youth), Malipiero did not think that that was enough. He introduced the young abbé, precocious in body and mind, to the cultured society that frequented his house, and so the youth achieved a modicum of social polish, and learned how to talk. He liked being free of the Senator's luxurious table, and had no objection to the presence of a delightful girl of eighteen, Thérèse Imer, for the care of whom the old man reaped no reward but the dubious one of being able to ease his emotion in tears and abortive rages.

Soon Malipiero proceeded to launch the promising abbé in his career, and managed to have him nominated to preach a sermon, which, in spite of the opposition of the curate of the

chosen church, Casanova insisted upon writing himself, con-
senting only to change the text from a Horatian titbit to one
more congruous with the place, if unrelated to his theme. He
learned his script up carefully, and delivered it brilliantly,
indeed with such grace that the plate set aside for offerings to
the preacher contained not only an inordinate number of
sequins, but a quantity of billets-doux as well. Here, then, was
the indubitable career for him: Casanova, the world-famous
preacher. . . . Full of confidence, he prepared his next oration
too flimsily, and confused in the head by a luncheon where the
wine had flowed liberally, he lost his thread, broke down
physically, and had to be carried from the pulpit. Drowned in
mortification, he bolted off to Padua for a few days to continue
his legal studies, and never preached again. Thus revising his
view of a career, he in due course mastered enough of the code
to be received Doctor in 1742 (unfortunately there is no trace
in the University Registers of this degree being granted him),
but at that point he deserted the law. Not for him the dust and
the routine, the excessive concentration of that arduous and
sedentary profession, which, like Faustus, he regarded as fit
only for a mercenary drudge. Better the Church than that: and
after all, was he not marked out for it?

In the meanwhile he enjoyed Venice, at that time one of the
best towns in the world for pleasures, especially during Carnival,
pleasures from which taking young abbés with perfumed hair
were by no means excluded. It is not surprising that at his age,
in that seductive atmosphere, Casanova began to feel the insidious attraction of the other sex, and to experience what was
perhaps his last moral battle. *Sequere Deum*, yes; but where with
us, temptations apart, it is often difficult to know exactly what
is *Deus*, with Casanova it was always impulse, which in natures
such as his is so strong as never to be misleading. Deus first
manifested himself at Paseano, where Casanova was staying
with some rich friends. There he was looked after in his room
by a charming flowering girl called Lucie, brimful of life and
the gaiety of life, adorned with as much fresh beauty as man
could wish, and whose very innocence, whose virginal trustful-
ness, threw her into the arms of the boy-abbé. He loved her,
she declared her love for him; who could resist? But Casanova
did resist. Heroic resolutions sustained him through white

nights of struggle, reticences of youth to which, he confessed, fear of consequences lent support. But what perverse moral lessons does life not teach! A year later, going back to Paseano full of eagerness (for through experience he had lost his puerile fears), he found that a fortnight earlier Lucie had vanished in company with a courier by whom she was with child. She was lost, irretrievably sunk—and it was all his fault! Had he quenched Lucie's fires, had he even allayed them, she would never have been seduced by this infamous courier. Casanova, who had been so proud of his conquest over himself, was now ashamed of his silly, of his fatal continence. He vowed that he would never repeat the offence, and immediately adopting 'a different system', one from which he never departed (except once, when frightened), he seized the opportunity of being in a chariot with a lady alarmed at a thunderstorm to put it into practice.

For by then he was no longer innocent; he had tasted the joys which he was to pursue all his life till time brought about its doleful revenge. For during that year he had his first adventure, falling victim to the not very great charm of the niece of the churchman who taught him languages and philosophy. She, however, was inflexibly unkind; marriage was her goal: but she had two friends, Marton and Manette, sisters, daughters of people whom he visited. They were beautiful, of noble birth and considerable wit, who after a first trial cunningly contrived, found Casanova so delightful a companion that they gave him a wax impression of the key of the room they shared. He did not love them; he did not pretend to love them; there was about this episode none of the spring freshness of his love for Lucie, none of the

> 'Ah, how sweet it is to love!
> Ah, how gay is young desire!'

rapture: it was merely, one would think, opportunity. But then, at the age of sixteen, love is not essential to enjoyment, and by the time Casanova returned to Paseano, he was thoroughly initiate, if not yet past master, in the mysteries of Venus.

By now he was already independent. His first visit to Paseano had been cut short by the illness and subsequent death of his grandmother; and his mother, established in the theatre at

Dresden, had bidden the Abbé Grimani look after her family, and install Giacomo in a furnished apartment she possessed. The daughters were otherwise lodged, and her second son François was apprenticed as pupil to Francesco Guardi, already famous as a painter. The other sons? Well, Casanova is always somewhat vague about these other brothers whom he disliked. Grimani was inadequate to the situation. 'I could never make out', Casanova said, 'whether he was good because he was a fool, or whether the foolishness was part of his goodness.' At all events he could not curb his eldest charge, and a crisis came when Casanova sold the linen and furniture to pay his debts and gamble. It was difficult to know what Grimani could do with this idle, unattached abbé, whose only serious occupations seemed to be occasionally to scribble an heretical thesis—such as the one which argued that any being of whom one could have nothing but an abstract idea could only exist arbitrarily—or to dabble in a dilettante way with chemistry. Even his serious social occupation was gone, for the revered Malipiero having found his young protégé making unequivocal and unresented gestures to Thérèse Imer, had belaboured the young ecclesiastic with a stick, and cast him out of his house.

It is true that in the offing there was a monk about to be made a bishop, apparently if not very believably through the influence of Madame Casanova, and he was going to take charge of the youth. Casanova was delighted at the prospect. Here was the path to Church preferment, even, who knew? to the pontificate, so did his young fancy run away with him. But for the moment the bishop did not materialize, and in the meantime Grimani packed Giacomo off to a seminary. Casanova had no objection to this scheme; it appealed to his whim: but he fiercely resented the entrance examination. Was he not Doctor? He sulked, was put among the small boys; but soon, by accident, the extent of his knowledge was discovered, and he was promoted to the senior class. This matter had hardly been arranged, however, than he was expelled for an offence of which he declared himself before God to be innocent, and which, indeed, scarcely tallies with his predilection for the other sex. Grimani promptly had him shut up in the fort of St. Andrew. There he was tolerably free, free enough at all events to escape for one night and rejoice in thrashing the man who, he thought, had injured him in

Grimani's esteem; and to receive from another inmate of the fair sex an incommodity which mortified him. For six months he endured this existence, which was not without its amenities, since he dined with the prison governor; then, shortly after his release, being once more installed at Grimani's table, he met his bishop, who gave him instructions for meeting him in Rome, from which they would go together to his see in Calabria.

In good heart, full of ambition, with such a supply of clothes and money as to give confidence, Casanova set sail towards the end of 1743. The first stop was Chiozza, where the voyagers were to stay for a few days, an almost fatal few days. For almost at once the not yet subtle enough young abbé was fleeced of his money at faro; and what was worse, having pawned all his clothes, he lost them too. This was enough to sink any youth to despondency, but what added to his grief was a second experience of a humiliating disease, for he had not yet got to the stage where he could say with equanimity (after twelve such illnesses), 'I have often observed that for the greatest part of my life I have been trying to make myself ill, and then, when I had achieved this, in trying to get well again. I have been equally successful in both; and now that, as far as that goes, I enjoy perfect health, I regret being unable to make myself ill: but old age, an illness as cruel as it is inevitable, forces me to be well in spite of myself.' But now in his nonage his circumstances plunged him in despair. He suffered mental agonies which he never forgot, and was on the point of letting go every moral hold, of sinking into degradation and ignominy. He lay and groaned on the bed which he had been hospitably offered, and was only rescued from the pit by the sailor who came to fetch him on board. It was the severest crisis of his life; but by the time he got to Ancona, where he was delayed by a quarantine, he had completely recovered. He made his way on foot to Rome, in company largely with a scandalously predatory monk, who, however, kept him in food, only to find that his bishop, tired of waiting, had gone on to Calabria. He pursued him to Naples, where a message had been left. Near Naples Casanova retrieved his fortunes by a dubious piece of chemistry which increased the volume of mercury (though it debased it); and selling this secret to a merchant, he proceeded, once more well equipped with clothes and money, to join his bishop.

Casanova liked this prelate, a worthy, pious, and educated man;
but the see was a desert, the country, in Casanova's eyes, bleak,
society non-existent. The bishop, shrewd and kindly, saw at
once that the young abbé was not the assistant for him, and
after three days they parted amicably, Casanova armed with an
introduction to a grandee at Naples.

Naples was always kind to Casanova: he was petted, was
given clothes and money by a cousin, became a figure in society,
and was offered admirable posts in noble houses. But he refused
all offers, asking only for recommendations in Rome, to which
he travelled in company with an advocate, his wife, and his
sister. With the wife, Lucrezia, he fell in love, and, favoured by
the promiscuity incident to travelling in those days, achieved
such progress that in Rome he was made happy. It was the first
affair in which his heart had been engaged; he was really in
love, and his passion was returned. *Amour, je te remercie*, the
couple cried simultaneously in their transport, and Lucrezia for
ever retained a niche in the sentimental corner of Casanova's
heart.

But such delights were only for moments stolen from a
sterner system of education which he was undergoing with a
subtle Abbé Gama, in whose charge he had been placed by
Cardinal Acquaviva, and who, bidding him abandon such
acquaintance as Lucrezia's family provided, revealed to him the
mysteries of discretion, of dissimulation, and of pleasing, which
make for progress in the Church. He also made him learn
French. Casanova seems to have been attached in some
secretarial capacity to the Cardinal's court, and he throve
through his appearance, his wit, his diligence; and these
combined with a brilliance in scribbling verses, make him
equally successful in the gatherings of cardinals and their ducal
mistresses, in which he became more and more intimate. When
he saw Pope Benedict XIV, he was quite at his ease with him,
made him laugh, and extracted permission from him to read
the books on the Index, and to treat fasts lightly, though
neither grace was given in writing. It looked as though he
would thrive in the Church; more than one cardinal had his eye
on him, the Abbé Gama felt his pupil was bringing him credit
but alas! just as the road to preferment seemed open, Casanova
helped an eloping couple to escape the law and the Inquisition

by harbouring the girl, disguised as an abbé, in his quarters.
The affair made so much noise that Acquaviva was forced to part
with his promising recruit; and asking Casanova what he would
like to do, sent him on some vague mission to Constantinople
to cover his expulsion from Rome.

It was unlike Casanova to have an unadventurous journey,
and his transit to Venice, from which he was to sail for the
Sublime Porte, provided matter as fantastic as it was unforeseen,
apart from the amorous extravaganza interwoven with it. The
journey involved a love-affair with a ravishing Thérèse, a
singer masquerading as a *castrato*, the loss of a passport, semi-
imprisonment, his sudden departure on a bolting horse he had
innocently mounted, entering and leaving Rimini as a muleteer,
and finally his casting away the cassock in favour of a smart
blue and white, gold and silver officer's uniform of his own
designing. Perhaps, after all, the Church was not the most
glamorous career. The journey also involved a deal of philosophic thought and introspection, but neither, though they
taught him carefulness, weakened his impulsiveness, as was
shown by his superb aplomb when his runaway horse was caught
by guards and he replied to the question of where he was going
so fast by saying he was carrying an urgent message to the
governor of Rimini, and thus ensured his being sent to the town
where Thérèse, or Bellino, then was. Introspection was
prompted by Thérèse herself, who at the conclusion of this
period, and while he was separated from her, wrote to say that
she had been made a good offer by a Duke to appear at a
Naples theatre, but that before accepting, she wished to offer
Casanova the first refusal of her person and her future. Or,
should she go to Naples and wait for him there? when he appeared, she would support him. 'For the first time in my life,'
Casanova wrote, 'I found myself forced to think before making
a decision. . . . Two equally powerful motives held the balance
even—self-love and love.' And, somewhat queerly, magnanimity
entered into it. Had he the right to prejudice Thérèse's career,
which, he foresaw, would depend more upon her charms than
upon her talent? For he did not see himself in the rôle of
complaisant lover or husband. Husband! the word had a horrid
sound, especially at eighteen; besides, it would have meant
abandoning the splendid future for which he felt himself destined.

And again, how could he bear the shame of appearing among his
aristocratic friends at Naples as the kept husband of an opera-
singer? No! impossible!—and if he was enamoured, he wa
past the first fevered rapture in which one can renounce the
world for love. So he advised her to go to Naples, where, no
doubt, some day he would join her. Thérèse was disposed of.

Thereupon, in his new soldierly character, Casanova slipped
through the quarantine, and appeared in his native town.
Grimani was horrified, but Marton and Manette, with whom
he lodged, were in ecstasies, and though his imagination was
filled with Thérèse, he did not disappoint them. He was guilty
of no inconstancy towards Thérèse, only of an infidelity, a pretty
distinction he was careful to make. Venice on the whole was
delightful, but since his career had to be seen to, he entered the
Venetian army as an ensign, and was sent to Corfu, from
whence he was granted leave to fulfil his 'mission' to Constantinople. This consisted merely in presenting a letter of
introduction to Achmet Pasha, who as a Christian had been
known as the Comte de Bonneval, one of Prince Eugene's
famous generals, and who now as a Moslem was a noted
diplomat. Casanova amused himself by making observations of
Turkish manners, which was all there was for him to do, since
he stupidly missed a sole opportunity for an amorous intrigue,
and then returned to Corfu. There, passing the time chiefly in
gambling, and in making a little summer love, he became involved in a disciplinary misdemeanour, and to evade what he
thought a humiliating punishment, he escaped to a neighbouring island, where he made himself for some time into a
sort of bandit chief surrounded by faithful soldiery—for such
the peasants became if sufficiently trained by largesse—but was
eventually induced to return. Soon after, in 1745, he went back
to Venice, where, disgusted at not getting the promotion he
had been promised, and feeling that he was not built for a life
of discipline, he threw up his commission.

Then for a while, after a brief experience in a lawyer's office,
he became a complete rapscallion. He who had dreamed of
being Pope, and had aspired to command an army, eked out a
bare living by playing the fiddle in a theatre orchestra; a
humiliating position for a Doctor of Laws, who from moving
in the most dazzling society had thus sunk to be the companion

ɔf dire rascals. What a crew! They got drunk every night after ̩he theatre, haunted brothels, roused honest citizens out of bed ɔn false pretexts, cut bell-ropes, slipped gondolas from their ̩noorings, sounded tocsins, and even kidnapped terrified ɔourgeois; and into this life Casanova drew his brother ̩François, now becoming a painter of battle-scenes. Such a life ̩would inevitably have led to prison; complaints against this ɔand of rogues were becoming too frequent: but then Casanova ̩ad a stroke of luck which reorientated his whole existence.

Leaving a festivity very late one evening, the violinist saw ̩going downstairs a venerable red-robed senator, who in ̩drawing out his handkerchief dropped a letter. Casanova ̩astened to pick it up, and, in thanks, the patrician offered to ̩ake the young man back to his lodgings in his gondola. They ̩ad hardly started when the senator was seized with an ̩apoplectic fit. Casanova rushed in panic to find a surgeon, who ̩at once bled the stricken man, Casanova tearing strips off his ̩hirt to make bandages. The youth then took the invalid to his ɔalace, another doctor was called, and Casanova quietly installed ̩imself as nurse. It turned out that the senator was a certain ̩Zuane Bragadin (more correctly Bragadino), who after the ̩wild youth proper to a handsome man was now at the age of ̩ifty-seven living a life of wisdom, in company with two old ̩wiseacres, Messieurs Dandolo and Barbaro. These, the next ̩evening, told Casanova he might go if he had business else-̩where, but the young man sententiously replied, 'I will stay ̩here tonight by the bed; for if I go the patient will die, whereas f I stay I am sure he will live.' The friends were staggered by ̩this assurance, and Casanova stayed. Moreover, his prophecy ɔroved true. For during the night the invalid began to suffer ̩agonies from a mercury poultice the doctor had placed on his ̩hest; in some way it was suffocating him. Casanova at once ̩roused the friends and said that it was essential to remove the ɔintment, and he did so, washing the chest with warm water. The patient forthwith revived. When the doctor bustled in ɔetimes the next morning he was overjoyed to see his patient ̩o well, but furious when he found what had been done. Doctor,' Bragadin said, 'the man who relieved me of the ̩nercury is a physician who knows more of medicine than you ̩lo', and he indicated Casanova. Both doctor and amateur were

astounded; it was all Casanova could do to keep his face, but
with his magnificent presence of mind he at once stepped into
the position. The doctor, of course, resigned the case, Casanova
took charge, and sensibly recommending a low diet, improved
the occasion by laying down the law, and quoting medical
authorities whose works he had never read. Bragadin and his
friends were in raptures over the young man; the senator
indeed declaring that he could not at his age know so much
unless he had supernatural aid. The suggestion appeared
brilliant to Casanova, and with inimitable swiftness he mounted
to the top of the situation. He confessed that he had indeed
some acquaintance with the occult sciences; more, he had a
familiar, an oracle, who would answer questions put to him. In
fact, it was owing to this oracle that he had been on the steps
when Bragadin had dropped his letter. In illustration of his
necromantic skill, he proceeded to erect pyramids of numbers
'Why, this is Solomon's Key,' Bragadin cried, 'what the vulgar
call the Cabbala', as he listened to the answers which Casanova
produced, extracting at will replies either clear, ambiguous or
unfathomably mysterious. 'Where', Bragadin asked in tremu-
lous delight, 'had he got his knowledge?' 'Oh,' Casanova
answered readily, 'from a hermit.' The three preposterous old
men fell into the trap, craving as they did for something more
esoteric than the Christian religion, in which they implicitly
believed because they found it all quite natural. Thus Casanova
became their joy: his oracle, called Paralis in the family circle
was their mentor; and soon they would do nothing without
the young man's advice. Bragadin made him a son of the house
clothed him, fed him, made him a handsome allowance.What
could be better? Casanova had not the heart to undeceive them
he fooled them to the top of their bent.

'I was not quite open and above-board with them', Casanova
confessed: but then, what was he to do? Would not Bragadin
have died but for him? Could he be so mean as to leave them
all in the lurch? And besides, they were such obviously easy
prey, that if he did not cheat them, some one else would. It was
his duty to go on, he felt; it would be unpardonably rude to tell
them they were silly dupes, and then leave them; it would not
cure them of their folly. Besides, pride forbade him to avow
himself unworthy of their distinguished friendship. 'It seems

o me,' he wrote in his unregenerate old age, 'that I chose the
better part, the most noble, the most natural.' After all, he was
twenty-one, and full of high spirits; the situation promised an
infinity of fun. And it gave him a position in the world, besides
securing him from poverty. And if the world puzzled its head
as to how three venerable old men could give countenance to a
notorious rakehell, it was no business of his. Thus Casanova,
if not settled in life, was at least provided with a base from
which to conduct those operations which fill us with amazement,
and seem at times incredible.

II

Various Facets

Fate, it is clear, had arranged to give an unshackled temperament just the education, just the introduction to life, to form a
prince of adventurers, cherished by Fortune in a shape 'which
offered him no temptation to tread the paths of moderation and
prudence'. He was an apparition, who for the next forty years
was to make more or less dazzling descents upon all the capitals
of Europe, to astound all classes from king to beggar, being
equally at home (like death's dancing feet) in palace or
tavern; a companion who could amuse men of intellect such as
Voltaire and Winckelmann, debating with them on level terms,
keep a cultured dinner-table in roars of laughter, or divert a
collection of crooks. In honour with statesmen, he was treated
with respect by rascals as master of their own crafts. Living most
of the while in luxury, travelling like a *grand seigneur*, he would
occasionally have to eke out a pittance in a garret: at some times
looked upon as a man of power, at others in prison, he raided
all Europe, now in the guise of a bird of paradise, now as a
hungry tiger restlessly seeking whom or what he might
devour. He was never still for long. Urged by the need to find
new fields to display himself in, but impelled at least as much
by curiosity, he could not bear to stay any length of time in
one place. Fresh manners and customs, new books and old
manuscripts, works of art, antiquities, and especially different
people, these lured him on: and if he was sometimes expelled
from the places he graced, he never minded setting out again
on his travels.

Of Herculean build, they said, very tall, unusually strong,
capable of athletic feats as well as of Gargantuan meals, he
could impose, by a happy swagger, on any company. Yet he
was no Adonis. His complexion, dark brown in his youth,
became 'African' as he grew older, while certain initial roughnesses, smallpox marks and scars, deepened with the years. A
high receding forehead, a long aggressive nose edged with an

nquisitive nostril, a lover's mouth, and a soft chin falling away
o a bull neck, do not seem to constitute the most fascinating
of masks. But fascination does not reside in formal beauty, and
his eye has yet to be taken into account, a large, rapacious,
black-lashed eye, a little protuberant under brows arching
outward, a light-lidded eye in which the iris seems to be set
ow down. It could flash, it could soothe, could warm to love,
could freeze to fear. But it was in the whole man rather than in
he face alone that the power lay: he seemed to radiate energy,
o be imbued with magnetic attraction. Abundantly vital, his
strength promised generosity, his gaiety kindliness, in spite of a
vestige of hardness. Perhaps he was over-confident, over-
assured, sometimes explosively so; but then he was permeated
by a belief in his good genius, his *esprit familial*, which though
t sometimes betrayed him, usually prompted him for his good.
It inspired and advised him, steeled his will, gave him infinite
resilience, and, most significant of all, rid him of scruples. His
social talents were enormous. Not only was he a good talker,
overflowing with unusual knowledge, a born orator, a poet
able to quote poetry inexhaustibly, and, since he was moved to
tears while he quoted, able to move his hearers; an inimitable
story-teller; but, being agog with curiosity, eager to pick up
knowledge of men or things, he was a good listener. And this
is a quality that makes for popularity.

Talents, sensibility, physical courage, and a personality
which attracted numerous friends—and made a few implacably
bitter enemies—to what end, we ask, did he use these precious
gifts? The answer is, to living, which, with him, meant princi-
pally loving, for he had early discovered that his mission in life
was to be, in his own phrase, a votary of Venus. Abnormally
endowed with procreative gifts—he has been described as 'a
sexual athlete'—he never lost an opportunity of being on
intimate terms with a woman, of any age or class, so long as
she had charms. It was his supreme bliss, it never palled, though
he confessed that as he grew older he became less delicate, and
no longer experienced the delicious excitement of his early
adventures. How should he, indeed? But he was no mere
animal. It is true that he was sometimes led into venal relations,
orgies to which as a rule he was incited by others, but he
obtained no pleasure unless his companion (or companions)

felt it too. He would have no grudging acquiescence; the idea
of force horrified him. Without sympathy, without real attraction on both sides, to act the beast with two backs (he was fond
of the Shakespearian phrase) meant nothing to him. First
attracted by a woman's face, he would be enraptured by her
conversation, her wit, till his passion was inflamed. Or so
seemed to him; but perhaps after all he did not know himself
very well. Sometimes he seems to have loved wholly, with
delicacy and constancy; he never ceased to have warm feeling
towards a woman he had really loved. But his peculiar kind of
constancy did not preclude his loving others at the same time
the appearance of any new beauty at once aroused his con-
cupiscence. He panted to possess every she whom he found
attractive, and was delighted with every one he conquered: all
had peculiar beauties; not one of them, in his own favourite
term, but could have served as model to Praxiteles.

Had you asked him if he never wearied of the diversion, he
would have stared at you and asked in return if you ever got
tired of reading books? All books were much the same, and so
were all women; but just as every book is unique, so is every
female creature. Declared bibliophile in both sorts, he made the
comparison at length. Women, like books, must first attract by
the title-page, which is to be read from top to bottom; and just
as the real amateur of women takes as great a delight in the feet
as in the face (he was something of a fetichist as regards feet)
so the bibliophile appreciates the printer's name at the bottom
of the page. He is taken with the outside, then he wants to read
the book. 'Moreover, just as great readers seize upon any
fresh book, good or bad, so the curiosity of a man who has
known many women, all lovely, is aroused about even ugly ones
when they are quite fresh to him . . . the work may be better
than the title-page suggests.' Habit, curiosity, then, as much as
anything else, impelled Casanova to his continual conquests, as
well as the urgency of his overheated temperament. Indeed it
became with him a question of self-respect. Not to have offered
to seduce a woman who came his way would have been to fail
in his mission as a high-priest to Venus: indeed it became his
duty to seek out sacrifices to offer on the altar of love. Thus his
course throughout Europe is marked by scores of Paphian rites,
of which only a trifling percentage can be mentioned here

everywhere over the Continent were to be found women not only whom he had adored, but who had adored him. Love was his happiness, he followed it, he sought it out wherever he could. More than anything else, if pleasure was his aim, love was his profession.

Moralists habitually condemn the pursuit of happiness, though what else man does in his multifarious activities it is hard to determine. There are, of course, many ways of obtaining happiness—in asceticism, in devotion to hard tasks, in power, in self-sacrifice, in the search after truth, in abandoning one's self to the will of God—and moreover it is fairly clear that to pursue the obvious, easy happiness by direct means is to court failure. Indeed man is so complex that he often has to perform the most intricate evolutions, undergo the most rigorous mental discipline, before he can be even contented, for it is hard to know in what, precisely, happiness consists. But Casanova suffered no mental tortures; happiness for him lay in obedience to impulse, in the immediate gratification of the senses—not excluding the senses of the brain and the delight of intellectual mastery—and his nature was so simple, so direct, even abnormally so, that he asked for no spicing to the dish, though indeed he was not averse from a little danger, a touch of mystery, a hint of secrecy, at any rate a trifle of difficulty. But that was all. Baudelaire's remark that the single and supreme delight of love lies in the certainty that one is doing evil would have been incomprehensible to him, for he had no atom, not the smallest residue of a sense of sin in making love. He experienced none of the delicious fears of the unknown, that 'panic terror of consequences which might disastrously affect the future', for alas, 'an ill philosophy lessens what we call prejudices to too small a number'. He pursued the obvious easy happiness as directly as he could, and the astonishing truth is that he caught it.

Money counted for nothing with him. It was meant to spend, lavishly, to obtain the best food and drink (and plenty of both), consideration from other mortals, splendid clothes, and love. For even when he does not buy his loves, a man must be set out in a certain way to be attractive to women; he must be able to afford to do amusing and expensive things, to shower unexpectedly lovely gifts on them, and above all, to be in a position to make sacrifices. Money meant living splendidly, and what was the good of living at all if one merely dragged through a sober, honest, and industrious life? Moreover, the world was like a kaleidoscope, full of gloriously coloured interesting things and people; the only difference was, that whereas a kaleidoscope revolves before you, you yourself had to do the revolving through a static world. And travelling, especially travelling in dashing style, needs money.

Casanova, then, got money. He was sure of never starving, for the good Senator Bragadin would see to that; but money from that source was the merest insignificant percentage of what he needed. His main fount of revenue throughout his life was gambling; he hated, he declared, to spend money not obtained in that way; but once his pockets were full, he scattered their contents broadcast, in clothes, jewelry, horses and chariots, in meals that would have gratified both Lucullus and Trimalchio, in orientally princely gifts to women, and in generosity to servants which staggered the recipients. He made many poor families happy, from vanity indeed rather than from virtue, though it gave him pleasure to make people rejoice; and he often gave, not lent, large sums to fellow-adventurers who were not so lucky as himself. But if he gambled to get money, he also gambled for love of the game: it was in his blood. He confessed that he could not live without it, could not resist punting at faro, his most usual game, though he preferred to keep the bank, as the odds were in its favour. He could not even always stop playing when his better judgment told him he should; and thus, sometimes beginning the evening a rich man, he would end it destitute. After all, gambling was part of his philosophy of life; indeed, life as he saw it was nothing but a gamble— but the way the cards are shuffled is predestined. Of course, as a Christian (for such this arrant pagan thought himself) he did not believe in Fate, yet it is extraordinary how often the word Destiny occurs in his memoirs. There was something which ruled the ways of men, as it did the fall of cards, for time and again he did things which according to all reason were follies and should have led to dire results, but which turned out happily; while, on the other hand, actions he had undertaken after hours of prudent thought had led to disaster: the sad story of Lucie of Paseano was a case in point. Clearly there was a

Providence which ruled the affairs of men. Who were they, poor mortals, to attempt to govern their ends? *Sequere Deum.* Thus Casanova took to the faro table all the boldness, the faith in providence, that he carried with him elsewhere. He was an incomparable player, cool, alert, never betraying himself by his face, which even when he was losing heavily radiated enjoyment in the game. He never cheated—not seriously—cards were far too deep a passion with him, and was always hot against those who 'corrected fortune', though indeed, if he never himself tampered with the cards, he did not mind on occasion going halves in a bank with those who did. As far as cards went, he piqued himself on being a man of honour. And his luck was amazing. Again and again he would break the bank; time after time he would, as banker, retire with his pockets bursting not only with gold, but with notes and bills of exchange. Fortune smiles on those who are not afraid of her, and whose nerves are of iron.

Once, however, it was not a question of nervous, but of physical endurance. At Sulzbach, in 1762, he lost a trifling sum at piquet to a certain Entragues, who offered him his revenge. 'I am not very eager for it,' Casanova answered, 'for I play for the fun of it, and you play to win.'

'You insult me.'

'I did not mean to: but every time we have played, you have stopped after about an hour.'

'You ought to be grateful to me for that; since not being up to my standard, you would have lost a lot of money.'

'Perhaps, but I don't believe I should.'

'I can prove it.'

'Very well: but whichever of us stops playing first will forfeit fifty louis.'

They began to play at three o'clock. At nine Entragues suggested supper. 'I'm not hungry,' Casanova said; 'but of course you can go away if you want me to pocket the stakes.' No more was said. The spectators went to supper, and came back to watch, leaving the gamblers to themselves at midnight. At six the water-drinkers congratulated them; at nine the combatants were persuaded to drink some chocolate; at four, a little soup. At supper-time it was suggested that they should divide the stakes; but Entragues being well ahead in winnings, Casanova would not consent. So on they played, all through the second

night, Casanova, less collapsed than his rival, winning back his
losses. At about nine o'clock it was suggested they should give
over: but now Entragues would not. Soup was given them,
but this was the end of Entragues. Tottering from his chair,
yellow as a corpse, pouring with sweat, he fainted. After forty-
two hours' play Casanova had a refreshing sleep, and unlike
his rival, who did not recover for some days, appeared his
usual radiant self at three-o'clock dinner.

But gambling, sponging on Bragadin, and once for a short
time more or less honestly earning money, as we shall see,
were not Casanova's only sources of revenue. There was magic,
a theme which runs like a ribbon through the memoirs, by
means of which he caused extraordinary sums of money to flow
from the coffers of his dupes into his own leaky pocket. A good
memory, amazing mental agility in erecting pyramids, a shrewd
insight into men—and women—a fund of common sense, and
a certain amount of esoteric medical knowledge, were his
weapons; but beyond these aids he was acquainted with the
recondite erudition of the cabbalists, knowing enough to impose
on others, though, as befits a scoffer, his learning was not much
more than superficial. And besides, he had astonishing good
luck. Normally he professed himself utterly sceptical, especially
where the work of other magicians was concerned; but ever and
anon things turned out so oddly that he wondered if there were
not something in it: he would find himself making unlikely
prophecies which came true! Once a slip he made in drawing the
numbers led to an answer which alarmed him by its recklessness,
but which led to the happiest results when acted on: and sometimes the sediment of superstition he was never able to rid
himself of, would swell and possess him. How could he not
believe when things happened so pat? Why, even at the very
end of his life, had he not found himself stating that a certain
pregnant cat would have six black kittens, and had she not
done so? 'There are more things in heaven and earth . . .', he
was fond of quoting. If he knew that Paralis was a fraud, he still
felt that he had a familiar that prompted him. Thus, to the
lover, the gamester, the wit, the man-of-the-world, the student,
the charlatan, and the poet, must be added as a constant
ingredient the make-believe sorcerer who half-believed in his
own spurious magic.

III

The First Odyssey

(1746–1753)

Casanova's lucky adoption made no difference to his moral being; it merely gave him extra advantages as a gay young rapscallion; for those who wanted anything from Senator Bragadin found that the easiest path to his good graces was through this tall, handsome, giddy, and perhaps rather flashy young interloper. Life was obviously a superb affair, and Casanova squeezed the utmost out of its joys, made love, gambled—at this stage too avariciously—fought a duel in which he pinked his man, and altogether behaved as though existence were one long Venetian Carnival, with as much significance as a Commedia dell' Arte farce.

There were one or two little disagreeables to add flavour to what might have been too sweet a dish, such as a charge of assault which he was able easily to rebut; for though he had indeed given a girl a sound drubbing with a broomstick, she had refused him her favours after he had compensated her mother for the loss of a trifling toy. There was also an affair, while he was staying in a merry prankish house not far from Venice, in which the general feeling was, he could not understand why, against him. He had merely taken a mild revenge on a man who had treacherously tumbled him into a muddy ditch, by presenting him in bed, in the dark, with a hand and arm which he had hacked off a corpse buried that afternoon! The man was prostrated, and never fully recovered his reason; there was a terrific to-do, and Casanova was howled back to Venice, assured that a charge of blasphemy would follow him there. Pooh! Absurd! they couldn't prove anything: and that was as far as the episode seemed to affect him. Remorse? Well, he was sorry; but after all, the trick the man had played him might have killed him, so they were quits. The story, true or not, and Casanova wished it thought true, grimly reveals

the basis of savagery upon which the social Casanova was built
He could see nothing loathsome in the horror he had per-
petrated; it was not among his prejudices to respect a corpse
any more than a living man; but even so, might it not have
revolted the fastidiousness of most good livers, most epicures
or Lotharios? To do such a thing from passion, or from half-
madness, as Ferdinand in *The Duchess of Malfi* did, is understandable; but for a sane young man to do it for a joke is, to say
the least of it, abnormal. He, no doubt, would have argued that
it showed supreme health, superiority over a sense of the grue-
some, freedom from the nonsense of superstition. But at all
events it was religious desecration, and Bragadin advised him
to fly; all would be arranged in a year or so. Those are the
reasons Casanova gave for his abrupt departure early in 1748;
but it appears that he was about to be charged with magic
practices, and that he fled to escape the Inquisition.

No warning, however, could deter Casanova from doing
anything that suggested itself to his madcap mind, and within
a few weeks he was deeply engaged in the first of many fantastic
sorceries. Some gullible old fool, who thought he owned the
knife with which St. Peter had sliced off the ear of the soldier,
had told him of a fortune buried near Cesena; and Casanova,
who saw here a chance of unlimited fun (and of extracting a
little money from the superstitious buffoon), egged him on, and
elected himself magician in chief. Besides, there might be some
one interesting at the treasure-dowered farm; and indeed there
was, a delightful, if unwashed, girl of fourteen. But Casanova
could see to her cleanliness, and promptly declaring that the
help of a virgin to cut out his magician's clothes was essential
to his success, lodged her with him. To an accompaniment of
comic ceremonies which he invented as he went, he got himself
made a cloak, a tall hat covered with alarming symbols, a wand,
a magic circle . . . and in the meantime he carefully prepared
the girl for the double part she was to play, which she soon
came to understand, and to agree to without reluctance. The
night of the full moon was chosen for both the conjuration and
the consummation of love, and the necromancer descended
majestically into the courtyard, laid his circle, gyrated round it
three times, and pronouncing fearsome, meaningless words,
jumped into it. But then a terrific thunderstorm swept over the

ountry; lightning flared all around the courtyard, seeming to
ly over Casanova, and to strike into the ground about him.
'ear began to seize upon him; he grew terrified, and wanted
o bolt back into his room; but the idea came overwhelmingly
•ver him that the reason why the lightning could not touch
im was because he was in his circle. 'Thus,' he was to say, 'I
dored my own handiwork!' Funk kept him in the storm, in
he torrential downpour; his rational system of philosophy
rumbled away, and he cowered before an avenging God about
o blast him for his wickedness. He repented, but finding
imself paralysed by fear, judged his repentance useless. How-
ver, the storm passed, but Casanova's state of mind was not so
leeting. The sight of the expectant virgin filled him with
error; even the next morning a curious state of inhibition
•ersuaded him that the girl's innocence was protected by God;
nd giving plausible reasons for his failure to extract the buried
reasure, he rode away sadly to Cesena, hastened by a wisp of
ear that the Inquisition might be after him.

But his depression did not last long. For, by blustering, he
lmost immediately saved from trouble a Hungarian captain,
vho, though he could speak only Latin, German, and Czech,
vas travelling with a young officer who could speak nothing
ut French. Suspicion, immediately confirmed by a charming
ead peeping out from the bedclothes, told Casanova that the
'rench officer must be a young woman. Her cavalier was
lderly, they spoke no language in common, and she was
dorable; there was only one thing for a man of honour to do,
nd Casanova did it. There was no difficulty. The Hungarian
vas a man of sense, and moreover had not the means to entertain
he lady properly, and the latter was agreeable to the exchange.
'asanova carried her off to Parma in a sumptuous coach he
ought for the occasion.

Followed three whole months of unalloyed bliss, for Hen-
iette, sublimely beautiful, added the keen edge of a fine
ducation to the charm of perfect manners. Her story was a
ttle vague. Somehow she had embroiled herself with her
'rovençal family, and was being conducted to a convent in Rome
y her father-in-law (though why in male costume is not
xplained) when she escaped. She dreaded lest the festivities
1en agitating Parma owing to the arrival of its new lord

(thanks to the War of Austrian Succession), the Infant Philip, should bring to the court some visitor who would recognize her. She preferred seclusion, Casanova's company was enough for her, and they never went out except in a carriage. Once indeed they did risk discovery by going to an entertainment given by a medallist whom Casanova patronized, an evening during which Casanova was melted to tears by discovering in Henriette a skill in 'cello-playing that amounted to genius, but no harm came of it. But at last, fatefully, Henriette's dolorous prognostication came true: she was recognized, negotiations were entered into with her family, and she was forced to agree to go back to it. Why, oh why, had he not taken her to England? Casanova mourned. They would have been safe there. Yet after all, perhaps it was just as well: he was at the end of his financial tether, and made no scruple of accepting the rolls of gold coins she pressed into his hand when they parted at Geneva. It was a terrible parting, all the more so as she had, unbeknown to him, scratched on the window of their room in the Hôtel des Balances with a diamond he had given her, 'Henriette also you will forget.' Ah! never! never! And indeed till the end of his days the thought of their love brought balm to his spirit.

He returned to Parma, ill from grief, and took to his bed, refusing food. But for the urgings of a certain De la Haye, whom he had employed to teach Henriette Italian, he would have died of starvation; however, in a few days he was so far recovered as to have a quarrel, and to seek relief in the arms of a casual lady. And then sickness of the soul was replaced by sickness of the body, with curious results. For the mercury which he took as part of his cure made cavities in his brain (the analysis is Casanova's), into which entered vigorous seeds of religious bigotry, blown there by De la Haye. The ribald blasphemer became pious, prudish, a puritan abhorring the flesh. He wrote to Bragadin, telling him about De la Haye, and a young protégé of his who had given up his worldly prospects to become a Catholic: and then Bragadin, who had smoothed out Casanova's difficulties with the Inquisition, told him it was safe for him to return to Venice.

The Senator and his cronies were delighted with the change that had come over the young man: mass every day, sermons often, evil company never. No gambling, paying his debts, studying when he was not engaged in edifying conversation with them, why, it was miraculous! De la Haye, and his young convert of twenty-five, Baron Bavois, were invited to live with Bragadin. They came, and Casanova was to find once more that good actions lead to repentance as often as bad ones. For De la Haye turned out to be quite different from the honest fellow he had seemed; he was a 'Jesuit'—the most opprobrious term in Casanova's vocabulary—for he wormed himself into Bragadin's confidence, so that Paralis and the whole authority of the cabbala had to be invoked to check his influence. Bavois was different, and by leading the gay life proper to his years, soon helped Casanova to fill those lamentable cavities in his brain, till before very long he was leading as wild a life as ever. Once more it was too wild, and after a short period, owing to an eager interest taken by the magistrates (enlightened perhaps by De la Haye) in an abduction which made some noise, Casanova found it wise to have an irresistible desire to see Paris. Luckily he had plenty of money; he had saved Bragadin's allowance, won a State lottery, and been lucky at the tables. So on the first of June 1750 he set off for France, arranging to meet on the way his actor friend Balletti, who was going to Paris to join his mother, the famous Silvia, for long the darling of the Parisian populace on the boards of the Italian theatre.

To Paris, then, the seat of a baroque royalty, with its vain but delightful pomp, its mistresses, its music, and its theatre. He hardly paused on the way, except to enjoy a gala at Turin, and to enter into the mysteries of freemasonry at Lyons—not completely, however, for it was not till later that he lit upon the inmost mystery, which is secret because it is incommunicable; and the moment he got to Paris he was plunged into its social joys. For Silvia was charming to him; and since she was petted by the best society (for to her art she added a virtue unique in her profession), she was able to introduce Casanova to the cream of the capital. By great good luck, one of the first whom he met was old (to distinguish him from young) Crébillon, the tragic dramatist, and Censor-Royal. The moment they met, Casanova cried rapturously that he had wanted to know him for eight years, and followed up the compliment by declaiming to him his translation into Italian blank-verse of a tirade from one of the Censor's tragedies. Crébillon, irresistibly charmed, recited his own version of the passage, and pointed out the places where the translation bettered the original. The old man paid great attention to Casanova's talk during dinner, and then told him that he had all the conversational talents except that of being able to speak French correctly: he was too inclined to dress Italian idiom in French words. Casanova agreed; he said that one of his objects in coming to Paris had been to learn French well, but even if he could find a master equal to the strain of so 'unbearable, questioning, curious, importunate insatiable a pupil', he would never be able to pay him. 'I have been looking for such a pupil for fifty years', Crébillon assured him, and offered to be his teacher. So for months Casanova went to learn French at Crébillon's lodgings, where the colossal old man—he was much taller even than his pupil—would sit with his leonine face blurred by the fumes of his incessant smoking, and surrounded by a menagerie of animals, which included more than twenty cats. Casanova even took him his verses. 'These', Crébillon would say, 'are good; they are correct, the idea is beautiful and highly poetic, the language is perfect; but all the same the poem is bad.' 'But how?' Casanova would ask. 'I can't say. It lacks the *je ne sais quoi*.' And to make his criticism plain, he told Casanova to imagine a man who seems to have every charm, but of whom a woman will yet say, 'I can find no fault in him, but somehow I do not like him.' Thus Casanova soon came to speak well, for he knew that society will pass over a man's vices, but will be merciless if he is ridiculous; and although this prevented him from making those amusing errors which by their happy indecency brought him a certain notoriety, he was very grateful. But Crébillon did more, and it was through him that Casanova came to know the famous literary figures of his time (for it was as a man of letters that he took his place), such as d'Alembert, with whom he felt much sympathy, the Marquise de Tencin, his reputed mother, whose works are now forgotten, the Abbé Guasco, the historian and friend of Montesquieu, and, after some months, the great Fontenelle, then over ninety years old. How raw Casanova still was may be judged from his telling Fontenelle that he had come from Italy solely to see him. 'Admit, sir, that you have taken your time about it', Fontenelle answered amiably, pricking the empty compliment and at the same time administering a reproof in a way which could not but please his visitor.

The Casanova of these years at Paris departs, in his outward life, far less from the average young man eager to enjoy himself than the Casanova of any other period: there are no extravagant pranks. He did not, certainly, omit to pay tributes to Venus, and once he was haled before the police on a charge of seduction, from which he emerged scatheless since he was able to turn the charge back upon his accusers, mother and daughter. There is the odd episode of the young Murphy, whose bared beauty he admired so greatly that he had her painted by no less a person, it would seem, than Boucher, but whom he spared, thinking indeed that she set too high a value upon a bauble. The picture was seen by the King, who, anxious to decide whether the portrait flattered the original, had her brought to Versailles—where she stayed. The Casanova that emerges, however, is the eager student of literature, of life, and of manners. He was fascinated by all that he saw and heard, yet all the while his mind was critically alert. He was astonished at the trick the French had of putting their writings into blank-verse of twelve syllables before turning them into prose; he argued decisively as to whether in songs the words or the music should be written first; he was a judicious haunter of the stage, an enthusiastic critic of dancing. He never lost an opportunity of meeting the distinguished and recording their conversation. Thus when the Abbé Voisenon told him that the King was coming to attend a Parlement to hold a bed of justice, he asked, 'Why bed?' 'I really don't know—unless it is that justice sleeps there.' He was extremely curious about the French character, and though he admired it wholeheartedly was alive to its ridiculous side; as, for instance, their excessive following of fashion, or their complacency in believing that the sundial at the Palais Royal cast the sun's shadow more correctly than any other. He was full of political observations, and his acumen told him that should royalty ever summon an Assembly, its days were numbered. In sentiment he was reactionary, yet at times he was oddly democratic, an attitude which peeps out in his description of the Queen's luncheon, where she sat alone at table surrounded by exalted courtiers.

13

Liking a dish she had been given, she had some more of it, and then ran her eyes around the circle in front of her, no doubt to see if among her observers there was not one to whom she should acknowledge her pleasure in food.

She found him, and said, 'Monsieur de Lowendal.'

At that name I saw a superb man come forward bowing, who said: 'Madame.'

'I think that ragout must be a chicken fricassée.'

'I thinks so too, Madame.'

After this answer, given in the most serious tone, the Queen went on eating, and the Marshal returned backwards to his place. . . . I was charmed to have seen the famous warrior before whom Berg-op-Zoom had been unable to stand; but it pained me to see so great a man have to answer a question about a chicken fricassée in the same tone of voice that a man pronounces a sentence of death.

How active his mind was, however, is to be judged from the long midnight conversation that he had with La Vésian, a lovely young Italian who, with her brother, had come to establish herself in France. Casanova, touched by her beauty, did everything in his power to set her in the right way to become the mistress of some rich seigneur. The talk ran upon the nature of happiness, upon what real pleasure consists in, upon the foundations of moral prejudice, upon the success of philosophers in attaining the happiness they preach; and if Casanova's philosophy was based upon Gassendi (as Molière's was) rather than upon austerer philosophers, it was none the less reasoned for that. Nor, during his stay, did he let his magic rust for want of practice, and if his greatest feat was to cure the Duchess of Chartres of acne (Paralis knew something about unguents and diet), he gained a vast reputation, and a tangible reward, by revealing that a certain unknown lady's illness was feigned from a desire to deceive her husband. The Duchess, who had asked the question with a very definite lady in mind, to Casanova's alarm betted heavily that she had not got the cancer she advertised, and found herself triumphantly right.

But though Casanova was enjoying himself hugely, he could not stay in Paris for ever; funds are not inexhaustible; and in August 1752[1] he decided to accompany to Dresden his eldest brother, whom he had brought to Paris to study painting, but whose efforts had been greeted as schoolboy daubs. He must

[1] So he says; but there is reason to believe that he stayed a good deal longer, and also a strong suspicion that he paid a visit to London, about which he is silent.

study more elsewhere before assaulting the Academy. So they went off together to join their mother at Dresden, where Casanova wrote a skit, which was acted, on a play of Racine's, and received a present from the King of Saxony. From Dresden he went on to Prague, and from Prague to Vienna, the beauty of which was ruined by the activities of the 'Commissioners of Chastity', horrid kill-joys established by Maria Theresa, whom, however, he managed to cheat. He met many old friends, including De la Haye, whom he happened upon in the public library, and made new ones, most important of all the great poet-librettist Metastasio, with whom he made a lasting friendship, infinitely admiring not only the quality of his inexhaustible works, but also the vast labour expended on them. Then he went home to Venice, where one of the first people he met was Thérèse Imer, now Pompeati, on whose account he had been flung out of Malipiero's house many years before. She received him in bed, according to the innocent custom of the day; her son who was with her had the tact to leave the room, and Casanova spent four hours with her, the last of which, he declared, was delicious.

IV

Convent and Prison

(1753–1756)

Casanova's discreet self-exile had not altered his character a jot. He was essentially the same man as before, only more assured, more experienced, and so more boldly determined to squeeze the utmost out of life's pleasures. His was not the type that gets satisfaction out of responsibility, from constructive work, from developing itself in any particular direction. He was learned, yet did nothing with his learning except shine in conversation; he had limitless energy, but could only dissipate, not direct it; he was blessed with more than common intelligence, but did not care to concentrate it—enough for him that it should prick the fat complacent bubbles of current religion and morality. All these are traits born of his genius for living in the present.

The police soon became interested in this tall figure, with the flashing, almost mad eyes set in the olive countenance, and had little good to say of him for the next two years. They were aghast at his having imposed himself upon, and half-ruined, the excellent Senator Bragadin, whom he had made believe in the imminent appearance of an 'Angel of Light'; he lived, they noted, at other people's expense, chiefly by clever imposture; he misled patrician youths by making them gamble, blaspheme, and lead riotous lives; he had a footing in every kind of society, from Venetian grandees and foreign ambassadors to the spume of the stews; he professed, they said, to live according to Epicurus, and was with it all a furious libertine; he wrote satires and atheistical poems; he was a magician and a free-mason. In short, 'You can tell by talking to the said Casanova that he carries unbelief, shamelessness, and debauchery to such a point as to arouse horror'—and the Venetian spies were not squeamish. The only thing in his favour was that he seemed incapable of cheating at cards, though, had they known, it was

at this period that he consented to pool resources with a
certain Croce to run a faro table, at which, it is true, Casanova
acted merely as croupier, but was aware that Croce 'corrected'
the luck. It was highly successful; but then, as the police said,
all his strokes were on the large scale. He was himself on the
large scale; meanness and pettiness are the last things one
associates with him; his generosity, indeed, was fabulous.

It seems a grimy world, harsh, hurtling, indifferent to the
values by which society exists; but Casanova lived in it sustained by a kind of lyricism which picked the flower and
ignored the midden from which it sprang, a lyricism which
became vocal as he described his love-affairs, with a wealth of
detail, a caressing touch, which might be offensive were he not
so uniquely free from a sense of guilt: there is no trace of a leer
in his writing. An affair to him was like living an amorous
passage in Ariosto: it was a poem—of the fleshly school, no
doubt, but the flesh seems to have no taint of corruption in it.
Thus it is that C. C., in spite of the favours she granted him,
shines from his pages with all the fresh brightness, the gay
laughter, the graceful gambolling beauty of the fifteen summers
that were hers.

C. C., whom history has decided to be Catherine Campana,
came into Casanova's life through her brother, as obvious a
scoundrel as ever flaunted, and who, hoping to profit by
Casanova, to all intents thrust his young sister into his arms.
For a time, checked by admiration and respect, Casanova was
all honour, objecting angrily to the brother's indelicate goadings.
But she was irresistible, he loved her, she returned his passion,
and would hear nothing of his being too old for her. Still
Casanova hesitated, but the memory of Lucie of Paseano came
to his mind: if not he, then another! Besides, this time he meant
marriage, and if in their ardour, in the springtime of their lives
and of the year, at Carnival time, which with the brother's con-
nivance offered so many gracious opportunities in island
gardens, they forestalled the ceremony, still Casanova was set
upon marriage. At least, he persuaded Bragadin to promise to
settle him in life, and to make a formal offer for the girl's hand.
But her father was obdurate; Catherine was to go to a convent
until she was eighteen: then they would see. Is it possible that
Casanova gambled on this refusal? 'I have often loved women

to madness,' he remarked in another place, 'but I have always
preferred my liberty.'

So C. C. departed to a convent at Murano, but she found
means to correspond with her 'husband', while he took to
going to mass at the church where the nuns went, where,
though he could not see her, she could look at him. But if she
could see him, so could the nuns, and he attracted the attention
of a certain M. M. (most probably Marie Madeline Pasini,
afterwards Abbess of the convent), who skilfully arranged for
him to meet her at the convent grating. He was exalted with
amazement at her beauty; she was the most lovely person he
had ever seen, and cultured, and witty. He found also that she
was rich, so could bribe; she had a lover who too was rich,
and therefore also able to bribe; and as a result the peccant nun
had the servants and the gardener in her confidence, and possession of the key of a small door that gave on to the water. The
lover, moreover, had a *casino* not far away, *casino* being the name
given to the little arbours of love or private gambling paradises,
rented by seekers of pleasure. The lover also had perfectly safe
gondoliers, discreet servants and cooks, besides an admirable
collection of aphrodisiac engravings; all of which, not being
jealous, he allowed M. M. to use as she wished. Thus Casanova
and M. M. had no difficulty in meeting. But had Casanova no
casino? she asked. He had; at least he obtained one with all
speed, in Venice, and the Turk was not more sensual in his
pleasures than the man who had designed it, the bedroom being
completely lined with mirrors, floor and ceiling as well as walls.
Sometimes M. M. would come to Venice disguised as a man,
and then Casanova would take her to the opera, or to noble
gambling establishments. And soon he met M. M.'s other lover,
who turned out to be M. de Bernis, French ambassador, a man
of a most amiable disposition with a knack at verse-making,
who whenever he went away left Casanova the key of his
casino and the ordering of his servants. Then one day that
Casanova went to a rendezvous with M. M. at their bower,
the person who greeted him as he came in was not M. M., but
C. C.! She was, it appeared, intimate, very intimate, with
M. M., and knew all about her latest intrigue. In a few days
he was meeting both the ladies together; but then M. de Bernis
stepped in, and declared himself in love with C. C. Casanova

could not object, and rendered up the girl whom he still looked upon as his 'wife'.

At last, however, Bernis went away on a diplomatic mission: he gave Casanova the use of his *casino*, but his boatmen were no longer available. So Casanova used himself to fetch M. M.; but this gave rise to some terrible alarms. Once a storm broke out, and he was only just able to make headway against it, and with help, itself dangerous, reach the door of the convent in time; once some one stole their boat, and rushing about in agony, he was only by the greatest luck able to get another so as to make his mistress safe. And then Bernis left finally for Paris, giving up his *casino*, so that intercourse became impossible. Casanova, however, took rooms near by, provided by the sympathetic convent laundress; and since the laundress had a daughter who looked after him, he consoled himself, merely seeing M. M. at the grating. Gradually, however, Casanova went to Murano less and less; and when C. C. told him that her father had found a husband for her, but that she would run away with him if he wished, he answered that he had no position, and advised her to marry the stranger. There were tears; both M. M. and C. C. felt that life was over for them; but Casanova's heart soon healed, and he was away on another intrigue.

Not that his life was all love. His boundless vitality carried him into every society, and he was a well-known figure, too well-known. Leader of a clique of young men who respected nothing, saying whatever came into his head, full of himself, giddy, pleasure-loving, hating prudence, jeering at everything that seemed to him stupid, whether sacred or profane, calling all which raised civilized man above the savages by the damning name of 'prejudice', having the word 'honour' ever on his lips through pride rather than through respect of principles, he was ready to break all laws which interfered with his pleasure or his spite. He never failed anyone, he said; he did not disturb the peace of social circles, he had nothing to do with politics or the quarrels of others. Thus judging himself he could find nothing amiss; if he was a libertine, that was his own affair; and he lived by the curious theory that nothing was wrong so long as one did not deceive one's self as to one's motives. Certainly a hypocrite was the last thing that he was.

But unfortunately he took sides in literary factions. There

was a certain Abbé Chiari (a rival of Goldoni) who wrote plays which Casanova ridiculed in a number of satires, to such effect that the theatre began to empty, to the indignation of Signor Condulmer, who was financially interested, and who, having just entered upon a period of office as Inquisitor, was an ill man to offend. The Inquisition had long had its eye upon Casanova, the difficulty had been to catch him on any indictable charge: but now, egged on by Condulmer, one of the spies, Manucci, lighted upon the magic books in Casanova's possession—books which he is quick to say he did not believe in, but which it amused him to turn over. The matter was made easier for them since at that time Casanova was living in a suburb, the heat of a Venetian summer being too much for him, he explained to Bragadin, though his concern really was to cure a beautiful girl of the virginal anaemia which made her as pale as a statue, a good deed in which he was eminently successful. Returning to his lodging on the morning of July 25th, 1755, he found that his quarters had been raided by *Messer Grande*, the chief of the archers, on the pretext of finding contraband salt. Casanova, who dined with Bragadin every evening, told his protector, and the old Senator, who doted upon Casanova like a son, was dreadfully alarmed. 'Make no mistake,' he begged; 'they don't break into houses to find salt: it is you they're after. I have been an Inquisitor, and I know.' But Casanova pooh-poohed the matter; he refused to fly, as Bragadin earnestly implored him to do; he would not even shelter in his palace for a few days. He was conscious of no guilt; what was worrying him much more was his debts. So he went home, and the next morning was awakened by *Messer Grande*, who, with an escort of forty archers, dragged him off to the prison known as 'the Leads'.

Casanova declared he never knew what he was charged with; he was never tried, though the records show that evidence was taken against him. It was stated that he had bewitched Bragadin, that he had in his possession a curious article which resembled the aprons worn by the so-called freemasons in their so-called lodges, that he was a corrupter of youth, and that seeing he consorted with both patricians and foreign ministers, he probably gave away State secrets. Then, on the ground that he was a notorious enemy to religion, he was condemned to five years' imprisonment.

He was not informed of the sentence, and for some time daily
expected to be released from the noisome hole under the leads in
which he lay in half-darkness, roasted by the heat, excoriated
by the fleas. He was a man of action, and he had nothing to do.
He was a man of intellect, and there was nothing to read; there
was no one to talk to. The authorities sent him books, not at all
to his taste; but even so, though there was hardly light enough,
he waded through them, even through *The Mystic City* of the
ecstatic theolept, Sister Agreda; but her outpourings seemed
to him such monstrously silly lucubrations, that far from making
him more religious, they turned him still further from the faith,
though not before he had himself been infected for a while by
visionary exaltation, an experience which taught him that
strength of mind was only relative, and that the judgment is
affected by what it has to feed on. Mental and bodily fever
produced by such reading, by a natural despair, and bad food,
laid him low. Life hardly seemed worth living. But a doctor
cured him, as much by substituting Boetius for Sister Agreda
as by physical remedies; and gradually as he recovered his
health he regained his spirits, and, like the man of mettle that
he was, began to think of escape.

Luck helped him. Being after a while allowed to take limited
exercise in the attic next his cell, he found, among a pile of
rubbish, not only a bolt about eighteen inches long, but also a
small slab of marble which he found would serve as a grindstone.
Working desperately for a fortnight, he succeeded in making a
small octagonal pike of the bolt, and having achieved this, he
decided to cut a hole in the planks under his bed. But then, they
swept under the bed. He therefore told the guards that the dust
affected his lungs, and when they persisted in sweeping, he cut
his finger, and producing a blood-stained handkerchief, swore
that the blood had come from his lungs, a diagnosis confirmed
by the doctor, who forbade the sweeping to continue. So far
good. But it grew very cold, in spite of the warm things
Bragadin sent him; the light, even with the lamp he managed
to make, was very inadequate; he was continually delayed by
other prisoners being put in his cell, and it was not till May
that he got to work. When would he finish? A priest who came
to confess him told him that he would be freed on his saint's
day; but which was his saint's day? He tried St. John of

Compostella; but the day passed: he then pinned his faith upon St. Mark, patron of all Venetians, but his day also passed. Other saints were fixed upon, but all with the same negative result. Clearly he had not hit upon the right saint; it would be better to trust to his own ingenuity.

With infinite patience he gouged out a circular hole in the planks, getting rid of the chips in the attic, but then he found himself faced by slabs of marble concrete. Thinking of Hannibal crossing the Alps, he proceeded to soften this with vinegar, and succeeded in making a large enough aperture both through the concrete and another layer of planks, working furiously, in a constant state of semiconscious prayer, swelling to fervent thanks to God as he saw the end of his labours approach. Then, most inopportunely, another companion was introduced, to whom pride forced him to reveal his plan, for how else could he explain his not minding the filth and the fleas under his bed? In due course the newcomer went away, keeping the secret, and Casanova decided to make a bolt for it on the night of August 27th. But on the 25th his gaoler appeared bursting with good news. Casanova was to be transferred to a better cell, in which he could walk about, and which had two windows with views over Venice to the Lido! The blow was terrific; and there was no protesting. He staggered sadly to his new abode —keeping his eyes open all the while—the only thought buoying him up being that his chair was transferred with him, and hidden in the chair was the ever-blessed pike.

Casanova did not admit defeat for a moment, and at once regained confidence when he found that he had silenced the gaoler, who came in raving when he discovered the hole in the floor. 'Where did you get the hatchet? Where is the hatchet? I shall report this, and you will be terribly punished.' 'If you report me,' Casanova answered, 'I shall swear that every implement I had came through you.' Thus effectively blackmailed, the gaoler soon softened, and, rather than buy books with the surplus of Casanova's food allowance, which he regarded as his perquisite, he put him in touch with the prisoners next door, who had a good library, not of novels, Casanova was relieved to find, but of scientific and philosophic works. In exchanging books the neighbours soon got into correspondence, and Casanova, transferring his pike by a sublime

trick to the monk Balbi who languished next door, arranged
the preliminaries of escape. Balbi was to cut through his
ceiling, covering the hole with pious pictures, pierce through the
party wall, and descend through Casanova's ceiling on the night
decided on for escape. The scheme progressed smoothly; but
what night was Casanova to choose? He decided to interrogate
Fate through the medium of Ariosto. Erecting cabbalistic
pyramids upside down, he was directed to the first line of the
seventh stanza of the ninth canto of *Orlando Furioso*. There he
read:

Tra il fin d' Ottobre e il capo di Novembre . . .

'Between the end of October and the beginning of November!'
Nothing could be clearer. Besides, November 1st was All
Saints'; and if Casanova had a patron saint, he was bound to be
commemorated on that day. Affairs were complicated by
Casanova once more being given a companion, a rascally,
treacherous spy, whom, however, he terrified by superstitious
fears into joining in the venture, and all was ready by October
31st.

At the concerted moment Balbi appeared through the ceiling,
and Casanova, with a pack of clothes and a bundle of ropes
made from his sheets, clambered into the next cell. There,
however, his companion said he would go no further, as did
Balbi's co-prisoner; so Casanova investigated the roof alone,
and found he could make a hole in it. Unluckily there was a
young moon, which made enough shadow to attract the attention of the crowd in the square of St. Mark's below, and they
had to wait till it set. At last, at midnight, precisely at the only
moment between the two months, while the clock was still
striking, Casanova hoisted himself on to the roof beside his
fellow fugitive. The latter at this stage did nothing but upbraid
him for not having a cut-and-dried plan, as he had said he had;
but Casanova took no notice, and using the pike managed to
turn the edges of the lead slats on the roof enough for them to
cling to with their fingers, and draw themselves up on the
ridge. Then what? Crawling along, Casanova investigated the
gable windows, which were above the chancellery. They would
have to climb through them. He let Balbi down inside by the
ropes, but found the drop was too great for himself. He

explored again, and with great good luck found a ladder, which
by herculean efforts, he got to the window; but in trying to
force it in he slipped, slid to the edge of the roof, and only
prevented himself from plunging fatally over the cornice by
clinging with his elbows. He levered himself up, and then for a
few moments was paralysed by cramp. At last he got the ladder
in, and rejoining Balbi, collapsed into coma for two hours.
Then Balbi, dithering with funk, awakened him. They investigated the loft, found an open door and a staircase, then
another staircase, which took them into the chancellery, where
they were held up by a locked door. The pike again came in
useful, and they managed to bash in an upper panel, through
which Casanova thrust Balbi, and then himself wriggled
through, tearing his flesh mercilessly on the jagged edges. They
found themselves in another room, where Casanova changed
his clothes and bandaged his knees. It was now light, and,
looking out of the window, he was seen by some people, who,
astonished at anyone being there, told the doorkeeper, who
proceeded to come up to them. 'Don't utter a word,' Casanova
told Balbi; 'when the door is opened, just walk out quietly
with me.' The doorkeeper was so dumbfounded at seeing two
men come calmly out, that he neither said nor did anything.
The fugitives strolled to the canal bank, where Casanova,
talking loud to attract attention, engaged two gondoliers to
row them to Fusina. Where the canal divides he asked, 'How
quickly can you get us to Mestre?' 'To Mestre?' the gondoliers
exclaimed; 'you said Fusina.' 'No, no! Mestre!' But the
stupid Balbi supported the gondoliers, and Casanova, forcing a
laugh, said he must have made a silly mistake; he meant
Mestre. He was almost free, and burst into tears, to the
amazement of the insensitive monk. They landed, and got clear
of the immediate neighbourhood, but not before Balbi's idiocy
had provided some moments too thrilling to be pleasant.
Casanova saw he must part from Balbi, which he did only by
dire threats, and began to make his way on foot to the frontier.
But he was exhausted; his wounds were troubling him; he
must rest. Asking a peasant whose were the houses he saw
round about, he was told that one of them was the home of the
chief of the archers, the very man whom Casanova must most
diligently avoid. But something impelled him to that house, a

ascination he could not resist; he walked towards it in a daze.
There, inventing some cock-and-bull story, he was taken in,
ended, fed, cured of his wounds by a country balm. When in
fter years he was accused of inventing the tale, he said, 'Why,
he archer's house was the safest place. It was the last spot he
would think of looking for me in. He was twenty miles away
hasing me.' Whatever had caused Casanova to go there, the
nove was triumphantly successful. Nourished and recovered,
e slipped out of the house the next morning, and after
ravelling another two and a half days, with sundry adventures,
e crossed the frontier, and was safe.[1]

[1] There are some Casanovist scholars who deny the truth of all this story:
hey say Casanova escaped by means of Bragadin's bribery! I cannot stay to bandy
vords with infidels. The existence of the bills for repairing the holes Casanova
nade should convince them.

V

The Great Odyssey Begins

(1756–1760)

When the Ballettis received him in Paris with open arms, they
told him they had expected him ever since they had heard of
his escape. Where else should one come to make one's way in
the world? For if the whole of eighteenth-century Europe was
individualistic enough, no town, as Casanova realized, offered
such opportunities for advancement 'if you took it in the right
way'. Therefore not now for him the undirected life, or rather
the life directed wholly towards pleasure he had led on his last
visit: this time he would settle in respectable rooms of his own,
select his acquaintance with an eye to business, and become—
well, Fate would show. He called immediately upon M. de
Bernis, who, a favourite of Madame de Pompadour, was
secretary to the ministry of foreign affairs, and was soon
himself to become minister. Bernis received him generously
(with a roll of gold), carried him to the Pompadour, sent him
to the great Choiseul, introduced him to the subtle diplomat
the Abbé de la Ville, and most important of all, recommended
him to one of the chief treasury officials, M. Duverney, as a
brilliant financier.

A financier? Casanova had never thought of himself as such,
but after all, why not? If Bernis said that Casanova had a
scheme for increasing the revenue, well, then, he had one.
Duverney invited him to dinner to meet the most exalted
economists, for Casanova had told him he had a project. 'I know
what it is', Duverney said. 'I am sure you do not,' Casanova
answered, 'for I haven't breathed a word about it to anyone.'
Indeed he had not, even to himself. The dinner was extremely
boring, for Casanova could not understand the technical jargon
talked; he hoped that his silence would give an impression of
sapience. But after the meal Duverney took him aside, and
showing him some papers said, 'There's your project!' Casa

nova saw at a glance that it was some form of lottery, and replied, 'Well, yes; but not altogether.'

Soon, then, Casanova was associated with the brothers Calsabigi, who, though international financiers, were not always in the most honourable repute. One of them never appeared in public, for he was afflicted with a kind of 'leprosy' which insistently demanded unmannerly scratching. He believed in God and His works, he said, and being convinced that God had given him nails as his only relief, he would use them. 'I see you believe in final causes,' Casanova told him, 'and I congratulate you; but I think you would all the same scratch even if God had forgotten to give you nails.' The sally put Calsabigi in a good humour; Casanova's boldness, his financial daring, and an unexpected knowledge of the mathematical laws of probability, did the rest. The scheme, with his modifications, was passed by experts, including d'Alembert; Casanova was granted a valuable concession which gave him more than an honourable income; and being the only one of many owners of ticket-offices to have the entrée into society, and having the wit to promise payment the day after the draw instead of a week later, he scored heavily over his colleagues.

Here, then, was a new career opening up before him, one which would lead to wealth and honour. But alas, he noted regretfully, one essential was lacking—constancy of purpose. For the moment, however, he was fitfully employed, first as a government spy on some French men-of-war, in which he dined; and observing shrewdly, drawing out his hosts, and writing an admirable report, was well paid. A farcical business, he thought; any one of the junior officers would have written the report for nothing; but ministers have a mania for spending other people's money. Then he was sent to Holland, to discount, it seems, large amounts of French *actions*, success depending upon whether foreign capitalists could be induced to believe that the war would soon be over. (It is only by such indirect references that we are reminded that we are now in the period of the Seven Years' War.) He seems to have been successful, and when he came back to Paris was congratulated by Choiseul, petted by the Pompadour, and erected into the lion of the hour.

And yet, was it really so? for Casanova's account of his life at this time is so skilfully confused that it is impossible to

unravel fact from brilliant fiction. Either his memory was con-
veniently at fault, or he deliberately falsified dates, persons,
and events: the narrative is a masterly and baffling mixture of
truth, lies, and a clever raising of the probable to the rank of
fact. Unless he could be in two places at once, a feat of which
even a fairy is incapable, some of his stories burst at the prick
of historical criticism. This is as true of his social life as of his
political escapades. Certain realities, however, emerge. Socially
he lived as a rich man, with a town lodging and a country
house, two coaches, plenty of horses, and a retinue of servants
to tally with his being always overdressed. Apart from
ministers such as Bernis, at whose levées he was assiduous, he
frequented chiefly such great ladies as were interested in sorcery,
such as the Comtesse du Rumain and the unbelievable old
Marquise d'Urfé. At the latter's house he met the self-styled
Comte de Saint-Germain, the most notorious necromancer of
his age, patronized even by Louis XV, a more sinister because a
more consistent charlatan than Casanova, whose butt and rival
he was. He went to such lengths as never to eat in public,
because, he said, the food provided was unsuitable to his age;
and this, since he credited himself with three centuries, was
not unlikely; and it was with Madame d'Urfé that Casanova
visited Rousseau; they took him some music to copy. But the
main prop of his social life was the Balletti household, where he
fell violently in love with the daughter Manon, whose accepted
fiancé he was. Less permanent erotic adventures were not
lacking, especially the astonishing one with X. C. V. (actually
Justiniana Wynne, daughter of an English gentleman of
position), whom, after the application of a magic abortive
known as 'aroph' (to apply which should have been the
privilege of a husband), he spirited away to a nunnery for her
lying-in. The affair brought Casanova into conflict with the
police, from whose clutches, however, he was saved by Madame
du Rumain, who was party to the secret.

His life in Holland was less glorious, but, though steadied
by high masonic ceremonies, none the less exciting. He says
he was sent there officially, under the aegis of the great Choiseul,
and worked hand and glove with M. d'Affry, the French
ambassador. The official correspondence, however, indicates
that though Casanova called on Affry, Choiseul warned the

ambassador against the adventurer; and it seems that Casanova's protector was not the Duc, but the Vicomte de Choiseul, an insignificant person. The affair is a mystery, which time has not yet cleared up.

It is certain, however, that his friendships among Jews and bankers were facilitated by Madame d'Urfé, who almost worshipped him as half-supernatural; and her giving him a large sum of money to negotiate from one currency into another led him to the home of a merchant of the well-known family of Hope or Hop. M. d'O, as Casanova calls him, was a good business man, but his daughter Esther was a miracle, and thus Casanova, while yet remaining constant to Manon, was inevitably enraptured. He taught her cabbalism, which so fascinated her that she insisted upon her father being instructed, only, of course, up to the point that Casanova thought discreet. He convinced them by finding a lost notebook containing several thousand pounds sterling; but since Casanova had himself accidentally caused the package to slip between the stairs, Paralis was favourably placed for discovering where it lay. Casanova refused the two thousand pounds he was immediately offered, but he was made free of the house, and given every commercial opportunity.

Ghosts of the past met him in Holland, such as Lucie of Paseano in the form of a loathsome decayed bawd, into whose hand he thrust some gold and hurried away. Less ghostly was Thérèse Imer, who, now a widow (her husband Pompeati had committed hara-kiri in a fit of madness), was eking out a living by singing at concerts. With her was her son, a handsome youth, but a dreadful little beast, brought up to horrid dissimulation; and a little daughter, who, it was obvious to every one, was the image of Casanova. When was she born? Casanova calculated hurriedly. Why, of course, she was his daughter! He offered to adopt her, but Thérèse would not part with her, though she gave him the chance of educating her son, which he accepted. The meeting between the old lovers was affectionate, but Casanova was not to be entangled. Instead he gave Thérèse some money to finance her projected descent upon England.

He might have stayed in Holland. M. d'O offered to take him into a partnership of magic-directed business. Esther would become his wife—she professed herself more than

14

willing, and Casanova certainly desired her possession—but it
would have meant settling down at Amsterdam, or at The
Hague, and Casanova could not bear so static a prospect. Also,
he confessed, he was idiot enough to want to cut a dash in
Paris; besides, was he not engaged to Manon Balletti? So he
went back to Paris, taking with him the young Pompeati, who
was for a short time stolen from him by the Marquise d'Urfé,
who was convinced that this was the virgin youth, born of the
union of a transcendental with a mortal, through whom she
would be regenerated. Then, however, he was sent to school,
where he managed to pass himself off as the Comte d'Aranda.
He was a promising youth.

Paris, however, was changing for Casanova. Silvia Balletti
died; Bernis, after becoming the Cardinal de Bernis, was
dismissed the ministry, and left Paris; treasury officials who
knew not Casanova came into power. He must try his hand at
something new. Thus, since there was at that time much talk
of being able to print silks (then an unknown art), Casanova
started a factory, to the lasting amusement of Madame d'Urfé,
who thought this was only a blind to cover necromantic
proceedings. The factory, however, did not go well. For one
thing, Casanova was always making presents of dress-lengths
to charming ladies; moreover, there were twenty girl hands
in the factory, all young, all lovely: they were books of which
the title-pages were so inviting that he had to read every one
of them, to Manon Balletti's not unnatural fury; and this
proved expensive. Besides, the dyes printed on the silks simply
would not stick; they ran at the first washing. Difficulties
accumulated, and Casanova, who had already sold his lottery
office, parted with some of his interest in the business to the
factory doctor, immediately after which there was a robbery,
followed by a lawsuit, and, swiftly, an arrest for debt. Casanova
was flung into prison, from which he circularized all his friends.
Some sent money, Manon brought the valuable diamond ear-
rings her lover had given her, Madame d'Urfé laughed, and
invited him to dinner that very day. She was convinced that this
incarceration was only an original kind of advertisement. But
soon she brought the necessary money, and in four hours
Casanova was free, shortly afterwards showing himself in the
theatre. And then, since M. d'O would not lend him money to

pursue the silk-printing business, but repeated his offer of a partnership, the adaptable Venetian thought he had better go back to Holland. He was not making his way in Paris.

Thus Casanova's memory told him; but he forgot a little matter of an action over a letter of exchange which he had backed and could not pay; he forgot that he had spent, not four hours, but two days in prison; he forgot, especially, some fraudulent letters of exchange he and his brother François (now becoming a famous painter of battle-pictures) had palmed off, concerning which legal action was imminent, making hasty flight imperative. History, backed by police records, has not been so kind as Casanova's autobiographical muse, and has remembered these things, besides pointing out that Casanova did not stay in Paris until December 1st, 1759, but disappeared from it in September.

However, whenever it was, he set off gaily enough in a chaise, preceded by his valet on horseback; and as he went he read Helvétius's great book *De L'esprit*, wondering as he read why it had been censored, seeing that after all there was nothing in it that had not been said before, notably by Pascal, who had handled the subject much better. The book refreshed him, however, and it was no abashed or daunted adventurer who returned to Holland to bask in the smiles of Esther d'O, and to call brazenly on the French ambassador, who, he says, received him most amiably. This time Saint-Germain was also there, selling, he hinted, the French crown jewels; but Casanova, who found that this was a rival far too near the throne, routed him by means of Paralis. He spent most of his time, however, with Esther d'O, now madly cabbalistic, and nearly succumbed to her chains. For just then Manon Balletti wrote to tell him that all was over between them; she was going to marry someone else; and this news, whether it was a shock to his vanity or to his heart, shattered the rejected lover so completely, that for three feverish days he refused food; whereupon Esther supervening as a ministering angel, he gave her all Manon's touching love-letters, many of which still exist. Esther made sure of capturing this almost superhuman figure, and indeed Casanova was so seriously in love with her that he did his best to disillusion her as to his magic powers: but still she thought him the most marvellous man in the world. But no, the mercuric Casanova would not bind himself: it would be better to travel a little in Germany.

It is impossible to follow Casanova's now dizzy peregrinations through Europe, to note, even, the adventures of heart and body in which he dared Fate, or his wildly novelistic love-affairs, or his princely entertainments contrasting with the moments of penury when he had to pawn his clothes. We must pass by the occasion when, intrepid as ever, he escaped over the walls of Stuttgart, as we must the period of ten days when he dallied, seriously, with the idea of becoming a monk. This was in Switzerland, where, taking eight unappropriated letters of the alphabet, he made himself known as the Chevalier de Seingalt. Where was the harm? Plenty of other people took names they preferred to their own; Metastasio or Voltaire to begin with: and the name Casanova—well, there was an actress so called, and a painter; besides, there were certain unlucky papers signed with it; it was better not to draw attention to that name. So it was the Chevalier de Seingalt who, armed with letters from Madame d'Urfé and the Duc de Choiseul (which put him in the good graces of M. de Chavigny, the French ambassador), gave the impression to the learned of a remarkably speculative man, interested chiefly in natural history and medicine—they wondered even if he were not the Comte de Saint-Germain—a haunter of libraries, deeply interested in politics, the army, and social customs, and anxious to meet the world-famous scientist Haller, whom he charmed. Others, especially a certain syndic in Geneva, saw a less intellectual side of the Chevalier: but then there were always these two Casanovas; the one ruled by his frantic body, the other governed by his enquiring mind; on the one hand the eroto-maniac, on the other the curious and accurate observer, the sage commentator, the wit and poet. Nor were the two in conflict with each other, so that it is not at all incongruous in reading the memoirs to break off a love-affair in the middle to follow a philosophic dissertation on 'form', and the impossibility of defining 'beauty'. One Casanova was necessary to the other if full development of either was to be attained; for himself, at least, he seems to have solved the problem of harmony. Or was it merely a division into separate emotional compartments?

His heart was still aching from the conclusion of a stirring

Swiss love-affair (he had relinquished the lady, according to his honourable wont, to some one better able than himself to look after her) when, going to Geneva to see Voltaire, in the room he was given at the hotel he saw scrawled on the window: 'Henriette also you will forget.' His hair bristled with his emotion, and he flung himself down on a sofa. Noble and tender Henriette! Where was she now? The memory roused a train of self-examination. Ah! he had not the delicacy, nor the probity, of those happy days; nor, most horrible notion of all, the vigour. Yet the idea of Henriette fanned his waning flame into a blaze; his heart being free, he was sure that if he knew where she was he would dash off to find her. Instead, within two days, he interlarded his Voltairean conversations with a debauchery so gross that even he did not dare describe it fully.

Voltaire had been expecting him, and received him with ceremony at his court of Les Délices. But the opening did not augur well between the wizened gimlet-like intellectual, and the gigantic, flaunting, overwhelmingly physical Chevalier de Seingalt. 'This, M. de Voltaire, is the great moment of my life. I have been your pupil for twenty years, and my heart is full of joy at seeing my master.' 'Sir, do me the same honour for another twenty years, and promise me to bring me my fees at the end of the time.' Everybody burst out laughing, and hardly heard Casanova's retort, 'Willingly, if you will promise to wait for me.' Barbed conversation ensued, on Algarotti, on the sonnet, and then on Ariosto, where Voltaire saved all by reciting, without a hitch, several stanzas of *Orlando Furioso*, and then retracted all he had ever said against Casanova's poetic divinity. Yet Casanova was not won over; more sharp words passed between them, till M. de Seingalt was persuaded to recite his favourite passage. He did it with so much feeling, he put so much emotion into his rendering, that the tears gushed from his eyes, his auditors sobbed, Madame Denis, Voltaire's niece, fell on his neck, and Voltaire himself embraced him. Sublime moment! After which the scene concluded so well, that on Casanova's saying that he was going away on the morrow, he was implored to stay in Geneva at least three nights more, and dine at Les Délices every day.

But when Casanova went to Les Délices the next morning, the major honours were for the Duc de Villars, an effeminately

decayed old debauchee of whom Casanova has left a well-bitten
etching; the Chevalier de Seingalt held his tongue during
dinner. His egotism was jarred, and when Voltaire spoke to him,
he was contradicted. The Venetian government tyrannic? Far
from it; one could live more freely there than anywhere else;
such was the type of interchange. After the meal Voltaire took
Casanova by the arm and did the honours of his garden, of the
beauties of the mountains, and showed him 'the Rhone which I
send off from here to France'. 'A transaction which does not
cost you much', was the acid answer. Voltaire imperturbably
did all he could to soothe his ruffled guest, held forth at length
on Italian literature, with great wit and erudition, Casanova
admits, 'but he always drew a wrong conclusion. I let him
chatter his nonsense.' Still Voltaire behaved charmingly, took
him to his room, informally changed his wig for a cap, talked
while Casanova behaved like a petulantly fractious schoolboy,
and even showed him his vast repository of correspondence.
And somehow, in the end, Casanova was tamed. The next
morning he sent his host a book of macaronic poems, accompanied by some blank-verse of his own. But when ('after a
delicious night, feeling as fit as a fiddle') he went at midday
to Les Délices, Voltaire was not visible. Madame Denis
entertained him, but not sufficiently well to conquer his huff,
and he refused to tell her the story of his escape from the Leads,
which at other places he was only too willing to embark upon.
When the great man appeared at five o'clock there was a
prettily acerb talk on Italian literature, only saved from ruin
because they agreed in praising Goldoni. Finally, at the last
visit, Voltaire was in a thoroughly bad temper. He and his guest
bickered ceaselessly; first about the macaronic verses, which
led to poisoned shafts about Voltaire's then unowned *Pucelle*;
about whether Casanova or Martelli had been the first to write
Alexandrines in Italian, in which Casanova proved to Voltaire's
discomfiture that Martelli's verses were not Alexandrines at
all. Voltaire grew warm, Casanova warmer, as the latter argued
that it would be folly to abolish superstition since it was
necessary to the existence of humanity, a standpoint which
naturally infuriated Voltaire, whose dream it was to do so,
though it is not certain that he got the better of the argument,
which led to another about government, in particular the

government of Venice, about which Casanova was always loyally sensitive. The Chevalier seems then to have lost his manners, for when Voltaire expressed great admiration for Haller, his guest regretted that Haller had not the same high opinion of Voltaire. 'Ah, ah! It is possible that we may both be mistaken', Voltaire retorted: and soon after, without saying another word except the formal ones of departure, Casanova withdrew, to spend the night and most of the next day in writing down these conversations, of which the record in his memoirs are but 'a feeble extract'.

The curious thing about these conversations is that in them it was Voltaire, not Casanova, who asked the questions. Self-centred, Narcissistic even, Casanova had gone, overdressed as it were in mind as well as in body, 'to point out some of his errors to Voltaire', especially his great error of being too idealistic in his view of mankind: and he had done so. He had tackled the great mind of his age on his own ground, and Voltaire had not seemed to appreciate it! A little later Casanova sent the sage a translation of *Les Écossaises* into Italian verse, and Voltaire said the translation was bad. Thus for ten years Casanova inveighed against Voltaire, wrote a book to cut up the *Éloges* published in his praise, did all he possibly could to injure his reputation. But in after years he admitted he was wrong—he had that sense and that degree of greatness—and made such 'humble reparation' as he could. 'If we meet again in the Shades, freed perhaps from the acidity of our mortal natures, we will come together agreeably: he will receive my sincere apologies, and we shall be, he my friend, I his sincere admirer.'

VI

The Inventive Magician

(1760–1763)

Then at once off again, accompanied by a gay, impudent young Spanish valet taken bodily out of an eighteenth-century French comedy. But why, it has been asked again and again, this ceaseless movement? so much of it without any evident motives. Was he a spy? Was he a secret emissary of the Grand Orient, the subversive masonic society of Europe? The question has never been answered, and to the outward eye the film unrolls itself as a constant succession of amorous intrigues, of gambling exploits, cast against an inimitable background of eighteenth-century friezes. Amorous intrigues! we are apt to get tired of them, and feel inclined to say with Lorenzo da Ponte, Mozart's librettist, that we listen eagerly to Casanova's conversation for the many interesting, witty, and even sage things that he says, and for their sake put up with what is disagreeable. Yet on second reading we find that each affair has its own special flavour, its sidelight on psychology, its revelation of manners and customs. Unlike Casanova, we begin to forget Casanova, and think instead of the multitude of people mixed up in his firework existence.

And after all, some of his most interesting loves are those where he was unsuccessful, as that of the Mademoiselle Romans whom he met at Grenoble. She was a perfectly dazzling creature, but her unconscionable price was marriage, do what Casanova might to break her resolution. Casting her horoscope, Casanova found that it was her destiny, if she went to Paris before she was eighteen (she was already twenty-three, but he had a mania for reducing the ages of his heroines), to become the King's mistress, and bear him a son who would be the hope of France; so he abandoned his pretensions, and strongly urged her to go. She went, and did become the King's mistress, giving Madame de Pompadour many qualms, and bore a son which the King so far acknowledged as to call him Louis-Aimé de Bourbon. Casanova consoled himself with others at Grenoble, and then went on to Avignon, where, amid scabrous joys, he gave a day to sensibility, and went to Vaucluse to weep over the relics of Petrarch and Laura. Then Marseilles, then Genoa, where he translated *Les Écossaises*, and sent Haller the news that he had had him elected to the Arcadians, a literary society in Rome; then Florence.

There he met his early preceptor, the Abbé Gama, who asked him to represent Portugal at the forthcoming Congress of Augsburg, for no clear reason except that this is a fairy-story; and he also ran into the arms (literally) of one of his very earliest loves, the Thérèse who had passed as the *castrato* Bellino. With her was a young man of seventeen, whom she presented to the world as her brother Césarino; and as she looked only twenty-four, nobody suspected that he was her son —and Casanova's. The likeness to the father was striking, but the two kept the secret, Casanova giving his fatherly feelings outlet in private. The youth filled him with delight, but he spoilt conversation when supping with Thérèse, for 'the presence of Césarino gave the meal a serious, if agreeable tone. Youth, pure and lovely, diffuses an inexpressible charm into life, and its innocence imposes respect and restraint.' Only, one would gather, however, when youth is male. He enjoyed Florence, was made much of by the famous Marquis Botta-Adorna, twice visited the virtuoso collection of Walpole's Sir Horace Mann, but was, unfortunately, ordered to leave Tuscany at short notice on account of a spurious letter of credit, even though he had been quite innocently drawn into the business. So to Rome, where he stayed with his brother Jean, then working under the famous painter Raphaël Mengs, engaged chiefly in making drawings for Winckelmann, with whom Giacomo had many scholarly conversations.

In Rome Casanova moved in the best society, as became a man with a coach and four, a valet and a secretary, and who made magnificent presents of rare books to cardinals. He visited Pope Clement XIII to beg his help in obtaining forgiveness from Venice, but the Pope, choosing an easier part, fobbed him off with the Order of the Golden Spur and appointed him apostolic protonotary *extra urbem*. Why? Well, that is another

Casanovian mystery, giving weight to the suspicion that he was a Jesuit. Whence the decoration, whence Augsburg, and the frequent call he felt, but never obeyed, to go to Portugal. And had he not been educated by the Jesuits? The idle-minded may linger over the unlikely supposition, before wondering why Casanova should suddenly have dashed off to Naples.

Whatever the reason, Naples procured him a very curious adventure. The girl who there captured his heart and his senses was the mistress (though only formally, since her lover was impotent) of the Duc de Mantalone. Leonilda was indeed so ravishing and so well dowered that Casanova at last determined to marry and settle down, to which end the girl's mother was sent for. To Casanova's delighted surprise she turned out to be the Lucrezia who had been his first passionate love: but, oh horror! she declared that Leonilda was his daughter! It was too much even for Casanova. Though he saw nothing contrary to nature in incest, yet a loathing of it was a human prejudice he could not help sharing. There was, of course, no evil in it if parent and child were not aware of the relationship, so 'incests, eternal subjects of Greek tragedies, instead of making me weep, make me laugh; Phèdre, indeed, makes me shed tears, but then that is Racine's doing'. So back to Rome, safely bachelor, having resisted the offer Lucrezia had made him of joining her life to his on a Neapolitan estate.

Rome, in spite of varied pleasures, did not hold him long. He sped back to Florence, but not being allowed to stay there, he left immediately with a young dancer, La Corticelli, who kept him company amid the gaieties of Bologna till she went to a theatre at Prague, leaving him free to investigate Modena. Turned out, without explanation, after two days, he went to Turin, where, advised by the Abbé Gama, he awaited the Congress of Augsburg, there again to be warned to leave, an admonition he successfully resisted with the aid of the foreign minister, the Chevalier d'Osorio. Then to Chambéry for a short stay marked by erotic adventures more amusing but no more edifying than those which had occupied him in Turin, and thence to Paris, where he at once reported his presence to the Marquise d'Urfé—for had he not come to Paris solely to engineer her avatar as a man?

We spent the next three weeks in making the preparations necessary to this divine operation, and these consisted in worshipping in a special way each of the genii of the seven planets on the days consecrated to them. After these preparations I was to go to a place revealed to me by these genii to find a virgin, daughter of an adept, whom I was to fertilize of a boy by means known only to the Rosicrucian brethren. This son was to be born alive, but only with a sensational soul. Madame d'Urfé was to receive him in her arms at the moment of his birth, and to keep him next her in her own bed for seven days. At the end of this time she was to die with her mouth glued to that of the child, who, by this means, would receive her rational soul. After this permutation it would be for me to look after the child by the magic means known to me; and as soon as the child should be three years old, Madame d'Urfé would regain consciousness of herself, and I would begin to initiate her in the perfect knowledge of the Great Science.

Well, if the credulous old woman asked for this outrageous nonsense (and she was very rich), why not give it her? Would scruples on Casanova's part save her? Not even the threat of death, which he had hopefully advanced, would deter her. If not he, then another, say Saint-Germain, would reap the benefit of her lunacy. 'Fraud is a vice; but honest guile can be regarded as the husbandry of wit. To be sure, this virtue looks like roguery; but one has to accept that: and the man who, at need, cannot practise it nobly, is a fool.' That would seem to settle the point of conscience, but it does not dispose of the question of veracity. The whole thing, even so far, seems incredible; what is to follow, a magnificently inventive phantasmagoria, tries faith still further. But then, if Casanova embarked on this business for gain, he did it also for the immense amusement to be got out of it. If his fertile mind projected a fantasy, there was nothing in the world to prevent his carrying it out. He was an artist, in the burlesque if you like, but an artist none the less.

His stay in Paris was, however, cut short by his running through the body a rascal of his acquaintance whom he thought would die: he made for Augsburg, where, he told Madame d'Urfé, he would meet the Portuguese minister who would be able to release from the dungeons of Lisbon the Rosicrucian adept Quérilinte, who was essential to final enlightenment. Augsburg and the neighbouring Munich were fatal, for there, through a failure of will, Casanova allowed himself to be robbed of both money and health by a woman too clever for him. Worse, since he had left Paris in a hurry, Madame d'Urfé had not been able to supply him with the quantity of clothes, jewels, and money necessary to his enterprise. She had sent them after him by his valet-secretary Costa, and Costa had decamped with the treasure. Luckily a letter of credit was sent by other means, and this enabled Casanova to cut his usual figure in society, and, after his recovery, to amuse himself in his usual way. Yet amid these crude enjoyments, Casanova the thinker snatched the friendship of the admirable Count Lamberg, philosopher and man of letters, with whom he corresponded for the rest of his life. The Congress was cancelled.

For the half-immortal immaculate virgin to be the instrument of Madame d'Urfé's transformation, Casanova pitched upon his Florentine drab, La Corticelli, who was always up to any mischief. She was to impersonate 'Mademoiselle Lascaris', derived from the last of the Roman emperors, a name hit upon by chance. Madame d'Urfé was delighted, for the d'Urfés claimed to have Lascaris blood; she called the dancer niece and Princess, and treated her as such. The awful impregnation took place at the hour of the May moon; but Casanova declared it unsuccessful because, he said, young d'Aranda, Thérèse Imer's son, whom he wanted to get rid of (he was making eyes at the Corticelli), had peeped through a curtain and seen it all. However, the next moon would do, so long as the act did not take place in France. So the party went to Aix-la-Chapelle, Madame d'Urfé presenting the Princess Lascaris with a box of jewels, which, however, Casanova impounded in case the Corticelli should want to bolt. But at the June moon, just as the crucial instant of three minutes past four was approaching, the divine instrument fell into convulsions, and informed Casanova that she would go on having convulsions at crucial instants until she got back the jewels.

Casanova was in some difficulty. He could not leave Aix, for he had spent or lost all his money, had pawned his valuables, including the jewels, and was awaiting a remittance from Monsieur d'O. On his making a pyramid of numbers with Madame d'Urfé, the oracle revealed that La Lascaris was possessed by an anti-Rosicrucian demon, and would no doubt shortly give birth to a gnome; that she was mad, and not to be believed (a wise precaution this, as she soon carried out her threat of telling the marquise the whole story); that a new vessel of election would easily be found; and that in the mean time Madame d'Urfé should write to the spirit of the moon.

Thus on the day appointed by the phases of that powerful orb, Casanova and the old marquise enacted portentous rites in a consecrated room, next to which there was a bath, filled with warm water perfumed with various essences pleasing to Selenis. After appropriate ceremonies, the adepts stripped completely and advanced to the bath, on the edge of which was an alabaster bowl containing gin, and irradiated by the moon. Casanova, uttering mock cabbalistic words which the marquise repeated after him, set the spirit alight and burned the letter to be wafted to Selenis, Madam d'Urfé declaring that she saw her very words slithering up the moonbeams. They then entered the bath, and a few moments later the answer from Selenis, written circularly in silver letters upon green transparent waterproof paper, appeared floating on the surface! The precious missive was taken out, placed on a scented cushion of white satin, and piously read. It announced that the old woman's hypostasis into a youth could only take place next spring, at Marseilles, in the presence of the great Quérilinte; that the Lascaris must be got rid of; and that Casanova was to take under his wing a widow and her daughter, and conduct them to Alsace. Thus Casanova disposed of La Corticelli, fobbed off the marquise, and was able to continue an intrigue which he had begun with the widow's daughter. All was well: he had in the meantime won vast sums in gambling, and was well equipped for further sallies. Indeed it was high time to go, for the Princess Lascaris was whirling in public like the ballet-dancer she was, and rumour was becoming ominous.

Until the spring of 1763, then, the Chevalier de Seingalt was free to live his life of ordered disorder, which he did to the full, gadding from Switzerland to Lyons, from there to Turin and Milan, happy in love, happy in gambling, winning enormous fortunes and spending them lavishly, everywhere in high fettle, superbly dressed, wearing wherever he went the cross of the Order of the Golden Spur which he had had set in diamonds. Not that he set any store by the decoration, except literally as decoration; yet because of it, fools, who did not know how little it was worth, gave him the greater honour. At Geneva (this time he did not visit Voltaire) he fell in love with a girl on account of her brilliance in theological discussion, a blue-stocking who carried learning so far that when divesting herself of her last garment she quoted St. Clement of Alexandria on the relation between clothing and shame. It was in connection with that affair that he warned parents that it was far easier to seduce a girl if she was accompanied by another than if she was alone; in the latter case the fierce barriers of virgin modesty would give ample protection; in the former, one would egg the other on. It was, however, in Milan and its neighbourhood that he had his most glorious adventures, and there his chief triumph was over a girl to whom he introduced the best literature, and this forms the centre point of a maze of scintillating intrigues, among which stands out the glorious fancy-dress ball to which he took two ladies as 'beggars', dressed in the most sumptuous clothes torn to tatters patched with the most expensive brocades. Otherwise amusing is the occasion when, having displeased a countess, he found in the back room of a shop an indecorous image of himself about to be pierced with pins to his eternal undoing, which, to be quite safe, he destroyed.

Then for the great operation to be performed upon the Marquise d'Urfé, who waited for him at Marseilles at the heaven-appointed time. The fun for Casanova was to cap her extravagances with better ones of his own. Might he not have spared her out of pity? Well, she would never be cured of her folly until she was ruined, so what was the good of having scruples? 'Had I worked merely to enrich myself at her expense, I would have been a scoundrel, and would have despised myself. But my intention was only to indulge my fancy and I considered that I was justified in using a madwoman's money to carry out my pranks.' To impersonate Quérilinte, Casanova employed a third-rate rascal called Passano, who, blacking his eyebrows, freely rouging his cheeks, and putting on a white wig, at first considerably impressed the marquise, who greeted him in a ludicrous costume weighed down with jewels. Unluckily she informed the pseudo-Quérilinte that she destined him a valuable casket of jewelry, a fact which Casanova had, for obvious reasons, wished to keep secret. Indeed, as a result, when the next day Passano fell ill, he threatened to write to Madame d'Urfé giving away the whole plot, and did so. Thereupon Casanova hastily told the marquise that the so-called Quérilinte was an impostor, to be answered calmly, 'Why, of course; didn't you know? My genius revealed to me during the night that it was Saint-Germain.' So making a swift journey to Aix, she interviewed the Duc de Villars, governor of the province, who had been in love with her fifty years before, and had Passano expelled.

What happened next is doubtful; for though Casanova gave his fancy full rein at Marseilles, he did so again when he wrote his memoirs, so that two distinct versions exist. In both, however, the scheme now was that Madame d'Urfé should herself be impregnated with the youth through whom she was to be regenerated; and, Quérilinte being out of the question, the task would fall to Casanova. A part of the operations, how-ever, and a very important part, was to get possession of the extremely valuable casket of gold and jewels, which, originally prepared for Quérilinte, was now to be offered as a gift to the Immortals. To this end Casanova fabricated a copy in painted wood which he easily substituted for the real casket; but then, how to convey away the replica so as to make the old lady believe that the Immortals had received it? However, a small point that did not baffle Casanova's inventiveness. Madame d'Urfé having told him that she had once had the water-sprite of the Seine for a lover, he decided that a female water-sprite should be the pivot of his piece of magic; and instructing his then mistress Marcoline, a frolicsome Venetian, as to what she was to do, he staged an ingenious scene. At the hour indicated by the motions of the celestial orbs, Casanova would, though in all decency, share the marquise's bed, after putting the sham casket on a pile of wood in the fireplace. Then the water-sprite (who was dumb) would enter, suitably clothed, or unclothed, offer the marquise some tinder soaked in spirit which the old lady would light, carry it to the fireplace and set the wood ablaze. All went according to plan. Marcoline appeared, in due course lighted the fire, and the casket with its contents were rapt by the flames to the destined recipients in ethereal spheres. Then a certain operation took place, and the sprite transferred 'the verb' to the old lady, who was thus impregnated to her entire satisfaction. Marcoline vanished, Casanova joined her, and the real casket was triumphantly filched away.

The greatest of all magic operations being thus happily in-augurated, Casanova decided to go to England to take the 'Comte d'Aranda' back to his mother, and, if possible, to retrieve his own daughter. Travelling to Lyons with Marcoline, his carriage broke down near Aix-en-Provence. The inhabitants of the neighbouring château came to the rescue, and invited them to spend the night. The châtelaine was a woman whom the rest addressed as Countess, and she appeared to be charming though she zealously kept her face hidden by a hood. Owing to a trifling accident she twisted her ankle, and retired to her bedroom, where, it was announced, they would all sup. Surely now Casanova would be able to see her face. But no; she sat up in bed with the curtains so arranged that her features could not be distinguished in the gloom. She was gay, witty, and spoke Italian, and, what was more, Venetian Italian. It was dis-appointing not to see her, especially as she did not appear the next day. When the travellers got to Lyons, Marcoline drew from her pocket a letter the Countess had told her not to give the Chevalier till they had arrived. Casanova tore open the blank cover, and found beneath, as the only address, 'To the best gentleman I have ever known.' Opening the letter he saw that that also was blank, except for the name—'Henriette.' Casanova went white as a sheet. Henriette! He would go back. Alas! it was clearly her wish that he should not. He would respect that wish. Was he not the best gentleman she had ever known? So on to Paris with Marcoline.

VII

Downfall in England

(1763–1764)

The moment the Chevalier de Seingalt reached London in the summer of 1763, he drove to Carlisle House, Soho Square, to deliver the 'Comte d'Aranda' to his mother, Thérèse Imer. She, now known as Madam Cornelis, would no doubt greet him with that warmth which he himself always maintained for his old, but never discarded loves. He was full of pleasant anticipation; she would fly to meet him, as she had in Holland. But no; after announcing himself he was given a note by a flunkey, and read that he was to take d'Aranda to a house not far off. There he was met by a stout housekeeper, who was full of delicate attentions for the youth, but completely ignored the Chevalier. D'Aranda was given a suite of rooms, and provided with servants, while Casanova was relegated to a side-room, and his valet stuffed into an attic. It appeared that Madam Cornelis was a great figure, with a sumptuous town mansion, thirty-three servants, a coach and six, and a country house, and thus 'Mr. Cornelis' would also be a person of great account. Casanova was apparently looked upon as the boy's tutor, a paid pedant, a nobody! So telling his valet to carry in his boxes but not to unpack, he took himself off, fuming with rage, to explore London.

Striding along to appease his dudgeon, he soon found himself in a coffee-house at the bottom of the Haymarket, all unaware that it was the very one, the Orange, which he had been warned to avoid as the meeting-place of all rapscallion foreigners. Calling for lemonade, he picked up an Italian newspaper, but his eye straying, he found the man next him carefully correcting Italian imprint, changing the modern forms of words into obsolete ones. Irritated at this 'barbarism', he forthwith told his neighbour that it was centuries since *ancora* had been written *anchora*. 'I know,' he was answered, 'but I am quoting

Boccaccio, and quotations should be accurate.' A scholar! Casanova was enchanted, especially since it turned out that this was
Martinelli, whom Casanova knew by repute. He at once introduced himself, subscribed for four copies at a guinea each of
Martinelli's edition of the *Decameron*, and made firm friends.
He was regaining his temper. They sallied out together to find
Casanova a house, and in a short time he had rented a superb
furnished mansion in Pall Mall at twenty guineas a week, a
price agreed to without bargaining, for no good came of
haggling in London.

Comforted in his esteem, he faced the future hopefully, but
not in playing the part Madam Cornelis had suggested, nor
even in the better place she later proposed him of being steward
at her vast public entertainments, which 'at first scandalized
but soon drew in both righteous and ungodly', Horace Walpole
declared, himself not much bewitched by her palace of splendour.
No, his was a different rôle. The Chevalier de Seingalt, wearing
the cross of his Order, was at the moment possessed of a dazzling
wardrobe, with lace every woman envied, a good substantial
sum in cash and notes, and a sound reserve in jewelry, not to
mention such appurtenances as a French valet and a negro
footman. His letters to several bankers would, with the
introduction he had to Lord Egremont, Secretary of State,
enable an intelligent man to float a lottery scheme. There would
certainly be something maleficent in the air if he could not cut
a dash; certainly all would not be right with the tender sex if
great happiness should not result. A steward! the idea was
laughable. Seingalt, at the prime of life, would take London by
storm, as he had taken Paris, Milan, Geneva, and other towns
where he was already a legend.

And besides, London was interesting, the English very odd,
unlike anybody he had ever met, in manners, tastes, even in
build. Not only the men and women, but even the animals and
fish grew differently in this strange place; the very earth was
peculiar, and Thames water was water unknown elsewhere.
Martinelli took him about, showed him the City, introduced
him to Lord Chesterfield's friend, Dr. Maty of the British
Museum; so Casanova was able to make many curious observations about the English, and about their country, where everything except unadulterated wine tasted of salt, so aquatic was

the land, so maritime the people. They were prodigious meat-eaters, but soup, which luckily Casanova's valet could make, was not to be had, for it was looked upon as pap for invalids. Stout, however, was a great invention. Moreover, the English lived differently from any people he had ever met, and their pride was terrific. Every people, of course, thought themselves superior to all others—so that the difficulty was only to find which held second place—but the English outdid everyone else in this. Still, if they were disgustingly democratic, if a gentleman could not wear his best clothes in the street for fear of being dirtied by the mob, they were in many ways admirable. Their towns were marvellously clean, their roads and their posting service superb, while their faith in their paper money attested the solidity of their credit. Of course, if anything went wrong, the result would be bankruptcy . . . and Casanova the financier envisaged dark possibilities. Most admirable of all, perhaps, were their night-watchmen, who very quietly did the job it took a posse of archers to do anywhere else.

But somehow Casanova did not make the way he deserved; Madam Cornelis's greeting seemed symbolic in its coldness. Lord Egremont died soon after the Chevalier had presented his letter; the bankers did not jump at Casanova's lottery, and, indeed, that field was at the moment held by Lord Bute. Gambling, except for mere drawing-room stakes, was not to be had, for Casanova seems to have been warned off putting up for White's. Nor did he flourish in society. The acquaintance he had made on the way over with the Duke of Bedford by surrendering half his boat did not ripen; Lady Northumberland, though friendly enough, thanks to an introduction in the form of a portrait from her son Lord Warkworth, to whom Casanova had surrendered a mistress in Genoa, soon went to Ireland. Lady Harrington—did Casanova know that she was nicknamed 'the Stable-Yard Messalina'?—seemed to take him nowhere but to Madam Cornelis's aristocratic Assemblies; and if he knew the Hon. Augustus Hervey and Lord Pembroke, they seemed to regard him merely as a vivacious companion in a debauch. Was it possible that there was something hostile in this insular atmosphere?

Certainly Venus did not seem to favour the island; even venal love, which might serve between whiles, proved unsatisfactory, though well organized. Perhaps it was too well organized, with its lists of promiscuous ladies. One adventure, indeed, Casanova did have. His carriage not meeting him at Ranelagh one evening, a charming woman offered him a lift. He got into the coach, he pressed her hand, to have the pressure returned; he kissed her cheek, and was not repulsed; when he placed his mouth on hers, those gracious lips responded. At last, circumstances being propitious, he was able to give his fair companion indubitable proofs of the feeling she aroused in him. He introduced himself. 'Don't ask my name,' he was answered; 'we shall meet again', and was thereupon unceremoniously dropped at his house. Still, it was promising. Not long after he went to call upon Lady Betty Germaine, a woman of distinguished fashion: she was not at home; would he wait? He was ushered into the drawing-room, and there he saw his Ranelagh charmer reading the *Gazette*. 'Ah!' he exclaimed, 'perhaps you will present me to Lady Betty.' 'But I don't know you, sir!' 'But I told you who I was! Surely you haven't forgotten me?' 'No, I haven't forgotten you; but a frolic does not constitute an introduction.' And she went on reading the *Gazette*. This was more than Casanova could understand: it put him completely out of action.

But he could not live alone, for he was not, as he said, cast in the hermetic mould. The simplest solution would be to put up a notice in his window:

Second or third floor to let cheap, furnished, to a single and un-attached young lady who can speak English and French, and is at home to nobody either by day or by night.

His old housekeeper roared with laughing; spiced comments appeared in the papers,[1] to Casanova's delighted admiration at the freedom of the English press. A hundred or so young women of doubtful reputation appeared, but none of them really pleased the lonely hero of romance. At last there applied a most ravishing creature, in all ways beautiful with her pallor and her black hair, and nobility patent in every gesture. She got her board and lodging for next to nothing. Casanova promptly fell in love with her, really in love; she stirred his imaginations as well as his senses; and what made Pauline, as she was called,

---

[1] Mr. Bleackley has been unable to find them.

even more desirable, were her wise and witty conversation, her love of poetry, her skill at chess, and her knowledge of languages. This paragon had eloped disguised as a man from her native Lisbon, with her husband disguised as a woman; but the latter had been captured as he was landing in England, and, the marriage still unconsummated, had been dragged back to Portugal. The affair was in the hands of the great minister Pombal, and Pauline, eking out a miserable residue of money, was waiting for a favourable decision. In the meantime, well, Casanova was still irresistible, the conquest did not take long, and he added Pauline not only to the list of women he had really loved, but of women who had loved him, in this case so much that she almost regretted her marriage. It was a dream of paradise while it lasted, most aptly commented by passages from Ariosto; but then the long-expected summons to Portugal came, with a vast supply of *reis*. And Pauline, as she went weeping to her happiness, begged Casanova never to come to her unless she sent for him. For weeks he was under the influence of a 'Platonic' love for her; he could not, nor did he wish to, rid his mind of her graces, of those perfections of soul which equalled, even surpassed, her physical beauty. Perhaps he remembered her with peculiar vividness in his later years, for she was his last complete love.

When she had gone he passed his time as best he could, visited Lord Pembroke, and was astonished at his fighting-cocks; gave Dr. Maty a cameo; observed the Stock Exchange, where men knew each other's incomes but not each other's names; was presented at Court by the French ambassador; and got his own back on La Cornelis, not only by becoming one of her high guests, but by sending their daughter to a very expensive and aristocratic school, where he would go to visit her, and, with the juvenile inmates, stalk like a vulture among the doves. But meanwhile his funds were dwindling; there seemed no way of making them up, and worst of all, he heard that Madame d'Urfé was dead. That bountiful source was dried up.[1]

No doubt Fate would provide in due course; for the moment there appeared a strange and attractive creature to occupy his

---

[1] As a matter of fact, she did not die until 1775; but Casanova believed the report. At all events, she had died to him.

thoughts, La Charpillon. It was not in any way an affair of the
heart; it was rather as a priest of Venus that he approached her,
some time in September. Fatal day, that he was to look back
upon as marking the deflexion of his life, day that the curve of
his existence stopped rising, and began to decline. For La
Charpillon was determined to defeat, not merely to reject him.
He should have had forebodings, for the very first time she met
him she confessed that had her mother allowed it, she would
have answered his notorious advertisement, 'to punish the
impudent author'. 'How would you have punished me?' 'By
making you fall in love with me, and then making you suffer
abominably. How I would have laughed!' Casanova accepted
this as a challenge, thanking her incredulously for the warning.
How could this exquisite girl, with her chestnut hair, her blue
eyes, her delicately dazzling skin, and above all her candid
expression of benevolence, be such a monster? He was already
half-enthralled.

La Charpillon being well advanced in the trade of courtesan,
there should be no difficulty; and although Lord Pembroke
warned Casanova that she was a trickster, on the day appointed
he went to tackle her mother, her two aunts, and her grandmother. There was a surprising mutual recognition between
Casanova and the horribly decayed mother, for some years
earlier she had planted him with two bills that were dis-
honoured, and which he still held. She had not realized that in
M. de Seingalt she would meet a creditor! He found himself
in a nauseating nest of witches living chiefly on the immoral
earnings of the girl, and collaborating with various insufferable
rogues. Casanova was not long in coming to the point, and
gave the mother a hundred guineas to embark on the manufac-
ture of an 'elixir of life'. Perhaps it was this blatant purchase
that exasperated La Charpillon; at all events, instead of entering
into possession of this Circe, as he called her, he was led the
most extraordinary dance which lasted for weeks. At first she
seemed all willingness, but refused the final favours. He turned
over to her the spurious bills, besides vast sums of money, but
still she did not yield. 'You have been too brutal', she said.
'Woo me handsomely for a fortnight, make me in love with you,
and I will be yours.' For a fortnight, then, the wooing went
on, with theatres, supper-parties, expeditions, and expensive

presents of china. On the appointed night they shared a room; but she swaddled herself in a long gown, and hunching up her body, resisted strenuously. Softness, anger, pleading, cursing, were all ineffectual, and even rough handling which covered her with scratches and bruises. He retired baffled, swearing he would have no more to do with her. But when she approached him again he was weak; he relented. Why had he been such a fool? he asked himself in his old age. 'Ah, reader!' he apostrophizes us, 'were you never in love?' Love? we ask in our turn, deciding that his was a far more complex emotion. There was Casanova's usual lust, but also there was aroused in him a combative spirit, a deep male brutality, which stirred up a desire for possession quite apart from enjoyment, to which was added a determination not to be made a fool of. More money flowed, and he took a coy villa at Chelsea where she promised to live with him. But the first night there was the same obduracy; nothing would make her submit; and once during the struggle when he felt his hands about her throat, he was deeply tempted to strangle her. There was nothing to do but send her away the next morning.

Still he went on, still calling himself fool, still fatefully lured, till one day he went to the sinister house in Denmark Street to see her, and found her in the embraces of a barber! He stormed and belaboured the young man; La Charpillon screamed; the old harridans crept in; he smashed the furniture, the valuable china he had given, everything he could see, creating a pandemonium which attracted the night-watchman. Suddenly it was found that La Charpillon had vanished. The servants were sent out, but could not find her. What might happen next? What might not happen? Casanova, his feathers drooping, staggered back to his house.

The next day he was told that she had come home, but was dangerously ill. He called, was not allowed to see her, was told she was delirious and raving against him. Casanova's nerves were completely shattered: he could not sleep: he could not eat. Each day the bulletins grew more alarming; there was small hope for her life. He haunted the door, and seeing a man come out asked, 'Is that the doctor?' 'The doctor! She's past doctors now. That was a priest.' At the end of three days he was informed that she had only a few hours to live. He went home;

and then the animal in him took its revenge, for he suffered a
wholly animal collapse, against which the will and the reason
were powerless. He would go mad—and on such occasions the
only remedy is suicide. He made his will, leaving everything
to Bragadin, shut up his jewels and money in a case, put his
pistols in his pocket, and buying as much lead as his pockets
would hold, headed for the Thames.

But just as he neared Westminster Bridge he was accosted
by an acquaintance of his, Edgar (Wellebore Ellis Agar?),
who, seeing that something was desperately wrong, refused to
leave him, and eventually persuaded him to the refreshment
of oysters and Graves; then to the further refreshment of a
pretty little orgy, in which, however, Casanova, who had
touched no food for three days, was too weak to take part; an
incident which taught him that love is the result, not the cause,
of gaiety. Since he now owed Edgar some money, he deferred
his suicide to the next day, and was teased to go to Ranelagh.
Half-dead, with hazy eyes, he watched the dancers; and then
he saw a strangely familiar figure—it was—his mind was
wandering—it could not be—she turned her face—yes, it was
not a hallucination, but La Charpillon! So she was in her death-
throes, was she! The reaction was terrific. Edgar thought that
Casanova was about to have a fit; but in a few minutes he
recovered, the lights of Ranelagh, which had seemed dim, now
burned brightly, and the Chevalier de Seingalt was himself
again.

Still, the whole monstrous affair had broken something in
him, his faith, perhaps; for from that time Casanova, at thirty-
eight, felt that he was growing old. True, his morale was somewhat restored by five delightful Hanoverian sisters, who were
far from being monsters like La Charpillon, but his spirit was
permanently scarred: for the first time he realized in his bones
that all flesh was as grass. Nor was the affair quite over. He
had the disgusting old procuresses imprisoned for debt (Edgar,
who was more successful with La Charpillon, as Wilkes was
to be, redeemed it); and they, having him seized as he was
issuing in gala-dress from one of Cornelis's royally attended
routs, charged him with attempted disfigurement, an accusation
from which he was only dismissed after being bound over on his
own and other recognisances, and paying a short but horrid

visit to Newgate. The only revenge he took was to train a
parrot to shout in French, 'La Charpillon is a wickeder harlot
than her mother', which he offered for sale at fifty guineas on
the Stock Exchange.

In the early spring Casanova, checking his resources, found
that he was only just solvent. He had spent thousands in
England (La Charpillon had cost him more than one), had
made up nothing in gambling, and had been unable to engineer
a lottery scheme. He must retreat. Selling nearly all his jewelry
to pay his debts, he gave up his Pall Mall mansion, and with-
drawing to rooms in Greek Street, Soho, prepared to go to
Portugal. One day, however, he met an amiable cosmopolitan
gentleman who called himself the Baron de Stenau, in company
with a still more amiable lady, with whom he gambled, and
from whom he won fifty pounds. His opponent could not pay,
but gave him a bill for five hundred, which he took to his
banker the next day, and signed on its being accepted. He
returned four hundred and fifty pounds to Stenau, made the
intimate acquaintance of the lady, and got ready to go. But
within a week he found that the lady was not above reproach,
and taking to his bed, undertook a month's cure. No sooner
had he done so, however, than he received a note from the
banker to say that the bill was fraudulent, and that either he
must return the money or produce Stenau. Casanova, crawling
out of bed, put a brace of pistols in his pocket and went resolutely
to ferret out the baron. He had bolted! Casanova was thus
responsible for the forgery, and forgery was a hanging matter.
There was only one thing to do—to leave the country within
the twenty-four hours allowed him by his banker. But had he
the money? He sold his clothes, which enabled him to refuse
the offer his valet made him of his savings and his credit (a
touching tribute); and making all possible haste to Dover,
landed safely at Calais. Farewell to England, inhospitable and
fatal! In eight months, from being the conquering, rich Chevalier
de Seingalt, he had departed from it ill, penurious, and sad, a
fugitive with a noose about his neck.

VIII

The End of the Odyssey

(1764–1785)

He was never quite the same man again. Although, thanks to Bragadin and the Comtesse du Rumain, he was supplied with money, and maintained his funds by gambling, he was never to be rich any more. His illness was severe; it nearly killed him, and his convalescence was slow. Afterwards his love-affairs multiplied, but there was not the same glamour about them; the animal continued, that was all, and the animal was beginning to fail.

Not that adventures were lacking. First he met Saint-Germain, and the master-charlatan turned a base coin of his into gold, Casanova being unable to detect the sleight-of-hand. At Brunswick, to which he had carried a frolicsome young woman, trouble arose over a bill on Amsterdam. The Jew with whom he negotiated it doubted its validity, and the Duke of Brunswick, bidding Casanova a meaning farewell, seemed to share the broker's suspicions. This was intolerable! Casanova could not leave, because it would look as though he was expelled by the Duke; and he could not stay, because it would seem that the Jew was right. So he retired to the neighbouring town of Wolfenbüttel, with its magnificent library, where he buried himself in books and manuscripts for a week, studying mainly in and about Homer.

I can count this week amongst the happiest of my life [he wrote with a flash of self-illumination], for I was not for a moment occupied with myself. I thought neither of the past nor of the future, and my mind, absorbed in work, could not be alive to the present. I have sometimes thought since then that perhaps the delight of the life of the blessed must be something similar; and today I see that for me to have been in this world a really good and wise man, instead of a real mad-man, only a combination of petty circumstances would have been necessary; for to the shame of my whole life I must proclaim a truth which my readers will find it hard to believe, namely, that virtue has always seemed to me preferable to vice, and that I have been wicked (when I have been wicked) only from lightness of heart: a fact which many will no doubt find reprehensible. But what does that matter to me? Man, in his inward or moral relations, is responsible to himself alone here below, and to God after his death.

After the Jew, with abject apologies, had honoured the bill on Amsterdam, Casanova made his way to Berlin, where he fell in with the younger Calsabigi, still busied in State lotteries. But Frederick the Great, nervous about them, was renouncing that method of raising revenue, and Calsabigi appealed to Casanova for help. Surely Fate itself had sent the genius of lotteries at just the right time to overcome Frederick's doubts. But how to see the King? Luckily Casanova met his old acquaintance Marshal Keith (to whom he gave Saint-Germain's piece of transmuted gold), who said, 'Why, write to him; he sees everybody.' Frederick duly appointed a meeting at four o'clock one afternoon in the garden of Sans-Souci, and appeared there after his daily flute-playing, with only a reader (a kind of jester) and a spaniel. As soon as the King saw Casanova, he took off his shabby hat, and addressing him by name, shouted at him to say what he wanted. Staggered by this reception, for once Casanova was mute. 'Well,' the King roared, 'speak up! Wasn't it you who wrote to me?' The mention of Lord Keith's name, combined with a compliment, smoothed the scene, and the talk whirled on gardens, on hydraulics, on the naval and military forces of Venice, and finally on finance, upon which Casanova held forth long and ingeniously, but still could not persuade the King to go on with the lottery. At last, as a conclusion, Frederick, looking Casanova up and down with a soldier's appraising eye, said, 'Do you know, you're a very fine figure of a man?' 'Is it possible, sire,' the retort came instantaneously, 'that after a long scientific discussion, your Majesty can see in me the least of the qualities that distinguishes his grenadiers?' The King smiled; he liked Casanova, who soon applied to him for a post. But since after a few weeks he was only offered a paltry tutorship of Pomeranian cadets, he refused the offer; and engaging a rascal as valet because he knew some mathematics, he made for Russia.

But by the time he got to Mitau, extravagance had depleted his funds. However, he entered the town *en grand seigneur*, and delivered a letter of introduction to the Chancellor of the Duchy of Courland, whose wife entertained him, and offered him chocolate. He accepted, and the servant who brought the refreshment was so outstandingly beautiful, that with all his old impetuosity (*sequere Deum*) he slipped the last three ducats he had in the world into her hand. The impulse brought its reward, for the fame of the munificent tip spread so fast that by the evening a Jew had petitioned to lend him money! The Chevalier was once more on his feet. Introduced at Court, some chance remark led the Duke to suppose that his guest was an authority on mines. Would he inspect his? Well, why not? So Casanova made a three weeks' tour of Courland, threw out common-sense suggestions, and writing a report adorned with drawings by his mathematical valet, received an honorarium. Therefore the Chevalier, who seems at this time to have adopted his mother's name of Farussi prefixed with the syllable Count, made a sufficiently striking entry into Riga, and soon after descended upon St. Petersburg.

There, though he led his usual life of gambling, gaiety, and love (the salient feature of the last was a young serf whom he bought, and who in jealousy threw plates at his head), his main interest was Catherine the Great. She was strong-minded, he decided—her lovers would prove her free from prejudice—but she was not perfidious and cruel, so might be exonerated from the murder or murders attributed to her. She was big, well-built, and without being beautiful, was pleasing. She was gentle and easy, and above all endued with a calm that never abandoned her. She was gracious to Casanova, whom she talked with several times. They criticized the statues in the gardens, and then the talk turned to Frederick, during which Casanova had the opportunity of telling the truth and of flattering the Czarina, by saying that his Prussian Majesty's great fault was that in conversation he never gave you time to answer his questions. More important, however, was Casanova's suggestion that it looked ill for a modern monarch to continue to use the Old Style in dating: why did she not impose the Gregorian calendar? Even England had done so lately. At their next meeting she declared that she had undertaken the reform; that all official letters now bore both dates; and then there followed a long and learned discourse on chronology, which reflects great credit not only on the Czarina's erudition, but also on Casanova's memory. This part of the memoirs is also embellished by an entertaining dialogue of the dead with Catherine, over her sudden death. It is in the best manner of Fontenelle.

Leaving St. Petersburg, since he sought no post in a country which he did not like, in 1765 Casanova rattled away to Warsaw. There his flaring adventure was his duel with Count Branicki, the King of Poland's favourite; an affair of honour in which there was the greatest friendliness on both sides. Casanova was always inordinately proud of this duel. He had fought many before, and with his famous direct thrust, lunged home as soon as his adversaries were on guard (one of them complained that he had been hit before he was on guard), had always pinked his foe. This affair was with pistols; but what made Casanova so vainglorious was that by fighting with so fine a gentleman he had been tacitly ennobled. Branicki was severely wounded in the stomach, but was able to prevent his infuariated people from killing Casanova, who for his part had his left hand shattered. Seeking sanctuary in a convent, he was attended by doctors who insisted that his wound being gangrenous, he must have his hand amputated. Casanova refused, though his friends implored him to save his life by submitting: he said there was no gangrene. 'It will poison your arm, and you will lose that', he was told. 'Very well, if it poisons my arm, you may take it off', he answered. He was irritated by a note from the King (who promised him forgiveness even if Branicki died) expressing wonder at his lack of courage; but still he would not give in, and time proved him right. For although he carried his hand in a sling for months, perhaps for more months than were strictly necessary, it finally healed. As soon as he could get about he found it wise to leave Warsaw for a while, to visit the noblemen who clamoured to invite him; but when he came back he found that rumour had been so sadly rife about him, that the King withdrew his favour, and virtually ordered him to leave his capital.

So then to Breslau, to Dresden, where he saw his mother, to Leipzig, to Vienna (we are now in 1767), where he renewed acquaintance with Metastasio, but from which he was expelled for gambling, which he had not indulged in (a bitter enemy had trapped him there), in spite of the succour of the great Prince

Kaunitz. Then Augsburg, Louisburg, Cologne, Spa, in ever more rapid progression, everywhere meeting old friends, and ever asking for employments which were invariably denied him, and even offering to sell the secret of the transmutation of gold to the son of the Duke of Courland for a trifling sum, which was not sent: and finally Paris, where he learned to his bitter regret that his perennial benefactor, Bragadin, was dead. There, offering to fight a nephew of the Marquise d'Urfé who made insulting remarks about him at a concert, he was handed a *lettre de cachet* ordering him to leave at once; so he made his way to Madrid (on the way to Portugal and Pauline), where on arrival his possession of the *Iliad* in Greek aroused the darkest suspicions of the customs officers.

The Spaniards, he found, had more prejudices than any other race, were even more conceited than the English, and hated foreigners. Nevertheless, armed with letters of introduction, he leapt into the good graces of such grandees as the Comte d'Aranda—this time the real one, and so powerful as to be more king than the King—and of other notables. Why had he come? they asked guilelessly. To see if his talents could be of any use to the State. Would his ambassador, Mocenigo, introduce him at Court? Alas, no; he was ill viewed by the Venetian Inquisition. Well then, he might by all means stay to amuse himself in Spain, but he could expect nothing. His case was becoming desperate; he was no longer fortune's darling, and he wrote urgently to Dandolo, Bragadin's friend, imploring him to arrange matters with the Venetian government, and have him recommended to the ambassador.

In the meantime things did not go so badly with him, and he was made hopeful by the behaviour of the ambassador's secretary, the delightful young Count Manucci, who came to call. Manucci? the name seemed familiar. Why, of course, this so-called count was the son of the dastardly spy who had been the instrument of his confinement in the Leads!—the son of a shopkeeper and a servant-girl! However, he did not unmask him, and through Manucci's friendship was privately welcomed by Mocenigo, over whom the secretary had compelling influence. Moreover, Casanova was received everywhere; his polished manners, and his brilliant, well-informed conversation opened even princely portals. And there was Ignazia, the daughter of a hidalgo, who was a cobbler but not a shoemaker, for his nobility would not permit him to stoop so low as to measure the feet of plebeians, though he might mend their leaky slippers. Casanova took her to balls, for which, irrepressible young beau of forty-three, he learned to dance the fandango; so that the whole made a gracious but not exciting adventure.

Unlike the one which was exciting enough but by no means gracious. One day, signalled to walk under a lady's window, a note was dropped at his feet, making an assignation with him that night at a specified door. Meticulously toileted, he was there punctually, and, full of expectation, was led, delightedly conscious of perfumes and rustling silks, along a pitch-dark passage. Dolores, so she is named, took his hand, and they entered the dim candlelight of a vast scutcheoned room. 'Do you love me? Will you swear to do as I ask you?' she whispered, to be promptly answered 'Yes'; and then Dolores—he noticed she seemed agonized and was trembling—led him to the curtained alcove and, flinging back the hangings, revealed the corpse of a young man lying on the bed! Dolores had murdered the lover who had been false to her. And since Casanova had sworn to do as she asked, he was forced to carry away the body and slide it into the river behind the house.

Such is the story; but it occurs in only one of the texts, and it is more likely that when, two days later, a stranger warned Casanova that he was about to be arrested, the reason given was the true one, namely, that he was illegally in possession of arms. He rushed for refuge to his friend Raphaël Mengs, now painter royal to Charles III; but Mengs was timid, and only harboured him against the grain. Uselessly, for the next day Casanova was dragged off to the prison of Buen Retiro. He had never been in such a vile place, in company with such revolting human dregs. The atmosphere was greasily foul; there were no tables, and the few camp-beds so crawled with vermin that it was impossible to rest on them. Casanova went in continual fear that he would be murdered for his money, for his watch, for anything: so for two days and nights he stayed awake, sitting upright in discomfort and dread. Mengs, however, sent him food, and Manucci procured him writing materials, with which he sent four outrageously stinging letters

to men in authority, the most vitriolic being reserved for
d'Aranda. This masterpiece concluded: 'Therefore give instant
order for my release, or end my torture: you will thus spare
me the pains of doing away with myself.' And soon he was
let out, the confiscated weapons were returned; and what was
more, Mocenigo, acting on instructions, received him openly.
Triumph once again!

So his old life went on, gloriously enough, He met all the
distinguished people in Madrid, discussing with them mathematics, poetry, philosophy and the arts; he wrote the libretto
of an opera performed at the embassy, and if he once or twice
indiscreetly brushed up against the priests, a friendly conversation with the Grand Inquisitor set matters right. Most of all,
he interested himself in a plan for colonizing a part of the Sierra
Morena, and expatiated so well that the authorities concerned
provisionally offered him the government of the nascent colony.
But then a hideous blow fell. Calling on Manucci one day, he
was refused the door; a note he sent him was returned unopened.
He met with similar rebuffs everywhere—at d'Aranda's, at
the Prince de la Catolica's, at each house where he had been
effusively welcomed. He soon discovered why. He had blabbed,
inexcusably, about a shameful aspect of Manucci's private life;
and he having told Mocenigo, the ambassador gave out that
Casanova was a scoundrel no self-respecting person should
receive. Indeed he had betrayed a friend. He had also fouled
his own nest.

There was, then, nothing for him to do but to leave Madrid.
Not, however, for Portugal, for Pauline had stopped writing
to him. He went eastward, to Saragossa, to Valencia, lingering
on his way to shed tears over the glorious ruins of Saguntum;
for however distressed Casanova might be, the ardent scholar
was always awake in him; to Barcelona, where he spent six
weeks in prison owing to his old infamous partner Passano
betraying his intimacy with the mistress of the Captain-General
of Catalonia. Another gaoling, however, did not daunt him, and
while there he solved mathematical problems, and continued a
work he had begun in Madrid, the *Confutation* of Amelot de la
Houssaye's inimical history of Venice. Then, on his release,
across the frontier, pursued by murderers set on by Manucci, to
wander awhile in the smaller towns of southern France, where,

although living was cheap, he left a trail of debts rather than a succession of lovers. At Aix he was so ill that the last Sacrament was administered to him, but his life was saved by the devotion of a nurse who quietly appeared. Who had sent her? Nobody knew. At last he discovered who it was: Henriette! whom he had lately had much in mind. They exchanged letters. 'We passed in the street,' she informed him, 'but you did not recognize me. I have changed a great deal. Not that I have become ugly, but I have grown prematurely fat.' The letter reached him at Marseilles. Should he go back? No. She had told him it would be indiscreet. Perhaps if later . . .

And so the restless journeying went on, with no outward confession of weariness on Casanova's part, though his friends unkindly told him that he looked surprisingly older. But what was the future to be for an ageing man, who yet insisted on being young? Cast out of nearly every capital in Europe, where was he to go? Venice! He was homesick for Venice, with an ever-increasing ache. So as he meandered from place to place—to Naples, where he met Lucrezia and Leonilda; to Rome, where he once more disported himself, though less scandalously, with the Cardinal de Bernis, now French ambassador, and where he encountered Manucci, who insisted that they were friends; to Florence, from which he was expelled for complicity, which he denied, in a gambling plot to fleece Lord Lincoln; to Switzerland—he all the time kept his compass set for his beloved birthplace. As he went, gambling, conversing with philosophers, arguing about poetry, and still making love (though his stories now become less and less convincing), he wrote and worked, publishing especially the *Confutation* which might restore him to favour. At last, in 1773, after six years of purposeless straying, living meagrely, only occasionally finding something of the old luck and the old gaudiness, he reached Trieste. It was nearly his goal. Finally, in the autumn of 1774, after rendering the State some secret service, he was allowed, to his great joy, to float once more upon the happy canals of which he had never ceased to dream.

It is well to pass hastily, with averted eyes, over the next eight years of his life, during which the sublime adventurer, the meteoric millionaire, the fantastically excessive lover, eked out a mean living as spy to the Inquisition! Moreover, in the

16

whole of Venice, there was only one poor, faithful shop-girl to love him. And it was all to no end. In vain his reports bewailed the shocking immorality of the town, and contained lists of the impious or smutty books owned by his compatriots; his employers complained he never sent them any information worth having, and would give him no reward beyond a wretched pittance. He was, indeed, received at patrician tables, for his conversation was inimitably stimulating; but that led nowhere. He tried to exploit a company of French actors; he started a theatrical magazine of some merit, *Le Messager de Thalie*; but it failed. He published a series of *Opusculi*, which came to a premature end in a novel, of which he sent a copy to his old bright flame, X. C. V., Justiniana Wynne, now Comtesse de Rosemberg. He fulminated against the Deism of Voltaire; and he began to translate the *Iliad* of Homer into Italian *ottava rima*, but the venture petered out after eighteen cantos; and finally he compiled a vast work on the troubles in Poland, of which only three out of the seven volumes were printed. He did not thrive, though he was at one time secretary to the Marquis Spinola. 'Either I am not made for Venice, or Venice is not made for me', he lamented; and at last there was a characteristic explosion. In a quarrel at the house of a nobleman he found himself so placed that either he had to violate hospitality, or own himself a coward, a situation so intolerable that he took his revenge by publishing a scandalous libel on both parties, *Ne Amori, ne Donne*. His book was stopped; friendly houses were closed to him, and it was intimated that there was nothing more for him to do in Venice.

So once more, at fifty-eight, with yellowing teeth, and wearing a chestnut wig, the battered adventurer set off, protesting and poor, into a greying future. He pinned his hope on Paris, especially, for some reason, on d'Alembert; but d'Alembert had just died, and Paris was dolefully changed, Still, he put up a bold front, mingled with *cognoscenti*, attended meetings of the Academies, but soon left it with his brother François, now painter to the King, to go to Dresden, and thence to Vienna, where François, thanks to Kaunitz, flourished bravely. Giacomo was not so lucky. He did indeed for some time act as secretary to the Venetian ambassador, but it was no life for him, even in old age, still loving as he did to dally with the arts, to make new acquaintances and meet old ones, and to live in the appropriate way. Among his new friends was Da Ponte, of the same kidney as himself, who tells that one day when he was walking with Casanova, the latter, suddenly contorted, ground his teeth, and rushed upon a man across the street, yelling 'Villain, I have caught you!' It was Costa, the valet who had robbed him of Madame d'Urfé's trunk of valuables. Da Ponte dragged Casanova away, but Costa soon reappeared with a stanza of doggerel verses to the effect that he had, after all, only been Casanova's pupil in theft, and that the latter had better keep mum. Casanova laughed, whispered to Da Ponte 'The rascal's right', and parted amicably from his old valet, who gave him a cameo ring as the last relic of the marquise's jewels.

And yet, in spite of queer associates, in spite of his mean position, Casanova was still a figure, still petted by the great, so much so that he conversed with the Emperor, Joseph II, and in no spirit of humility. When the Emperor said, 'I don't think much of people who buy titles', M. de Seingalt innocently asked, 'And what about those who sell them, sire?' But such petty triumphs would not enable a man to live, nor would a work on the quarrel between the Dutch and Venetian Republics: nothing seemed to offer, and the world became, if not flat and stale—it could never be that to Casanova's eager mind—at least unprofitable, for he had lost even his secretaryship when his ambassador died. Then one day, dining with Count Lamberg, his Augsburg friend, he met the young Count Waldstein, whom he fascinated. Waldstein turned the talk upon magic. 'Oh, I know all about that', Casanova struck in. 'Then come and live with me at Dux', Waldstein said: 'I'm going back there tomorrow.' But Casanova did not fancy burying himself in the wilds of Bohemia, and for a year he struggled on, went to Berlin to get a post in the Academy, battled against his fate. But at last he accepted Waldstein's offer to become his librarian at a not ignoble salary, coupled with the promise that he would be treated like a gentleman.

IX

Twilight at Dux

(1785–1798)

Was the adventure to end at last, at anchor in the library of a
petty prince, with the cobwebs and the dust gradually covering
over the old decaying body, the mind rusting until the wheels
slowed down to a stop? Exile, forgetfulness by the world—the
tiger in a cage! Never again would the brilliant Chevalier de
Seingalt flash astonishingly through the capitals of Europe,
swaggering and irresistible; no more would the faro tables
hope or tremble at his approach; Venus Pandemon would for
ever lose the most constant, the most arduous of her votaries.
Impossible! or at least unthinkable! Could not life be made to
conform to desire, as he had said over and over again? And at
first, when the Count was in residence, there were gleams;
sumptuous dinners with entrancing food, and wines abundant
and select, upon which Casanova pounced wolfishly; talk something like the old talk; and balls with the delicious proximity of
beauty floating by amid the ravishing perfumes of the boudoir.
Sometimes there were visitors to drink the waters at Teplitz,
near by, such as the genially cynical Prince de Ligne, Waldstein's uncle, a great man of the world and man of letters; and
he, or others, or Lorenzo da Ponte, would come to gossip, to
listen, to be dazzled, for to the end Casanova was extraordinarily good company, flashing with wit, bubbling over with
anecdote, and dropping remarks of a staggering sagacity.
Moments of happiness, of illusion, for which the old adventurer
was always grateful to Waldstein. But, and it was to be tasted
almost at once, there was gall even in the sweet: if there was a
crowd at a banquet, the Count's steward, Feltkirchner, who
hated him, would thrust him away to a side-table; perhaps
rightly, for the society which came was not of his world, nor
of his age, and few of them understood the languages he knew.
He tried to speak German, they did not understand him, and

when he grew angry, they laughed. They laughed when he
showed them his French verses, as they laughed at his gesticula-
tions when he declaimed his beloved Ariosto. When he bowed,
as Marcel the famous Paris dancing-master had taught him to
do on coming into a room, when he danced a minuet in the old
stately fashion, when he wore the velvets, the plumes, the
buckles which had been the admiration of the companies he
had loved, they laughed again, immoderately. '*Cospetto!*' he
would cry; 'pigs that you are! You're all Jacobins!'

It was worse when the Count was away, and the marooned
ancient was left to the tender mercies of the steward and his
like-minded assistance. They could not abide this arrogant
stranger who did not speak their language, who seemed hardly
to be of the same species as themselves, who grumbled incessantly, and appeared to bark at them; and they took no pains
to hide their aversion. Casanova, fretted by an inaction so
foreign to his nature, exaggerated little rubs to fantastic
proportions; everybody was in conspiracy against him! He
became a prey to persecution mania, his nervous potential
burst out in terrific rages, and his need for action relieved itself
in daily storms. The cook had spoilt his coffee or ruined his
macaroni; his soup had, out of pure malice, been served too hot
or too cold; the coachman had deliberately given him a poor
horse to drive over to Teplitz with; a dog had barked all night,
a hunting-horn had driven him crazy, or the priest had been
trying to convert him. It was all the steward's doing. Who had
suggested that the servant-girl should use some of his manuscript to light the fire with? Feltkirchner. Who had told the
courier to jostle him at the street corner? Feltkirchner. And
who had incited the same courier to tear his portrait out of a
book and paste it up in the privy with obscene comments, if not
Feltkirchner? The steward was always setting people against
him, even the Count. Why, Waldstein had not said good-
morning to him first, had lent some one a book without telling
him, had failed to introduce him to a distinguished stranger who
had come to see the sword that had pierced the side of Wal-
lenstein, or had not reprimanded a groom who failed to touch
his cap to the librarian. Could it be borne? Sometimes it could
not; and Casanova would be commanded by God (such was his
belief) to obtain letters of introduction from the Prince de

Ligne to some ducal potentate, or certain Berlin Jews; and he
would slip off secretly, leaving a letter of farewell for the
Count, who would laugh and say, 'He'll come back.' But his
search for old friends, his attempts to link up with the old life,
or with his family, were doomed to disillusion: at Weimar, for
instance, all the attention went to a young man called Goethe;
there was no life for him outside Bohemia. Thus holding forth
against German literature, against the rascality, the superstition, and the ignorance of Berlin Jews (whose money, however,
he borrowed and upon whom he drew bills in Waldstein's
name), he would creep back after a few weeks. Waldstein
laughed, Casanova wept, and said that God had ordered him to
return to his chamber at Dux. And then he would delight the
company with a ludicrous account of what had happened to him
on this last trip.

And after all, as he had been fond of saying, while there is
life all is well; so his exhaustless vitality, which could find no
release in squabbles with servants, turned to other outlets. The
lover, the swashbuckler, the gambling adventurer, took to his
pen, and the output was terrific, if dispersed. He would show
the world that he was the equal of Voltaire; he would put that
charlatan Rousseau in the shade: poetry, politics, mathematics
—if he could not shine in these, who could? Thus in 1790 he
published his works on the duplication of the cube, with two
corollaries on that of the six-sided solid, which mathematicians
have found sensible if not epoch-making, besides thoughts on
the Gregorian calendar; he sent the Emperor a *Lucubration on
Usury*, a subject on which he undoubtedly knew something; he
delivered himself of a long critical essay on Manners, Art, and
the Sciences. Roused by detestation of the Jacobins who were
laying waste the Pompadour France that he loved, he produced
Reflections on the French Revolution. And as he sat in the library
at Dux, or in his own room, thinking, writing, dreaming, the
fever of scribbling grew upon him. The only way, he found, to
prevent black melancholy from eroding his existence or driving
him mad, was to blacken paper ten or twelve hours a day. So
he wrote and wrote—now projecting a heroic-comic drama, now
a musical comedy, or again a tragedy or a mime-ballet; but
none of these came to fruition except a dreary play *Polemoscope*,
acted at Dux, and *La Lorgnette Menteuse, ou La Calomnie*

Démasquée. He was always making notes, jotting down observations, memories, ideas, on scraps of paper, in a handwriting which grew ever shakier, the subjects varying from a philosophic dialogue between himself and God (no less), to notes on the kind of biscuit he best liked soaked in wine. The stupendously numerous large files are encyclopaedic in their variety: it is as though his mind, ungeared from his body, whirred round at ever greater speed. There are scraps of stories—about Roland, about an adventure with women in a cave; there are cryptograms, and a grammatical lottery; there are more snippets of Homer, and there is the *Icosaméron*, a philosophic fantasy, wild but unreadable, for which he got three hundred and thirty-five subscriptions, but of which his bookseller did not sell a copy. There is a work, pretending to be translated out of English, on the follies of human beings, a *Meditation on Sleep*, a design for discovering a perfect language, a long critique of Bernardin de Saint Pierre, a *Songe d'un Quart d'Heure*, and, in Italian, a treatise on the passions; in fact, the only thing which he seems to have left untouched was his *Dictionary of Cheeses*, which he had once projected, but which he found too large a subject for him. There are stacks of verses in Italian and French, often heavily corrected; and one quatrain in particular which seems to have given him enormous trouble, as well it might, seeing how contrary it is to his own nature:

Sans mystère point de plaisirs,
Sans silence point de mystère,
Charme divin de mes loisirs,
Solitude! que tu m'es chère!

Solitude! the thing he most hated in the world—so does man deceive himself in the search for happiness.

And when philosophy or poetry would no longer bring balm to his irritated nerves, there were letters, not merely the answers he would write to poets, prose-writers, men of science, and philosophers who still wrote to him, but more personal ones, to Henriette, to his brother, to the old Countess Waldstein, his patron's mother at Vienna, in which he complained of his treatment by the egregious Feltkirchner: and then letters to Feltkirchner himself, in which, unconsciously comic, he gave a loose to his rage, grossly, frantically, signing himself the steward's best friend, Jacques Casanova de Seingalt; and, pricked by the same spur, he dashed off a dialogue with O'Reilly the doctor, full of invective and scathing sarcasms on his ignorance, avarice, and idiocy. Old age made no difference to the temperamental explosiveness of the Venetian.

These works, with various jottings and maxims, such as considerations on pride, on whether a man who knew no Latin could compose a perfect hexameter, on Italianized French words, would have occupied the whole time and energy of most men; but these things were mere offshoots, leisure-moment productions, in the intervals of his great work, the *Mémoires*. They would be more than memoirs, they would be confessions, and would have been called such had not 'that charlatan' seized the title. He had already written a small section of them, published in a private edition for his friends, *My Escape from Prison*, but this had been done in self-defence. For he was often asked to tell the story, and could not refuse, for fear of being thought churlish; but it took two hours to do justice to it, and talking at length was becoming difficult, for how can one talk without teeth, and the superb set, with which he had delighted to crack ship's biscuits, had decayed to nothing. That, however, was merely a story, an adventure; there was little room for the mind, the soul even, to have play; but in these confessions everything would be there. He would tell the truth, for truth, he declared, was the one constant passion of his life; and it would be the truth about himself by a man who understood his own nature—*Nequidquam sapit qui sibi non sapit*. He would not spare himself, 'I have committed many follies in my time', he wrote; 'I confess it with as much openness as Rousseau, but I am not so vain about them as that unhappy gentleman is.' Yes, it would be candid, extremely frank indeed, and therefore it could not fail to be morally useful. Not that he himself had erred much, he thought; the only deed for which he felt remorse was his careless betrayal of Manucci; but he would abundantly reveal the crimes of other people.

Moreover, would it not be instructive to the tolerant—and he addressed himself to these alone—to have before them the portrait of a man who had always done as he wished, lived according to impulse? And if some of his pictures might seem too precisely, too vividly painted, well, prudes might miss them

out; and if, on the other hand, it should happen that such
scenes inflamed the ardours of some of his readers, again, well,
he could wish them nothing better. The book, of course, would
have a Preface; he would introduce himself to his readers
before he talked to them; it would be a résumé of his philosophy.
He tried several openings, especially one in which he endeavoured to relate himself to the universe; but little by little
throwing out the costive philosophy, he made the Preface into
a work of art, graceful, winning, and, surely, irresistible. It is
none the less a confession—his confession of faith; and it gave
him great difficulty, for however eager one may be for truth,
it is hard to be exact in stating one's belief about first and last
things. He wrote it again and again, the last draft being revised,
it seems, just before his death.

'There is not one Giacomo Casanova, there are a hundred'
—and even in this Preface, where the man tried with all the
concentration of purpose he could muster to create a unity,
several people seem to jostle in it, and exclaim: *Nequidquam
sapit* . . . but there were so many people to know: the man
who believed in God, knowing that he had prayed to Him, yet
who believed also in destiny; the Christian who believed in
immortality, but not that he would survive death. Nevertheless
one Casanova emerges clearly, the man who had loved life,
and all the things in it that had tasted strong—dried cod, high
game, cheeses in a state of putrefaction, spiced wines, and, he
adds without a pause, the perfume of women. And if the taste
may seem gross to some, he says defiantly, I can afford to
laugh at them, for all I know is that I have enjoyed life the
more for these things. Enjoyment—premeditated and remembered—was it not for this that man had faculties higher than
those of the beasts? To enjoy life thoroughly, sensually, was to
fulfil the purposes of nature, which had made man sentient.
It is odd that in his Preface he does not touch upon his intellectual pleasures: perhaps it is that the memory of those fades;
one cannot in imagination relive them as one can those of the
body, for that was where Casanova was sentimental. He did
not excuse his way of life; he saw no need for excuses. He told
his story for his semblables to read; they might be few, but
they were the only ones he cared for.

And, ultimately, what was he writing the book for at all?

Perhaps he would burn it before he died. He was scribbling it
to live again his old pleasures, and that he did to some extent
do so is obvious from the nervous warmth of the whole. There
was fun in telling the truth (with the few omissions he felt he
had a right to make), but the real delight was to turn over his
innumerable notes, the scraps he had jotted down, such as his
conversations with Voltaire, and the letters he had kept, those,
for instance, from Manon Balletti, which Esther d'O had given
him back. Yes, it seems as though in remembering he did
renew his youth. The old mangy tiger once more became the
splendid beast, burning bright. He forgot his aches, his im-
potence, the insults of Feltkirchner. After all, all life, all enjoyment, is memory: we do not live, we have lived. And what
a life he had led! memories of which brought back all the old
love of it. They were fools who said that life was not worth
living, that there was no happiness in it; they were criminal
fools who committed suicide.

So now he worked continuously; he would leap out of his
bed to write and to rewrite, revising all the while; it might
even be said, he told one of his still numerous correspondents,
that he wrote while he slept, for he dreamt of his book. Even
when he went for walks the business of composition went on.
The children who saw the tall, gaunt figure stalking along the
streets would scatter and flee at his approach, for it was not
merely his bony face, brown as a Moor's, that frightened them,
his receding forehead, his still lambent eyes that gazed before
him in such fixity, but the torrent of words that came from his
bitter lips, now a mouthing, now a passionate outburst; a
lonely melancholy figure, with a monstrous reputation behind
him, who seemed to be communing with spirits. It was not only
the children who got out of his way.

And then, when the work was about half-done, the itch to
publish came upon him, upon the man who had stated so
roundly that nothing should appear till after his death. Portions
of his memoirs were read by his friends, especially by the
Prince de Ligne, who, delighted with his frankness, his refusal
to gloze over details, urged him to make them known. The
Prince was no more shocked by the unhampered picture of
humanity than he was by the Italianized French; and besides,
he recognized in it a superb picture of the baroque aspect of

the society of the whole of Europe, filled with a delightful philosophy, crammed with vignettes of social life, stocked with sketches of people both famous and infamous, and which read like a masterpiece in the picaresque. Casanova hesitated no longer, and sent one volume of the manuscript to Count Marcolini at Dresden for him to print, saying that the success or failure of the book would determine him whether to continue or to burn. Marcolini, however, serious, dignified, prudent, and first minister to the King of Saxony, was afraid. The words Casanova used were too blunt; too many people still living were mentioned; he refused.

Perhaps it was this disappointment that made Casanova ill, brought him face to face with the only really disagreeable thing about life—death. But indeed his imprudences were finding him out in the shape of an incurable disease, for such in those days was considered trouble of the prostate gland. He was looked after by a nephew and by a blue-stocking lady, Élise von der Recke, who for a last pleasure brought him Malesherbes' daughter as a visitor. Casanova knew he was dying: his book was finished only up to 1774, so he burnt most of the remainder of the rough notes. He realized that his *Mémoires* were a work of art, the most complete revelation of a human being ever penned, and was determined that nothing imperfect should come from his hand. It was on June 4th, 1798, that the unrepentant old pagan died, rich in his memories, reluctant to leave them. His last words have all the old effrontery, all the old sense of the dramatic, the same queer tang of belonging to the hero of a novel that distinguishes all his life: 'I have lived as a philosopher,' he murmured, 'I die as a Christian.'

For a long time his grave was lost: how should a fairy have a grave? Only a legend remained that the metal cross which had surmounted it used to entangle the skirts of girls as they went to church. Research, however, has cast a cruder light; his grave, and even his bones have been found; and these last have only recently been disturbed to be carried to, and honourably buried in, that Venice which he had so fruitlessly loved, and which during his life had consistently rejected him.

BIBLIOGRAPHIES

These contain in the main the books that I used in writing these three lives; the lists hardly merit the title of bibliographies, and are, rather, guides to further reading. Unless otherwise stated, the place of publication is London, Oxford, or Cambridge.

1. SARAH CHURCHILL, DUCHESS OF MARLBOROUGH

The chief sources are, naturally, her own writings: *An Account of the Conduct of the Dowager Duchess of Marlborough, From her first coming to Court to the Year 1710*, 'arranged by N. Hooke' (1742): *Private Correspondence* (2 vols. 1838), which contains 'The Opinions of the Duchess of Marlborough, published by Lord Hailes' in 1788: and *Letters* (1875). On its appearance the Duchess's *Account* was frequently attacked with factional virulence, to be defended by Henry Fielding in *A Full Vindication of the Dowager Duchess of Marlborough* (1742).

Contemporary *Diaries* contain snatches of information, such as those of John Evelyn, Thomas Hearne, and Narcissus Luttrell, in his *Relation of State Affairs*, as does Swift's *Memoirs Relating to that Change in the Queen's Ministry in 1710.*

Letters also provide material, such as those of John Vanbrugh (Vol. IV of the Nonesuch edition of Vanbrugh, ed. G. Webb), Lady Mary Wortley Montagu, Horace Walpole, and those contained in *The Wentworth Papers 1705–1739*, ed. J. J. Cartwright (1883).

Background studies which are useful are *Letters of Two Queens*, by the Hon. Ben Bathurst (1925); *The Court of William III*, by E. and M. S. Grew (1910), G. M. Trevelyan's *England under Queen Anne* (1930), and *Walpole* by J. H. Plumb (Vol. 1, 1956).

Useful biographies of the Duke and Duchess include Archdeacon W. Coxe's *Life of Marlborough* (3 vols. 1818); Mrs. A. T. Thomson's *Memoirs of the Duchess of Marlborough* (2 vols. 1839); Lord Wolseley's *Marlborough* (2 vols. 1894). Straight biographies are: *The Queen's Comrade*, by F. Molloy (1901), and *Sarah Duchess of Marlborough*, by Mrs. A. Colville (1904). Recent more general works are: *Marlborough. His Life and Times*, by Sir Winston Churchill (4 vols. 1933–8), and *The Early Churchills*, by A. L. Rowse (1956).

2. JOHN WESLEY

The Journal of the Rev. John Wesley, A.M. was edited by Nehemiah Curnock (8 vols. 1914). There have been many abridged editions, such as the one by P. L. Parker, with an Appreciation by Augustine Birrell (2 vols. 1902), and an 'Everyman' edition in 3 vols. *The Letters of the Rev. John Wesley, A.M.*, were edited by John Telford (8 vols. 1931). *The Arminian Magazine*, now *The Wesleyan Methodist Magazine*, began in 1778.

Accounts of John Wesley by: J. Whitehead (1793–6); Robert Southey (2 vols. 1820, repr. 1925); H. Moore (1824) are the best earlier Lives. To be read also are *The Life and Times of John Wesley*, by L. Tyerman (3 vols. 1871), still to some extent the standard biography; and *John Wesley*, by C. E. Vulliamy (1931). Works of broader scope are *Wesley and the Evangelical Reaction of the Eighteenth Century*, by Julia Wedgwood (1870); *Wesley, Christian Philosopher and Church Founder*, by G. Eayrs (1926); *England: before and after John Wesley*, by J. W. Bready (1938); and *Young Mr. Wesley*, by V. H. H. Green, 1961.

Interesting collateral reading is provided by: *Hetty Wesley*, by 'Q', viz. Sir Arthur Quiller-Couch (1903; often reprinted in 'Everyman' up to 1931); M. L. Edwards's *Family Circle. A Study of the Epworth Household in Relation to John and Charles Wesley* (1949); and the admirable *A Tale of Two Brothers*, by Mabel F. Brailsford (1954).

3. JACQUES CASANOVA (DI SEINGALT)

Casanova's own writings published during his life consist of *Lana Caprina* (1772), *Le Messager de Thalie* (1780), *Isocameron*, etc. (1788), *Histoire de ma Fuite des Prison*, etc. (1788), reprinted in the Éditions Bossard by Charles Samaran (Paris, 1922). But the *Mémoires of Jacques Casanova de Seingalt* have an unlucky history. Written in French, they first appeared in a German edition in 1822; and when the first edition in French was projected in 1826, many of the people whom Casanova had put upon his canvas were still alive, and discretion was forced upon the publisher. Moreover, Casanova's French being Italianate, it was corrected and lavishly 'edited' by a Dresden professor, Jean Laforgue, who not only smoothed the style, but bowdlerized the contents. The MSS. remained in the hands of the firm of Brockhaus of Wiesbaden, from which texts offering considerable variations were offered, namely that by Paulin-Rosez (Paris, 1860) and Garnier (Paris, 1879). My text is based on the superb, magnificently illustrated, and well-annotated Édition de la Sirène (Paris, 1924–35), which appeared from the hands of the most devoted Casanovians led by M. Raoul Vèze. Recently a new authoritative edition from the MSS. has been coming out from the press of Messrs. Brockhaus of Wiesbaden. Though the phrasing is different, and here and there more vivid, it does not seem to make much difference to the 'facts' related by Casanova. A translation by Mr. Arthur Machen was published for the Casanova Society (12 vols. 1922 *seq.*), and later in Edinburgh (8 vols. 1940). A further 'unexpurgated' translation is now being produced, also by Mr. Machen.

There has been a multitude of books about Casanova, from which may be selected: *Casanova et Son Temps*, by Édouard Maynial (Paris, 1910); *Jacques Casanova*, by Charles Samaran (Paris, 1914); *Les Adventures de Casanova en Suisse*, by Pierre Grellet (Lausanne, 1919); *Casanova in England*, by Horace Bleackley (1923); *Casanova Loved Her*, the story of X.C.V., by Bruno Brunelli (1929); and *Casanova*, by Guy S. Endore (1930), which contains an ample bibliography as does *Casanova* by J. Rives Childs, 1961. *Casanova's Homecoming*, by Arthur Schnitzler, trs. Eden and Cedar Paul (1923), is not history, but is a work of art.

Essays on Casanova include those by Sainte-Beuve in his *Causeries de Lundi*, by Havelock Ellis in *Affirmations* (1915), by Arthur Symons in *Figures of Several Centuries* (1916), and by Charles Whibley in *Literary Portraits* (1920).

INDEX

INDEX

For convenience to the reader, the three subjects are indexed separately under each letter, a space being left to indicate the division when necessary.

PRINTED BY SPOTTISWOODE, BALLANTYNE AND CO. LTD., LONDON AND COLCHESTER